I0652474

THE SEVENTEENTH-CENTURY RESOLVE

The Seventeenth-Century Resolve

A HISTORICAL ANTHOLOGY OF A LITERARY FORM

Edited by

John L. Lievsay

THE UNIVERSITY PRESS OF KENTUCKY

ISBN: 978-0-8131-5337-7

Library of Congress Catalog Card Number: 79-4004

Copyright © 1980 by The University Press of Kentucky

Scholarly publisher for the Commonwealth,
serving Berea College, Centre College of Kentucky,
Eastern Kentucky University, The Filson Club,
Georgetown College, Kentucky Historical Society,
Kentucky State University, Morehead State University,
Murray State University, Northern Kentucky University,
Transylvania University, University of Kentucky,
University of Louisville, and Western Kentucky University.

Editorial and Sales Offices: Lexington, Kentucky 40506

For Norman Stanhope,
who will find many an old acquaintance here

Contents

Preface

The materials presented in this book have been gathered, desultorily, over several decades. In the process of transcription, of selection, and, finally, of choosing a suitable editorial treatment, they have undergone many changes. Elimination—or even detection—of inconsistencies in treatment has not been easy, but every effort has been made to achieve a readable text that is not modernized completely out of the seventeenth century. For such rough spots as may remain, I must crave the reader's indulgence.

My principal obligations along the way are to the directors and staffs of the libraries in which I have worked: the Henry E. Huntington, where the quest began; the Newberry Library; the Library of the British Museum (now the British Library); and the Folger Shakespeare Library, where most of the reading and writing was done. To all these institutions and to the helpful persons there whose services lightened the chore, I offer sincere thanks.

It is also my pleasant obligation here to acknowledge the aid of, and to render thanks to, several patient and well-disposed individuals. I have profited in various ways from their advice and assistance. Dr. Virginia Callahan helped me with some of the more obscure Latin references; Dr. Dale B. J. Randall, my colleague at Duke, gave me the benefit of his expert knowledge of the Fourth Lord North; and an unidentified reader for the Press, by suggesting some drastic excisions, has made the book more manageable and, I trust, more palatable to the general reader.

J.L.L.

Introduction

The seventeenth century, it is commonly agreed, witnessed a rich development in the writing of English prose. Old and familiar forms were pushed into a greater prominence: history, fictional narrative, biography, sermons, conduct-manuals, works of utilitarian instruction. And new forms, such as the essay and the "character," were either then invented or enormously popularized. These two latter, at least, have received adequate attention at the hands of critics and literary historians. With another seventeenth-century prose innovation, the "resolve," the case is different. It is the purpose of the present work to supply an anthology of representative resolves, a cursory history of the genre, and some critical and comparative evaluations of the resolve writers and their products.

Like much else that proceeded from that fertile and vexed period which stretches between the death of Elizabeth I and the Restoration, the resolve is preponderantly of religious inspiration, an instrument for the perfecting or reforming of private and public morals. It is the theological and ethical counterpart of those utopian inventions which looked toward the creation of the ideal Christian state and the achieving of perfection in the individual man. Naturally, among the multitude of rival voices all directed more or less to such ends, it had to compete vigorously for the attention of the reading public. That it did not succeed in establishing itself as a perduring literary form may be attributed to a number of causes, some of which will become apparent as we trace its history through its emergence, rapid near-success, and total decline—within a period of, roughly, sixty years. About the only modern residue from that past (or, rather, only modern rudimentary analogue) of the resolve is the New Year's resolution, our annual recognition of perfections not reached.

Basically, the resolve is a meditation in prose and, though less sophisticated and ritually elaborated, is thus akin to those holy reflections, exclamations, observations, prayers, and vows which underly the process of the unspoken or unwritten meditation and its religious congener in verse, so ably analyzed and illustrated in the studies of Louis Martz. But it is also akin to the essay, the sermon—even the character; and therein lies one of the elements contributing to its extinction. The resolve writers simply could not agree upon a single term to describe, and thus to isolate, what it was that they were trying to write. Witness the range of labels appearing on the title pages of works by representative re-solvers: "Meditations" (Hall, Stafford, Tuke, Rous, Henshaw, Warwick, Manley, Tubbe), "Vows" (Hall, Tuke), "Purposes" (Tuvill), "Resolutions" (Tuvill, Stafford, Struther, Warwick), "Essays" (Tuke, Brathwait), "Resolves" (Brathwait, Feltham), "Excogitations" (Feltham), "Observations" (Struther, Trench-field), "Discoveries" (Saltmarsh), "Flames" (Saltmarsh), "Con-templations" (Trenchfield), "Occasionals" (North). The state of confusion and irresolution mirrored in that variety of designa-tions is pinpointed in several titles attempting further discrimi-nation through alternatives, qualifying adjectives, or specified ends: Warwick's *Resolved Meditations and Premeditated Reso-lutions,* or Rous's *Meditations of Instruction, of Exhortation, of Reproofe.* Looking back through the mass of their productions, we can at this distance see perfectly well what was not so apparent to the writers of resolves. We can see, for instance, that in the col-lections of certain writers (Struther, Henshaw, Saltmarsh), even when the author demonstrates a command of the resolve formula, he feels at liberty to deviate from it and to place a gallimaufry of essays, brief hortatory sermons, and unresolved observations side by side with the authentic resolves. But whatever the label, they were all mainly trying to perform one simple operation, reducible to an easy basic formula. As we see it now, the resolve writer eyed a situation, either public or personal, adjudged it to be either de-sirable or undesirable, and *resolved* upon an appropriate course of action. The whole thought-process might be expressed in terms such as these: "I have observed that the situation is thus-and-such; I have approved or (more commonly) disapproved; and *I shall therefore* do so-and-so."

Obviously, this process in its barest form may be accomplished in a sentence or two; or it may be elaborated into a lengthy dis-course, depending upon the complexity of the matter discussed, the temper or wit of the writer, or the degree of exornation thought desirable to communication. An instance of brief delivery may be seen in the epigramlike resolve of Bishop Hall (XLVI): "Not onely commission makes a sinne: a man is guilty of all those sins he hateth not. If I cannot avoyd all, yet I will hate all." Other resolves, by other writers, stretch out to the length, almost, of a short sermon.

The formula admits of numerous variations, a factor that, in skillful hands, saves the resolve from the tedium of endless repetition. One of the terms in the process may be omitted, for example, or may be present only by implication. Or the resolution (*"I shall therefore"*) may stand by itself. Or, for the resolution, an equivalent ending in exhortation or prayer may be substituted. All these, and other, variations appear occasionally in the resolves here presented, as does also the full-fledged resolve (Waterhouse) inserted as part of a larger discourse directed to other ends than those normal to the more specialized form.

To a man, the writers of the resolve took a negative view of the morals of their own times. The normal temper of the resolve is that of the medieval (and later) *contemptus mundi,* its world view that of the *laudator temporis acti.* You may expect to find some puritans among the resolvers. The object of the writers was the reformation of manners, personal and national. Insofar as this attitude affected the form and mode of the genre, it tended to align the resolvers with the satirists, chiders, and epigrammatists, flourishing weeds in the literary garden of the time. This connection is especially evident in the works of the first two writers of resolves, Joseph Hall and Daniel Tuvill. Stylistically, the resolve unfortunately shares with its contemporaries, the character and the essay, something of the tendency to prettify its turns of speech with what then passed for "wit" or "conceit." And, as chiefly the product of preachers, it exhibits the characteristic reluctance of that conservative crew to abandon the worn-out devices of euphuism, especially wordplay, alliteration, and exemplary comparisons and clichés drawn from that "unnatural natural history," which, whether Plinian or biblical, provided such useful and deluding pabulum for the unwashed many. Even the best of the resolve writers—Hall, Rous, and Feltham—are occasional sinners along with the rest; but Feltham at least had given serious thought ("Of Preaching") to the nature of a decorous pulpit delivery.

I have referred to Hall and Tuvill as the first two writers of resolves; but the distinction of primacy must incontrovertibly be awarded to Hall. Nevertheless, before proceeding to a running history of the form, we shall not do amiss to consider a suggestion made by the always perceptive and sensible Douglas Bush. In discussing Feltham he says, "If the essays of Cornwallis partake of the 'resolve,' Owen Feltham's *Resolves* . . . often approach the pure essay." I have no quarrel with either half of that balanced proportion; but if a hasty reader should assume from it that the resolve form begins with Cornwallis's *Essayes* (1600, 1601) rather than with Hall's *Meditations and Vowes* (1605), then, clearly, a corrective statement is needed. My old friend Don Allen, who had an eye for such unregarded trivia of Letters as the obscure author and the neglected form, and who was not besotted with the hoity-toity obsessions of belletristic critics, credited Cornwallis rather than Bacon with being the real father of the English essay. And I have no quarrel with that proposition, either; but his *Essayes* definitely are not also the father of the resolve. Nowhere in his edition of the *Essayes*, neither in the Introduction nor in the Commentary, does Allen so much as mention the resolve. Had there been any essential connection, he would have been the first to expound it.

A reexamination of Cornwallis's *Essayes*, however, shows that Bush's statement, rightly understood, is correct: the *Essayes* do "partake" of the resolve. They do so to the extent that here and there in the course of his self-examining reflections, almost by accident rather than by intention, Cornwallis will see one of his own shortcomings and *resolve* to do something about it. That detached observation is a momentary stopping by the wayside, a diversion into an interesting side path. It is not part of the highway to a planned conclusion. "As conceits come into my Head," says Cornwallis, "I utter them" (Essay 25, "Of Fame"). What we have is a dribbling of resolves *in posse,* not *in esse;* there is here no effective formulation of a single fully mediated resolution. He does begin his essays with one "Of Resolution"; he does (like Shakespeare before him) use the word *resolve* as a substantive: "I do not poetically deifie Resolve, neither do I set up a marke impossible to hit" (ed. 1600, sig. A4 verso); many of his themes are such as can be found in the authentic resolvers—and elsewhere; and in writing an even fifty essays he achieves half of the "century" that the resolvers commonly affected. Further, Essay 25 ends in a resolve, as do several others (numbers 5, 9, for instance); but it is not *the* resolution toward which the whole drift of the essay's scattered observations inevitably leads—if such formlessness leads anywhere. The reader needs to remember that all resolves are meditations, but that not all meditations, or essays, are resolves. It is not in theme that the resolve is differentiated from the essay or the sermon, but in form. Cornwallis simply has not the form.

To step from negatives to positives, that form is full-blown and solidly apparent in the *Meditations and Vowes Divine and Morall* (1605) of Bishop Joseph Hall, one of the great religious voices of his day. Along with such figures as toothsome Hooker, bitter-mouthed Crakanthorpe, and endless Ussher, he represents the *via media* of Anglicanism; and similarly his humane, secular interests are in classical poise, in rational balance. The brevity and simplicity of his normal utterance are well reflected in his Resolve LXVI: "One saide, it is good to inure the mouth to speake well, for good speech is many times drawne into the affection. But I would feare that speaking well without feeling were the next way to procure an habituall hypocrisie: let my good wordes follow the affections, not goe before them. I will therefore speake as I thinke; but, withall, I will labour to thinke well, and then I knowe I cannot but speake well." If the resolve had kept on the even keel with which it was here launched, it might not have suffered its later shipwreck.

As the stamp of his Senecanism is upon Hall's resolves, so the stamp of his resolves is upon various ones of his successors—in content, form, and style. And upon none more clearly than upon the *Christian Purposes and Resolutions* (1611) of Daniel Tuvill. These are generally longer-winded than Hall's resolves—the effect of Tuvill's single-minded preacherliness showing through. In individual statements, however, Tuvill can be as neat and as strikingly aphoristic as the bishop himself. More importantly, he seems to have exercised some influence upon Owen Feltham's *Resolves,* the chief product of the genre. That exchange was not a one-way proposition. In his *Vade Mecum* (1629), a revision of his *Essays Moral and Theological* (1609), Tuvill indicates his acquaintance with the later writer's *Resolves* and acknowledges a few sentiments lifted from them.

The heyday of the resolve embraces the period from 1612 to

1634. After Tuvill there appeared in rapid succession Anthony
Stafford's *Meditations and Resolutions* (1612); Thomas Tuke's
New Essayes: Meditations and Vowes (1614), a title patently echo-
ing Hall; Nicholas Breton's *I Would and Would not* (1614); Francis Rous's *Meditations of Instruction* (1616); Richard Brathwait's
Essaies upon the Five Senses (1620); Owen Feltham's *Resolves*
(1623); William Struther's *Christian Observations and Resolutions* (1628), the title probably but not necessarily reflecting Tuvill's; Joseph Henshaw's *Horae Succisivae* (1631), and Arthur
Warwick's *Spare-Minutes* (1634). An introduction does not allow
space to give each of these separate attention; other information
about the authors and their works, their specific qualities and their
interrelationships, will be found in the headnotes to the selections
from each writer. At this point it may be sufficient to say that of
those listed above, only Breton, whose resolves are in verse, is a
questionable inclusion. With some hesitation I have nonetheless
decided to make place for him, partly because, like Yorick, he was
a fellow of infinite jest, but mainly because he was an egregious
popularizer in verse and in prose, one who was instantly respon-
sive to the current fad. It would have been remarkable had he not
responded to the resolve while it was a novelty about town—and
responded in his own novel fashion. Judging from his other prose,
unlike Milton, he might have done better with his left hand.

In 1634 appeared Donald Lupton's *Objectiorum Reductio: or
Daily Imployment for the Soule* (STC 16945), described on the
title page as "Occasionall Meditations upon severall Subjects." Although none of these meditations has been included in the present
selection, they are nevertheless closely akin to the resolve form.
And Lupton is worth reading.

After 1634, at an interval of six years in times of growing religious and political tension, signs of which inevitably creep into
their resolves, John Saltmarsh published his extraordinary *Holy
Discoveries and Flames* (1640); Dudley North, third Baron North,
his *Forest of Varieties* (1645), not represented in this anthology;
Thomas Manley his *Temporis Angustiae* (1649); Edward Waterhouse his *Humble Apologie for Learning and Learned Men*
(1653); John Spencer his *Things New and Old* (1658); Henry
Tubbe his *Meditations Divine and Morrall* (1659); and Caleb
Trenchfield his *Historical Contemplations* (1664). The final selec-

tions in this volume, the "Occasionals," from *Light in the Way to Paradise* (1682), a posthumous publication of Dudley North, fourth Baron (and son of the third Baron North) were probably written during the 1650s or 1660s.

In some of the later works the resolve has ceased to be the chief focus of the book and appears only incidentally, though still recognizably, among other matters; particulars concerning this change are reserved to the headnotes.

By about 1660 the thrust of the form had petered out, and the resolve was tabled. If others continued to write resolves—and that is yet to be discovered—they made no great splash in the world of letters. With the exceptions of the folio editions of Feltham, a scattering of "modern" reprints (Breton, Feltham, Saltmarsh, Spencer), and the anthologizing of Feltham for the use of college students and bibliophiles, the resolve has long been among the endangered species. Perhaps some would say that it has already joined the dodo and the coelacanth.

What accounts for the failure of the genre? One cause, already noticed, was the lack of a uniformly accepted name for it. There would probably have been no trouble on this score had Feltham been the first to write in this kind. But he was a late arrival. Notwithstanding the prior substantival use of *resolve* by Cornwallis and its appearance in a secondary position on the title page of Brathwait's *Essaies* (1620), the term did not catch on. Curiously, the magisterial *Oxford English Dictionary* (OED) takes no notice ("Resolve," *sb.* 1) of the term as a literary form, or even mentions Feltham in this connection: the Homers of etymology were drowsing.

Confusion over a name, however, was perhaps less damaging than a failure to establish exact boundaries. A form that had no consistent length, and could slip so easily into essay or sermon, was from the outset in peril of losing its identity. What the resolve desperately needed at its inception was a literary manifesto, a clear and formal declaration of its being and purpose. Several of the resolve writers do discuss this matter; but they do not do so with sufficient clarity and force—or early enough in the life of the genre.

In another direction, it might be said that the resolve failed for lack of heavy artillery. Hall, Brathwait, and Feltham are respectable figures and are remembered in our histories of literature. But they are still figures of the second or third rank; and some of the other writers included in this anthology are hardly more than names—barely that. Had a Shakespeare, a Bacon, a Donne, or a Jonson lent his name to the form, it might have enjoyed a longer life.

Speculating on what might have happened to the resolve under other circumstances is a little like locking the stable after the horse is stolen. What did happen was that the resolve emerged in an age when pious meditations were a familiar part of daily life, and the composition of these particular lucubrations was mainly left to the hands of preachers. Such a cargo of piety went well enough in an age that could digest endless sermonizing. That it should pall upon succeeding ages, "enlightened" and grown a bit blind and deaf to the spiritual, is hardly the fault of the good men who wrote, as they thought (and often declared), for the benefit of their own souls and those of their fellows.

In transcribing seventeenth-century texts, where no notice to other effect appears, I have observed the following practices. Exclusive of brief quotations in the introduction and headnotes, *i* and *j, u, v, vv* follow modern usage; the erratic capitalization and italics of the period are regularized according to modern practice; though all original spellings are strictly preserved. Obvious misprints are silently corrected, and any supplied or changed words are enclosed in brackets. Printing contractions, such as the nasal tilde in *whẽ,* are expanded; internal ampersand reads *and,* terminal ampersand reads *etc.;* ligatures or digraphs are not preserved. Where catchwords and text vary, I follow the reading of the text.

In the punctuation I have taken some liberties which will, I trust, annoy none but pedants. Apostrophes indicating possessives are supplied according to modern usage; apostrophes of omission in the original have been preserv'd. My general rule for treating the punctuation of the original text has been to let stand as much of it as will not cause confusion, hesitancy, or misunderstanding for the modern reader. The shift from a rhetorical system of punctuation, such as the resolve writers generally used, to one based upon syntax and logic, may occasionally result in an emphasis (or even a meaning) not intended by the writer. But the gain in clarity and ease of reading will commonly more than compensate for the loss of the intended vocal effect. I have not, therefore, scrupled to change punctuation where it has seemed to me likely to mislead. My notes record only the most drastic or dubious of such changes. But no change of mere punctuation can salvage some constructions. With them, the reader is on his own.

Joseph Hall, Bishop of Norwich

1574-1656

TEXT: *Meditations and Vowes Divine and Morall. Serving for direction in Christian and Civill practise. Devided into two Bookes* (London, 1605); *STC* 12679. There are two copies of this first edition in the Folger Library; the one I use for copytext is that from the library of King James I, with his Garter arms on the front cover. But despite this evidence of royal interest (or of author's hunger for attention), the little volume is printed with exquisite carelessness. The First Book (of an even 100 meditations) is dedicated to Hall's patron and parishioner, Sir Robert Drury; the Second (containing only 90 meditations—a defective "century"), to Lady Drury. Subsequent editions of the book appeared in 1606, 1607, 1609 "newly enlarged," 1616, and 1621. It is also reprinted in later collected editions of Hall's works.

Joseph Hall (1574–1656), bishop of Exeter and later (more famously) of Norwich, was educated at Emmanuel College, Cambridge. Under royal patronage he became one of the most eminent men in the kingdom. He was a staunch defender of the episcopal position, a controversialist of power (who tangled with Milton), an advocate of the *via media* in church ceremony and doctrine, and a prolific writer of both religious and secular works. Many of his individual writings have been edited in the past and present centuries; the first edition of the complete *Works*, and still the only complete one, is that of Josiah Pratt in 1808. Hall's position as the first (regular) English satirist after the Latin manner and his innovations and experiments in other forms have earned him a permanent and honorable place in English literature.

Each of Hall's resolves (or "vowes") consists, structurally, of a meditation—and Hall was both a theorist and a voluminous writer of meditations and "contemplations"—followed by a vow (or resolution). The intention of the book is to make personal and practical application of the Christian aphorisms it contains. Many of Hall's resolves are so brief as to suggest either epigrams or moral maxims. Many, if not most, open with an eye- or mind-arresting statement, such as one finds at the beginnings of Bacon's *Essays*.

It is to be noted that some of his spiritual exercises end rather in a direct prayer than in a formal resolution. But the effect is the same; and the device became common among later resolve writers. The diction of Hall's resolves is generally unpretentious, the syntax relaxed and informal. Always the "end" of his resolves is to effect moral improvement; and the application to the writer himself carries with it the implied injunction to the reader: "Go and do thou likewise."

These *Meditations and Vowes*, in the edition of 1609, were enlarged by the addition of a third "century." John Spencer's citations (below, p. 167) of Hall refer to this added century. The reader's attention is especially invited to Resolve XLVI of Book One, which, in its brief two sentences, is a stark paradigm of the resolve pattern.

MEDITATIONS AND VOWES
DIVINE AND MORALL

from BOOK ONE   I

In meditation, those which begin heavenly thoughts and prosecute them not are like those which kindle a fire under greene wood and leave it so soone as it but begins to flame, leesing the hope of a good beginning for want of seconding it with a suitable proceeding. When[1] I set my self to meditate, I will not give over till I come to an issue. It hath beene said by some, that the beginning is as much as the midst; yea, more then all: but I say the ending is more than the beginning.

VIII

I have often wondred howe fishes can retaine their fresh taste, and yet live in salt waters, since I see that every other thing participates of the nature of the place wherein it abides. So, the waters passing through the channels of the earth varie their savour with the veynes of soyle through which they slide. So, brute creatures transported from one region to another alter their former qualitie and degenerate by little and little. The like danger have I seene in the manners of men, conversing with evill companions, in corrupt places. For, besides that it blemisheth our reputation and makes us thought ill though wee be good, it breedes in us an insensible declination to ill and works in us, if not an approbation, yet a lesse dislike of those sinnes to which our eares and eyes are so continually iniured.[2] I may have a bad acquaintance; I will never have a wicked companion.

XIII

Constraint makes an easie thing toilesom, wheras againe, love makes the greatest toile pleasant. How many miles do we ride and run to see one silly beast follow another, with pleasure; which, if wee were commaunded to measure uppon the charge of a superiour, we should complaine of wearines. I see the folly of most menne, that make their lives miserable and their actions tedious for want of love to that [which] they must doo. I will first labour to settle in my heart a good affection to heavenly things; so, Lord, thy yoake shall be easie, and thy burden light.

XIV

I am a stranger even at home. Therefore, if the dogs of the world barke at me, I will neither care nor wonder.

XV

It is the greatest madnes in the world to bee an hypocrite in religious profession. Men hate thee, because thou art a Christian, so much as in appearance. God hates thee double, because thou art but in appearance; so, while thou hast the hatred of both, thou hast no comfort in thy selfe. Yet if thou wilt not bee good, as thou seemest I hold it better to seeme ill as thou art. An open wicked man dooth much hurt with notorious sinnes; but an hypocrite dooth at last more shame goodnes, by seeming good. I had rather bee an open wicked man then an hypocrite; but I had rather bee no man, then eyther of them.

XXIII

I will use my friends as Moses did his rodde.[3] While it was a rod, he helde it familiarly in his hande; when once a serpent, he ranne away from it.

XXV

An ambitious man is the greatest enemy to himselfe, of any in the world besides. For hee still tormentes himselfe with hopes and desires, and cares, which hee might avoid if he would remitte of the height of his thoughtes and live quietly. My onely ambition shall bee to bee in God's favour on earth, and to be a Saint in heaven.

XL

Not to be afflicted is a signe of weakenesse; for therefore God imposes no more on mee, because hee sees I can beare no more. God will not make choyce of a weake champion: when I am stronger, I will looke for more. And when I sustaine more, it shall more comfort me that God findes mee strong then it shall grieve me to be pressed with an heavy affliction.

XLIV

Hee was never good man that amends not. For if hee were good, hee must needes desire to be better. Grace is so sweete that who ever tastes of it must needes long after more; and if hee desire it, he will endevor it, and if hee doo but endevour, God will crowne it with successe. God's familie admittes of no dwarffes, which are unthriving, and stand at a stay; but men of measure. What ever become of my body or my estate, I will ever labour to finde somewhat added to the stature of my soule.

XLVI

Not onely commission makes a sinne: a man is guilty of all those sins he hateth not. If I cannot avoyd all, yet I will hate all.

LIV

There is nothing more odious then fruitlesse olde age.[4] Now for that no tree beares fruite in autumne, unlesse it blossome in the spring; to the end that my age may be profitable, and laden with ripe fruit, I will endevour that my youth may be studious and floured with the blossomes of learning and observation.

LX

Heaven is compared to an hill, and therefore is figured by Olympus among the heathen, by Mount Sion in God's Booke; Hell, contrariwise, to a pit. The ascent to the one is hard, therefore, and the descent of the other easie and head-long; and so, as if wee once beginne to fall, the recoverie is most difficult, and not one of manie stayes[5] till hee comes to the bottome. I will be content to pant, and blow, and sweat, in climbing up to Heaven; as, contrarily, I will be warie of setting the first step downeward towards the pit. For as there is a Jacob's ladder[6] into Heaven, so there are blind stayres that goe winding downe into death, whereof each makes way for other: from the object is raysed an ill suggestion, suggestion drawes on delight, delight consent, consent endevour, endevour practise, practise custome, custome excuse, excuse defence, defence obstinacie, obstinacie boasting of sinne, boasting a reprobate sence. I will watch over my waies, and do thou, Lord, watch over mee, that I may avoid the first degrees of sinne; and if these over-take my frailtie, yet keepe mee that presumptuous sinns prevaile not over mee. Beginnings are with more ease and safety declined, when wee are free, then proceedings when wee have begun.

LXII

I never loved those salamanders[7] that are never well but when they are in the fire of contention. I will rather suffer a thousand wrongs, then offer one; I will suffer an hundreth, rather then returne one. I will suffer many, ere I will complaine of one and endevour to right it by contending. I have ever found that to strive with my superiour is furious, with my equall doubtfull, with my inferiour, sordid and base, with any, full of unquietnes.

LXVI

One saide, it is good to inure[8] the mouth to speake well, for good speech is many times drawne into the affection. But I would feare that speaking well without feeling were the next way to procure an habituall hypocrisie: let my good wordes follow good affections, not goe before them. I will therefore speake as I thinke; but, withall, I will labour to thinke well, and then I knowe I cannot but speake well.

LXXVIII

As man is a little world,[9] so every Christian is a little Church within himselfe. As the Church therefore is sometimes in the wane through persecution, other times in her full glory and brightnesse; so let me expect my self sometimes drouping under tentations, and sadly hanging downe the heade for the want of the feeling of God's presence, at other times carried with the full sayle of a resolute assurance to Heaven; knowing that as it is a Church at the weakest stay, so shall I in my greatest dejection hold[10] the child of God.

LXXXIII

Every man hath a kingdome within himselfe: reason as the princesse dwels in the highest and inwardest roome; the sences are the gard and attendants on the court, without whose ayde nothing is admitted into the presence. The supreame faculties [such] as will, memorie, etc., are the peeres; the outward parts and inwarde affections are the commons; violent passions are as rebels to disturb the common peace. I would not bee a stoick to have no passions, for that[11] were to overthrow this inward government God hath erected in me; but a Christian, to order those I have. And for that I see that, as in commotions, one mutinous person drawes on more, so in passions, that one makes way for the extremitie of another (as excesse of love causes excesse of griefe upon the losse of what we loved). I will doo as wise princes use to those they may misdoubt for faction, so holde them downe, and keepe them bare, that their very impotencie and remisnesse shall affoorde me securitie.

XC

Christian societie is like a bundle of stickes layd together, whereof one kindles another. Solitarie men have fewest provocations to evil, but againe fewest incitations to good: so much as doing good is better then not doing evill, will I account Christian good fellowship beter then an eremitish and melancholike solitarinesse.

XCIII

The rules of civill policie may wel be applied to the minde; as, therefore, for a prince that he may have good successe against either rebels or forraine enemies, it is a sure axiome, Divide and rule: [12] but when hee is once seated in the throne over loyall subjects, Unite and rule; so in the regiment of the soule, there must bee variance set in the judgement, and the conscience, and affections, that what is amisse may be subdued; but when all partes are brought to order, it is the only course to maintaine their peace, that all seeking to establish and helpe each other, the whole may prosper. Alwayes to be at warre is desperate; alwayes at peace, secure, and over Epicure-like. I doo account a secure peace a just occasion of this civill dissention in my selfe, and a true Christian peace, the ende of all my secret warres; which when I have atchieved, I shall reigne with comfort, and never will bee quiet till I have atchieved it.

XCVI

It is not possible but a conceited man must bee a foole; for that overweening opinion hee hath of himselfe excludes all opportunity of purchasing knowledge. Let a vessell be once full of never so base liquor, it will not give roome to the costliest, but spilles beside whatsoever is infused. The proude man, though hee be empty of good substance, yet he is full of conceite: many men had proved wise, if they had not so thought themselves. I am emptie enough to receive knowledge enough: let mee thinke my selfe but so bare as I am, and more I neede not. O Lord, doo thou teach me how little, howe nothing I have; and give mee no more then I know I want.[13]

from Book Two   IV

That which is saide of the elephant,[14] that being guilty to his deformity he cannot abide to look on his owne face in the water but seeks for troubled and muddy channels, wee see well moralized in men of evill conscience, who know their soules are so filthy that they dare not so much as view them, but shift off all checkes of their former iniquity with vaine excuses of good fellowship.

Whence it is that every smal reprehension so galles them, because it calles the eyes of the soule home to it selfe and makes them see a glance of what they would not. So have I seene a foolish and timerous patient which, knowing his wound very deep, would not endure the chirurgian to search it; whereon what can ensue but a festering of the part and a daunger of the whole body. So I have seene manie prodigall wasters runne so farre in bookes[15] that they cannot abide to heare of a reckoning. It hath beene an olde and true proverbe: Oft and even reckoninges[16] make long friends. I wil oft summe up my estate with God, that I may knowe what I have to expect and aunswere for; neither shall my score runne on so long with God that I shall not know my debts, or feare an audit, or despaire of payment.

VII

Even griefe[17] it selfe is pleasant to the remembrance, when it is once past, as joy is whiles it is present. I will not therefore in my conceit make any so great difference betwixt joy and griefe; sith griefe past is joyfull, and long expectation of joy is grievous.

VIII

Every sicknes is a little death. I will bee content to dye oft, that I may dye once well.

IX

Ofte times those things which have been sweete in opinion have prooved bitter in experience. I will therefore ever suspende my resolute judgment, untill the tryall and event. In the meane while I will feare the worst and hope the best.

XII

There must not bee one uniforme proceeding with all men in reprehension, but that must varie according to the disposition of the reprooved. I have seene some men as thornes, which, easily touched, hurt not; but if hard and unwarily, fetch blood of the hand: others, as nettles, which, if they bee nicely handled, sting and pricke, but if hard and roughly pressed, are pulled up without harme. Before I take any man in hand, I will knowe whether hee be a thorne or a nettle.

XXIII

There bee three usual causes of ingratitude upon a benefit received —envie, pride, covetousnesse: envie looking more at others' benefits then our owne; pride looking more at our selves then the benefit; covetousnesse looking more at what wee would have then what wee have. In good turnes I will neither respect the giver, nor my selfe, nor the gift, nor others; but onely the intent and good will from whence it proceeded. So shal I requite others' great pleasures with equall good-will, and accept of small favors with great thankfulnes.

XXV

We pitie the folly of the larke which, while it playeth with the feather, and stoopeth to the glasse,[18] is caught in the fowler's net; and yet cannot see our selves a-like made fooles by Sathan; who, deluding us by the vaine feathers and glasses of the world, suddainly enwrappeth us in his snares. Wee see not the nets; indeede, it is too much that we shall feele them, and that they are not so easily escaped after, as before avoyded. O Lord keep thou mine eies from beholding vanitie, and though mine eyes see it, let not my heart stoope to it, but loath it a farre off. And if I stoope at any time, and bee taken, set thou my soule at liberty, that I may say, My soule is escaped,[19] even as a bird out of the snare of the fowler; the snare is broken, and I am delivered.

XXX

The world is a stage;[20] every man an actor and plays his part heere either in a comedie or tragedy. The good man is a comedian which, howe ever hee begins, endes merily; but the wicked man's acts a tragedy, and therefore ever end in horrour. Thou seest a wicked man vaunt himselfe on his stage, stay till the last act, and look to his end, as David did,[21] and see whether that be peace. Thou wouldst make strange tragedies,if thou wouldst have but one acte; who sees an oxe grazing in a fat and ranke pasture, and thinks not that hee is neere to the slaughter? whereas the lean beast that toyles under the yoake is farre enough from the shambles. The best wicked man cannot be so envied in his first showes, as hee is pitiable in the conclusion.

XXXIII

There be three things which of all others I will never strive for: the wall,[22] the way, the best seate. If I deserve well, a lowe place cannot disparage mee so much as I shall grace it; if not, the height of my place shall add to my shame, whiles every man shall condemne me of pride matched with unworthinesse.

XXXV[23]

Great men's favours, friendes' promises, and dead men's shooes I will esteeme, but not trust to.

XXXIX

Secrecies, as they are a burden to the mind ere they bee uttered, so are they no lesse charge to the receiver, when they are uttered. I will not long after more inward secrets, least I should procure doubt to my selfe and jealous feare to the discloser; but as my mouth shall bee shutte with fidelity, not to blab them, so my eare shall not be too open to receive them.

XLV

An honest word I account better then a carelesse oath. I will say nothing[24] but what I dare sweare, and wil performe. It is a shame for a Christian to abide his tongue a false servant, or his minde a loose mistresse.

XLVIII

I will not be so merry as to forget God, nor so sorrowful to forget my selfe.

LIV

The eare and the eye are the mind's receivers; but the tongue is onely busied in expending the treasure received. If therefore the revenues of the minde bee uttered as fast or faster then they are received, it cannot be but that the minde must needes be held bare, and can never lay up for purchase. But if the receivers take in still with no utterance, the mind may soone grow a burden to it selfe and unprofitable to others. I will not lay up too much, and utter nothing, least I be covetous; nor spende much, and store up little, least I be prodigall and poore.

LV

I will speake no ill of others, no good of my selfe.

LXIII

Nothing doth so befoole a man as extreme passion. This doth both make them fooles, which otherwise are not; and show them to be fooles that are so. Violent passions, if I cannot tame them that they may yeeld to my ease, I will at least smother them by conceal-ment, that they may not appeare to my shame.

LXIX

The Spanish proverb[25] is too true: Dead men and absent find no friends. All mouthes are boldly opened with a conceite[26] of im-punitie. My eare shall be no grave to burie my friende's good name: but as I will bee my present friend's selfe, so I will bee my absent friend's deputie, to saie for him what hee would and cannot speake for himselfe.

LXXIX

It hath beene saide[27] of olde, To doo well and heare ill is princely; which, as it is most true, by reason of the envie which follows upon justice, so is the contrarie no lesse justified by many experiments: To do ill, and to heare well, is the fashion of many great men. To do ill, because they are borne out with the assurance of impunitie. To heare well, because of abundance of parasites which, as ravens to a carkasse, gather about great men. Neither is there any so great miserie in greatnesse[28] as this, that it conceales men from them-selves; and when they wil needs have a sight of their own actions, it showes them a false glasse to looke in. Meanenesse of state (that I can finde) hath none so great inconvenience. I am no whit sorrie that I am rather subject to contempt, then flatterie.

LXXXI

There is nothing more troublesome to a good minde then to doo nothing; for besids the furtherance of our estate, the minde doth both delight and better it selfe with exercise. There is but this difference then betwixt labour and idlenes: that labour is a profitable and pleasant trouble, idlenesse a trouble both unprofitable and comfortlesse. I will bee ever doing something, that either God when he commeth, or Sathan when hee tempteth, may finde me busied.[29] And yet since as the olde proverbe[30] is: Beter it is to be idle then effect nothing, I will not more hate dooing nothing, then doing something to no purpose. I shall doo good but a while; let me strive to do it while I may.

LXXXVIII[31]

A man neede not to care for more knowledge then to know him selfe; he needes no more pleasure then to content himselfe, no more victory then to overcome himselfe, no more riches then to enjoy himselfe. What fooles are they that seeke to know all other things, and are strangers in themselves? that seeke altogether to satisfie others' humours with their owne displeasure? that seeke to vanquish kingdoms and countries, when they are not maisters of themselves? that have no holde of their owne hearts, yet seeke to bee possessed of all outward commodities? Goe home to thy selfe first, vaine hart, and when thou hast made sure worke there in knowing, contenting, overcomming, enjoying thy selfe, spend all the superfluity of thy time and labor upon others.

NOTES

1. *proceeding. When:* The edition of 1605 reads *proceeding: when.* The reader is to note throughout that where the colon in the original texts represents a full stop, it will be treated (in Hall and in all others) as it is here. 2. *iniured:* inured (not injured). 3. *Moses . . . his rodde:* Compare Exodus 4:3. 4. *fruitlesse olde age:* Compare this with Feltham's resolve XXXVIII. 5. *stayes:* halts, stops. 6. *Jacob's ladder:* Compare Genesis 28:12. 7. *salamanders:* Salamanders were fabled to be fire-resistant. 8. *inure:* 1605 reads mure. 9. *man is a little world:*

Hall employs the common image of man as microcosm; compare John Earle's nearly contemporary *Microcosmographie* (1628) and E. M. W. Tillyard, *The Elizabethan World Picture* (New York, 1944), pp. 84–87. 10. *hold:* remain, continue.

11. *for that:* because. 12. *Divide and rule:* Latin maxim, "Divide et impera." M. P. Tilley, *Dictionary of Proverbs in England*, D391, cites this passage from Hall as the first instance in English. 13. *want:* lack. 14. *the elephant:* A piece of the "unnatural natural history" much used by moralists. Probable origin: Aelian, *Characteristics of Animals*, IV, 31. 15. *in bookes:* in debt. 16. *proverbe . . . even reckoninges:* Compare Tilley, *Proverbs*, R54; Hall is not cited. 17. *Even grief:* Tilley, *Proverbs*, R73, cites this passage from Hall and attributes the original to Erasmus, *Adagia:* "Jucunda malorum praeteritorum memoria." But it is at least as likely that both Erasmus and Hall are remembering Virgil, *Aeneid*, I, 203: "Haec olim meminisse juvabit." 18. *feather . . . glasse:* These are lures to attract the lark. *Stoop* is a technical term in falconry meaning to swoop down on prey or descend to a lure. 19. *My soule is escaped:* Psalm 124:7. 20. *The world is a stage:* Shakespeare (*As You Like It*, II, vii, 139 ff.) had no monopoly on this idea. "Totus mundus agit histrionem." The idea that comedy ended happily and tragedy "in horrour" was a commonplace.

21. *as David did:* David's peaceful end is related in 1 Kings 2:1–10. 22. *the wall:* It was considered good manners to yield the wall (inside path) to one's superiors. Our ancestors were very touchy in matters of precedence. 23. Meditation XXXV: This brief resolve seems to be a conflation and adaptation of several proverbial motifs. For *dead men's shooes*, compare Tilley, *Proverbs*, M619. 24. *I will say nothing:* Compare the ending of Feltham's resolve C. 25. *Spanish proverb:* Tilley, *Proverbs*, M591, cites this passage in Hall. The original runs thus: "A muértos y a ýdos no hay amígos" (Minsheu, *A Spanish Grammar*, 1599). 26. *conceite:* notion, assumption. 27. *It hath beene saide:* Diogenes Laertius, *Lives of Eminent Philosophers*, "Antisthenes," VI, 3. Plutarch, *Parallel Lives*, "Alexander," attributes the saying to Alexander. 28. *miserie in greatnesse:* Compare Bacon, *Essays*, "Of Great Place." 29. *Sathan . . . busied:* Hall is recalling the old saying "The Devil finds work for idle hands (heads)." Compare also Tilley, *Proverbs*, D281: "He that is busy is tempted but by one Devil, he that is idle by a legion." 30. *the olde proverbe:* A direct translation of Erasmus, *Adagia:* "Satius est ociosum esse, quam nihil agere."

31. Meditation LXXXVII: A descant on the old Grecian adage "Know thyself," attributed by Diogenes Laertius, *Lives of Eminent Philosophers*, I, 40, to Thales.

Daniel Tuvill

ᵛᵞᗠᛃᗡᗺᵞᵛ

ca. 1584-1660

TEXT: *Christian Purposes and Resolutions. By D. T.* (London, 1622); *STC* 24152.5. My text is transcribed from a Folger photostatic copy of the originally unlisted *STC* Huntington copy. The listing in the second edition of the *STC* (24393.3), revised and enlarged, of a single copy (University of Glasgow) of *Christian Purposes and Resolutions* dated 1611 and hitherto unknown to me, has had the important effect of promoting Tuvill into the second place, chronologically, as a writer of resolves. The 1622 volume contains a total of fifty-eight numbered but untitled resolves, of which nine are here reproduced.

About Daniel Tuvill (or Touteville), ca. 1584–1660, whose works were published over the initials "D. T.," not much is known. The son of French Huguenot parents naturalized in London, he was educated at the newly founded Sidney Sussex College, Cambridge, and through much of his life maintained connections with the important and influential Montague family, his principal patrons. He began writing early, publishing two series of *Essays*, in 1608 and in 1609, the latter going into three further editions during his lifetime. In 1627, we learn from his own statement (*Vade Mecum*, 1629, preface) and from Bishop Hall that he took part (perhaps as a chaplain) in the unfortunate British expedition to the Island of Rhé "before Rochelle"; and in 1631 he preached in Sutton's London Charterhouse. In 1635 he published his last known work, *St. Paul's Threefold Cord*, a book of "domestic" manners. Under the Long Parliament he was deprived—for drunkenness, according to the infamous "Century" White. After that, silence.

Because some resolve elements appear in Tuvill's *Essays*, it would appear that he had begun to work in this pattern as early as 1609. That he was later, at least, aware of Feltham's *Resolves* is patent from several references in the *Vade Mecum*. Like Bacon's *Essays*—and Tuvill was a Baconian, of sorts—D. T.'s resolves often open with a striking epigrammatic or aphoristic statement. But in content they are closer akin to meditation and exhortation than to the secular familiar essay, contrasting in this way with the first century of Feltham's *Resolves*. In their brevity, they more nearly resemble those of Feltham's second century.

Of all the resolve writers, Tuvill comes closest to making direct use of the Scriptures. His illustrations and supporting arguments are strictly biblical. Indeed, his Christian "Resolutions" are little more than a skillful tesselation of passages from the Bible, sometimes quoted verbatim, sometimes modified to suit his topical discussion. A more exactly descriptive title for his collection might have been *Biblical Purposes and Resolutions*. The reader of these resolves will find himself seldom far removed from the Wisdom literature of the Old Testament, or from the Gospels and Pauline epistles of the New. Certainly, in effect they are more closely related to the sermon or religious "lesson" than to the looser ethical ends of the essay. Tuvill himself states (Dedicatory epistle) the seriousness of his purpose: "My chiefest intent in publishing these Papers, is the good of others; And it may be, that these imperfect Resolutions and Meditations, in the practise wherof my owne soule hath profited, may be availeble to some."

Further information about Tuvill and his resolves may be found in my article "Daniel Tuvill's 'Resolves,'" *Studies in Philology* 46 (April 1949): 196–203, and in my edition of his *Essays* (Charlottesville, Va., 1971), Introduction.

CHRISTIAN PURPOSES AND RESOLUTIONS

IX

Man's intention without God's assistance availeth nothing. Peter was but a while forsaken, and howsoever he did abound with love and zeale, yet was hee notwithstanding supplanted by the enemy. His faith was overwhelmed with feare; hee forsooke him for whom he swore to dye.[1] God's assistaunce without man's intention profits as litle. For what action, circumstaunce, or exhortation could be thought requisite for the reclayming of Judas,[2] which Christ omitted? But al was to no purpose; hee was a devill, and so he dyed. And heereupon the Lord himselfe complaineth in the 23. of Mathew, *Hierusalem, Hierusalem, which killest the Prophets, and stonest them that are sent unto thee; how often would I have gathered thy children together as the hen gathereth her chickens under her winges, and ye would not?* God pointes us to the springs of heavenly grace, but unlesse we stoope to the well we cannot be refreshed with the water. We lie wallowing heere in the mire of earthly cogitations, and in vaine shall he assay to raise us if wee be not willing to rise; if hee lende us his hand, wee must give him our heart, or rot and putrify in our own infirmities. In al humility therefore, and singlenesse of spirit, I will desire the Authour of my salvation that he would vouchsafe to second my holy resolutions, and so quicken mee according to his loving kindnes, that whensoever it shall please him to call unto me, I may be instantly ready to runne unto him, applying my selfe without delay to keepe his statutes and commaundements.

XI

The covetous man is like a Christmasse boxe;[3] whatsoever is put into it, nothing can bee taken out of it till it bee broken. Hee soaketh up the waters like a spung, and till death come and squeeze him with his iron graspe, he will not yeeld one drop. His hand is sound and nimble to receive, but when he shold use it to relieve the wantes of his distressed brother, it lyeth withered in his bosome and can by no meanes possible be stretched out. Hee weareth out himselfe in labouring for that whereof hee hath no use. Hee knoweth no God of Sabaoth, but his gold; his restlesse purchase of it is his rest, and with religious admiration doe his thoughtes adore it. Hee thinkes it sacriledge to diminish the least heape; but the time will come when he shall goe as naked out of the world as ever he came into it, and then those aungels[4] in which hee gloried heere shall bee so many devils to torment him there. Whereas he that dealeth his bread[5] unto the hungry, and bringeth the poore unto his house; his light shal break forth as the morning, and his health shall growe with speede. His righteousnes shall go before him, and the glory of the Lorde shall embrace him.[6] He shall bee like a garden that is watered, and like a spring that can never faile; his very bones shal fatten, and his soule bee satisfied in the midst of drought. I will continually therfore cast my bread[7] upon the waters, and, according to that portion which the Lord hath lent mee, bee alwaies ready to releeve the needy.

XIII

God is not an Italienated courtier,[8] nor doth hee ever entertaine us with lippe-courtesie. When he inviteth[9] us, we must in no wise say him nay: hee will pull us to him with the cordes of a man, and drawe us on eeven with the bands of love; and when he seeth that this is not sufficient, hee will sende his chasticementes and his corrections for us, who like faithful messengers, will not be satis-fied[10] with any vain excuses, but wil compell us by violence to come unto him. It is not the purchase of a farme, the buying of an oxe, nor the marrying of a wife, that will serve our turne. The Mayster of the Feast hath sent for us, and we must goe. His dinner is prepared; hee hath killed his fatlinges, and all thinges nowe are in a readinesse.[11] If hee see that his table bee not thorowly furnished with guests, he will instantlie grow exceeding wroth, and woe be to us, if once hee send his warriours forth. For then shall we bee given as dust unto their swordes, and as scattered stubble unto their bowes.[12] I will not therefore slightly regard his invita-tions. He shal no sooner call but I wil free my selfe from all en-cumbrances and come. Blessed, I know, is he that eateth bread in the kingdom of God, and sitteth at supper with the holy Lambe.[13]

XXI

The Prince of Darknes[14] is exceeding politicke, and much abounds with craft in his proceedinges. He knowes that things which were once bruised may bee soone broken; he knowes that wood which was somtimes kindled wil quickly burne.[15] And therefore hee still enticeth men to commit such sinnes as in former times they were accustomed unto. Hee is withall a cunning rhetoritian and doth use much sophistry. He never comes to the point but by insinua-tion: he usurps uppon them by degrees[16] and deales with them as the father of the Levites did with him; by little and little hee procures theyr consent unto that which, were it summarily pro-pounded, would peradventure be utterly rejected. There are twoe things which oftentimes enthrall and captivate the soule of man. The one is pleasure; which, when he saw that Christ resisted, hee did assaulte him with the other, which was griefe, the surer engin[17] as he thought for battry of the twaine. And lo he stirred al men up against him; his Disciples hee caused to deny their Maister; the

souldiers to deride their captaine; the passengers to blaspheme
their guide; and in a word, the Jewes to crucify their king. So that
hee forced him to cry out, Beholde all yee that passe this way, and
see if ever there were any griefe that may bee thought to parallel
this of mine.[18] But notwithstanding this hee findes him still in-
vincible. The cruell dolours of his torments cannot make him forget to praye for his tormentours. I will alwaies therefore strive to
fortify the weaker place; and where the foe shall have made a
breach, I will erect a bulwarke. Let the perswasions of that Abaddon,[19] of that *Bad one* be never so enticing, I wil imitate my
Maister Christ, and seeke to crosse them with a *Scriptum est.*[20]
When God hath given mee a precept, I will endeavour to performe
it. The spirite of untruth, though in the mouth of a Prophet, shall
not be strong enough to divert mee from it. The Lorde will sende
a lyon to devour the disobedient, and his carkase shall bee denyed
the sepulcher of his fathers.[21]

XXV

Profanenesse is the badge of basenes, but a religious and upright
heart is the ensigne of true gentry. Such as are the children of
Abraham will doe the works of Abraham. They will bring foorth
nothing to disgrace their birth, to prejudice their breeding. Their
actions shal have alwaies written in theyr fronts[22] the lively char-
acters of their progenitors.[23] Others may boast of their descent, but
they are no better then the spurious issue of an heroike father.[24]
They are a wilde and savage generation:[25] the Bond-Woman[26] is
their mother. They have nothing in them that is truely generous,
and shall therefore be cast out with Ishmael[27] from beeing part-
ners of the promise with the lawful heire. The father of Canaan
for his impiety shall be made a slave;[28] and the King of Babell[29]
for his pride shall become a beast. The wealth and glory of the
world, with those hydropicall and puffed uppe titles which are
the foode and fodder of ambition, what are they else but imagi-
nary and fantastick graces,[30] of slender substaunce, of short continuance? The feare of the Lord is the height of honour, and hee
that is vertuous is only noble.[31] I wil labor alwaies therfore to doe
righteously and teach my hart the way of God's commaundements.
The men of Berea were preferred by the holy Ghost before those

of Thessalonica, because they searched the Scriptures with more
diligence and received the word which was taught them with more
willingnesse. I will doe as they did and obtain the same stile
which they had. I will delight[32] in the statutes of my God, and
with his precepts will I solace my soule.

XXIX

The sunshine of the wicked lasteth but a while. It is quickly over-
cast, and the joy of hypocrites doth vanish in a moment; though
his excellency mount up to heaven, and his head do reach unto the
cloudes, yet shall he perish for ever like his dung, and they which
have seene him shall say, *Where is he?* The worldly pleasures
whereon he feedes with such a ravening and unsatiable appetite
shall fret asunder his entrails. His meate shall turne within his
bowels into the gall of aspes; and howe sweete soever it seeme in
his mouth, it shall bee most unsavorie in his maw.[33] Nor shal his
state and condition bee so wretched in this world, but it shall bee
more in the worlde to come. Such feare and horrour shall hedge
him in on every side in that dreadful day, that he shal not know
which way to runne, nor whether to retire. Above him shall hee
see an angry Judge, out of whose mouth commeth a sharp two-
edged sword;[34] and well may he then entreate the mountaines to
fal downe upon him, and the hils to cover him from the presence of
him that sitteth on the throne, and from the wrath of the Lambe;
but it shall little avayle him. At his right hand hee shall discover
the hideous and distorted brood of his transgressions, which challenge him for their patron and will by no meanes be induced to
forsake him. At his left will stand the Devill his accuser,[35] who
then unfolds his ephemerides[36] and leaves not the least of all his
sinfull actions unatomiz'd.[37] Hee quotes them like a cunning
register, with every particular circumstance, both of time and
place. Hee bringeth forth to his reproach and disadvantage those
filthy and polluted garments in which he took him, and as Joseph's
bretheren[38] to their father, so saith he unto the Lord: *Behold,
this have I found, see now whether it bee the coate of any of thy
sonnes, or no.* If he turne back his eyes into himself, he shal meete
there with the worme of conscience,[39] that doth never dye; if he
reflect them on the world, he shall perceive it to be nothing round

about him but a burning flame. If hee cast them downewardes he shall there descry, to his perpetual terrour and affrightment, that unquenchable lake of fire and brimstone, which is prepared for him. The plentiful years are past; the yeares of dearth and scarsitie are come, and nowe not so much as one drop of water[40] shall ever be granted him to qualifie the heat of his inflamed tongue. The moth-eaten robe[41] shall exclaim against the proud, and the cankered gold against the covetous; the stone shall cry out[42] of the wal against the usurer, that buildes his nest uppon the ruines of the oppressed, and the beame out of the timber shall answere it. The whole world and whatsoever is therein contained, shall stand uppe in judgement, and witnesse against the reprobate. Then shal they confesse that it had beene better[43] that they had never been borne, or that a milstone beeing tyed about theyr necke they had been taken from out their cradle and cast into the sea. While I have time, therfore, I wil wash my hart from all uncleannesse; I will take my leave of all iniquity and bid farewel for ever to al profanesse and impiety. I will altogether exercise my selfe to godlines, which hath annexed unto it the promise of the life present and of that that is to come.[44] The Lorde is my helper and deliverer in the time of trouble; he is my rocke and my defence; I will continually waite upon him and wil praise him more and more.[45] My mouth shall rehearse his righteousnesse, and my tongue shall speak of his salvation.

XXXVI

God is no respecter of persons. The ruler entreated him to come unto his sonne, and he would not;[46] the centurion did but sende unto him for his servant, and immediately hee went.[47] It is not the beauty of outward objectes that attractes his eye, nor the quality of ambitious titles that stirres up his respect. When he past thorough Jericho, there were many that came foorth to see him, more specious[48] to the viewe of weaker sence, and of higher place and ranke in the cittie then Zacheus was, yet hee alone was graced by him above the rest.[49] The Baptist was not clothed in soft rayment, nor fed with delicates. His meat was locustes with wilde hony, and his garment of camel's hayre, yet did hee make him greater then a Prophet. Peter was not arrayed in purple, nor did hee

live deliciously in courtes of kinges, and yet he made him prince
of his Apostles. So the body bee sound, hee cares not for the bark.
If the living⁵⁰ be good, let the outside bee as ragged as it will. I wil
not therefore greatly eie my present condition: though I bee rich,
I will not presume uppon my wealth; though I be poore, I wil
not despaire for my want. He that called unto the fisher-men that
were in their ship, mending their nets, not minding him, and sayde
unto them, *Come followe me,* will out of question give kind and
courteous entertainment unto him, who out of love and of his
owne accord doth humbly sue unto him for his livery.⁵¹ Againe,
I know that Dives was in torments, when Lazarus⁵² was in Abraham's bosom.

XXXVIII

Prayer is the minde's ambassador to God. It is the onely agent
for the soule; but if it have not faith and humility for assistants,
it will never bee admitted to his presence. The one⁵³ is so much
interested in him that whatsoever we desire⁵⁴ when we pray,
let us beleeve that wee shall have it, and it shall bee done unto us. The woman that had so long bin troubled with the fluxe
did but touch the hem of his garment, and without further en-
treatie he turned him about and said unto her: *Daughter, be of
good comfort, thy faith hath made thee whole.* His graces are
proportioned by this. *According to your faith, be it unto you* said
he unto the blinde that came and besought him for their sight;
and to the Captaine: *As thou hast beleeved, bee it unto thee.*⁵⁵
The other⁵⁶ is of that excellency, might, and power, that it maketh
way for our requestes, even thorough the regions of the ayre, and
commands their passage thorow the thickest clouds. It ushereth
them into the privy chamber of his imperiall Majesty, and obtains
both hearing and dispatch for them without stop or stay. The
prayer of the centurion, sent forth in the behalfe of his diseased
servant, was well accompanyed with both. *I have not found*⁵⁷
(saith our Saviour of the first) *such faith, no not in Israell;* and for
the last,⁵⁸ it was not to be parallelled: *I am unworthy,* said hee (O
humblenesse of mind), *that thou shouldst enter under my roofe.*
And by so saying, hee shewed himselfe worthy, not into whose
house, but into whose heart the Lorde might enter. By making

himself unworthy (saith St. Chrisostome)[59] to receive Christ into
his gates, he was made worthy to bee received of Christ into his
kingdome. But beside these, it had with it the encouragement of
charity, that with the more assurednesse and better confidence it
might appeare before him. To pray for our selves proceedes from
nature, but to pray for others is the worke of grace. Necessity
enforceth us to that, but brotherly love exhorteth us to this; and
it is indeede a far sweeter savour in the nostrils of the Lord, then
that which ariseth from the sensitive apprehension of our own
misery. *I advise you therefore* (saith Saint Paule to Timothy) *that
first of all supplications, prayers, intercessions, and thanksgivings
be made for al men.*[60] The word which we professe instructeth us
by precepts and examples that the conservation of duty to the
publique should bee much more unto us then the conservation of
eyther life or being, and that whatsoever good is communicative
should be preferred before that which is but private and particular. St. Paule desired[61] to bee anathemized for his bretheren; and
Moses to bee razed[62] out of the Booke of Life for the Children of
Israell, such was their zeale unto the Church, and such their feel-
ings of communion.[63] I wil continually therfore labour to lift up
pure handes to heaven without doubting. I will imitate the lowlinesse of the Publican;[64] and in my bosome will I cherish his meane
conceite. When I pray I will not stand in the synagogues, nor
kneele in the corners of the streets that I may bee seene of men;
but I will enter into my chamber, and having shut my doore, I
wil cal upon my heavenly Father. He seeth in secret and shall reward me openly.[65] In my prayers I will bee mindfull of my afflicted
bretheren, that so the Lord may be more mindfull of mee. God is
exceedingly in love with charity.[66] The very name thereof to him
is an oyntment powred out. She is his onely darling; hee dooth
kisse her with the kisses of his mouth; when shee commeth to him,
hee lodgeth her betweene his breastes and never sendes her from
him but with laden hands. The gaoler washed Paul[67] and Silas
from their stripes; and by so doing, himselfe was washed from his
sinnes.

XL

Sathan is a bolde intruder. Hee resides not alwayes in the graves,
nor is hee still abyding in the desertes. You shall finde him som-

times in the company of God's electe and chosen children: on a
day when they came and stood before the Lord, he likewise came
and stood among them.[68] Somtimes among his Ministers: Jehoshua, the High Priest[69] standes before the angell, and loe, the
Deceiver is at his right hand to resist him. Sometimes again with
his Apostles: *Have I not chosen twelve* (saith Christ), *and one of
you is a devil.*[70] He is a guest that will come without great bidding,
the least cast of our eie doth serve him for an invitation, and the
slightest complement will embolden him to be insolent. If we
make him our companion, he will be presently our master. If he
get but a foot within our doores, hee will cast us out, and like a
merciles disseisour[71] put us by[72] our right; nor shall it ought availe
us to plead our title when hee is in possession. I will bee alwaies
therefore verye carefull how I suffer him to approch me. If I can-
ot barre him my presence, I wil deny him my countenance and
make him knowne[73] by my lookes that he shall not lodge in my
heart.

NOTES

1. *Peter . . . to dye:* See Matthew 26:33–75. *Judas:* See Matthew
26–27. 3. *a Christmasse boxe:* A pottery box or closed container in
which coins were collected for presents to be shared at Christmas 4. *aungels:* British gold coins of the period, so-called from depicting the
archangel Michael slaying the dragon. 5. *dealeth his bread:* Tuvill's
marginal note reads "Mat. 25. 34." 6. *his light . . . embrace him:* Isaiah
58:8. 7. *cast my bread:* Adapting Ecclesiastes 11:1, "Cast thy bread."
8. *Italienated courtier:* One whose manners are over-nice, promising
much, but whose performance is small. Tuvill uses the phrase also in
his *Essays Moral and Theological,* ed. Lievsay, p. 107. 9. *when he inviteth:* Tuvill's marginal note reads "Hos[ea] 11[:1–4]." 10. *not be
satisfied:* Tuvill's marginal note says "Luke 14.13," but the relevant passage is in verses 15–23.

11. *fatlinges . . . readinesse:* Tuvill's note: "Matt. 22.4." 12. *as dust
. . . bowes:* Tuvill's note: "Esay. [Isaiah] 41.2." 13. *Blessed . . . Lambe:*
Tuvill's note: "Revel. 19.9." 14. *Prince of Darkness:* Shakespeare uses
the phrase for Satan, *Lear,* III, iv, 148. 15. *wood . . . quickly burne:*
Compare Tilley, *Proverbs,* W742, "Wood half-burned is easily kindled."
16. *usurps . . . by degrees:* Tuvill's marginal reference reads "Judg.
19.5"; but the whole passage embraces verses 1–9. And "the father of

the Levites" refers, less ambiguously, to the father-in-law of a Levite unhappily married. 17. *engin:* here, a battering ram. 18. *Beholde . . . this of mine:* Tuvill's marginal note reads "Lam. 2.12," but the correct reference is to Lamentations 1:2. 19. *Abaddon:* Compare Revelation 9:11, "angel of the bottomless pit; his name in Hebrew is Abaddon, and in Greek he is called Apollyon." Tuvill's pun has little to recommend it. 20. *Scriptum est:* "It is written"; Matthew 4:17, Jesus' reply to Satan. 21. *The spirite . . . his fathers:* Tuvill's marginal note reads "2 King, 13.18," but the right reference is 1 Kings 13:18–30. 22. *fronts:* foreheads (Latin, *frons, frontis*). 23. *Their actions . . . progenitors:* Tuvill's reference, "1 John 3.10." 24. *spurious issue . . . father:* Abraham's child by Hagar the Egyptian. 25. *wilde and savage generation:* Genesis 16:12. 26. *the Bond-Woman:* Hagar. 27. *cast out with Ishmael:* Genesis 21:12 (Tuvill's reference). 28. *father of Canaan . . . slave:* The curse of the offended Noah on Canaan, son of Ham; Genesis 9:25. 29. *King of Babell:* Nebuchadnezzar, king of Babylon; compare Daniel 4:33. 30. *fantastick graces:* Perhaps the word intended is *grasses*.

31. *vertuous is only noble:* A Renaissance commonplace in the theory of nobility; original perhaps Juvenal, *Satires*, VIII, 20 ("Nobilitas sola est atque unica virtus"). 32. *I will delight:* Compare Psalm 119:16. 33. *The sunshine . . . in his maw:* Compare Job 20:5–14. 34. *angry Judge . . . two-edged sword:* Revelation 1:16 (Tuvill's reference). 35. *the Devill his accuser:* For Satan as accuser, see Revelation 12:10. Milton alludes to this verse in *Paradise Lost*, Book IV, 10: "The tempter ere accuser of mankind." 36. *ephemerides:* Plural form of *ephemeris*, "a record of daily occurrences" (*OED*). 37. *unatomiz'd:* Probably meaning "reduced to separate items" or "unanatomized." *OED* recognizes neither form. 38. *Joseph's bretheren:* Compare Genesis 37:32 (Tuvill's reference). 39. *worme of conscience:* Compare Isaiah 66:24, Tuvill's reference, though it may be doubted that the "worm" mentioned there has anything to do with conscience. 40. *one drop of water:* In reference to the plea of Dives, the rich man, to "Father Abraham" from Hell; Luke 16:24.

41. *moth-eaten robe:* Compare James 5:3 (Tuvill's reference). 42. *the stone shall cry out:* Habakkuk 2:11 (Tuvill's reference). 43. *it had been better:* Matthew 18:6 (Tuvill's reference). 44. *godlines . . . is to come:* 1 Timothy 4:7–8 (Tuvill's reference). 45. *my rocke . . . more and more:* Psalm 71:3, 14–15. The ending of this resolve is typical of Tuvill's modifications and conflations of biblical materials. 46. *The ruler . . . would not:* John 4:46–50. 47. *The centurion . . . hee went:* Luke 7:2–10. 48. *specious:* Used in the obsolete sense of handsome, fair to the eye. 49. *Zacheus . . . above the rest:* Zacchaeus was a short

man who climbed a tree for a better view of Jesus; compare Luke 19: 2–10. The quaint old Primer rhyme, familiar to our ancestors, runs "Zaccheus he / Did climb the tree / His Lord to see." 50. *living:* Perhaps a misprint for lining?

51. *livery:* The official badge or uniform which identified a servitor's employer—and worn by the servant, of course. 52. *Dives . . . Lazarus:* Luke 16:23. 53. *The one:* I.e., faith. 54. *whatsoever we desire:* Tuvill mistakenly refers to Matthew 11:24. He is perhaps here conflating Matthew 8:13, Jesus' words to the believing centurion, and Matthew 7:7, "Ask and it shall be given you." 55. *the Captaine . . . unto thee:* Matthew 8:13 (Tuvill's reference). 56. *The other:* I.e., humility; *other* in the sixteenth and seventeenth centuries often had the meaning "second." 57. *I have not found:* Luke 7:9 (Tuvill's reference). 58. *the first . . . the last:* faith, humility. 59. *(saith St. Christome):* Chrysostom's commentary on the centurion's faith and humility is in the *Homilia* xxvii of his *Evangelium secundum Matthaeum commentarii.* 60. *I advise you . . . men:* 1 Timothy 2:1 (Tuvill's reference).

61. *St. Paule desired:* Romans 9:3 (Tuvill's reference). 62. *Moses to bee razed:* Exodus 32:32 (Tuvill's reference). 63. *communion:* unitedness, community of interests. 64. *lowlinesse of the Publican:* The Publican (tax collector) was so humble that in praying for mercy he would not even lift his eyes to heaven. Compare Luke 18:13 (Tuvill's reference). 65. *When I pray . . . openly:* Matthew 6:5–6. 66. *in love with charity:* Modified from Song of Solomon 1:2–3. 67. *The gaoler washed Paul:* Acts 16:33 (Tuvill's reference). 68. *on a day . . . among them:* Job 1:6 (Tuvill's reference); repeated in Job 2:1. 69. *Jehoshua, the High Priest:* Zechariah 3:1 (Tuvill's reference). 70. *Have I not chosen . . . devil:* John 6:70 (Tuvill's reference).

71. *merciles disseisour:* a dispossessor (with implication of thievery or injustice). 72. *put us by:* deprived us of. 73. *make him knowne:* make it known to him. For the sentiment, see Hall, Book One, resolve VIII.

Anthony Stafford

❦

1587-1645?

TEXT: *Meditations and Resolutions, Moral, Divine, Politicall. Century I. Written for the instruction and bettering of Youth; but especially, of the better and more Noble. By Anthony Stafford, Gent. There is also annexed an Oration of Justus Lipsius, against Calumnie; translated out of Latine, into English* (London, 1612); *STC* 23127. I use the Folger Library's Harmsworth copy, with which is bound Stafford's *Heavenly Dogge* (*STC* 23128) and Robert Newton's *The Countesse of Mountgomeries Eusebeia* (*STC* 18509).

Anthony Stafford (1587–1645?), descendant of a noble family, studied at Oxford and at the Inner Temple and was later (1623) created M.A. of the former. His other writings, mainly devotional, interestingly include two biographies—of a sort: *Staffords Heavenly Dogge* (1615), a "life-and-death" account of Diogenes the Cynic, and *The Female Glory: or the Life and Death of the Virgin Mary* (1635), a work that embroiled him in controversy with the puritans. The date of his death is not known.

Stafford's *Meditations, and Resolutions* is dedicated to Lady Frances, "Countesse of Hertford (Daughter to the Right Honourable, Thomas, Vicount Bindon)." In this "Epistle Dedicatorie" Stafford says (sig. A6 verso) "The truth is, Madam, that finding my Booke to have little spirit, or life in it, I made use of your Name to make it live"—a dubious compliment, at best. The reader will perhaps feel little inclination to quarrel with Stafford's assessment of his work. He adds (sig. A7 recto) a promise, or threat, of "a farre greater, and a farre better" work—possibly hinting at a further "century," or even centuries, of meditations. But if this (or these) reached print, no record remains thereof.

The brevity of the *Meditations, and Resolutions*, the "century" form, the simple numeration without captions, the temper all suggest that Stafford was following Hall as his model. If so, the reader may justly feel that he follows the model at a considerable distance. Actually, Stafford has not 100 but 101 resolves, a generosity of measure for which we need feel no extra gratitude. Stylistically, Stafford is a little overmuch given to playing with alliteration, antitheses, repetitions, paradox, and other word-juggling. The struggle to be "witty" makes him too often sound only precious. A linguistic peculiarity of these resolves is Stafford's practice of hyphenating verb forms, when compounded, to include prepositions or adverbs as an element of the verb itself.

As a sample of the unedited text I append Stafford's second epistle, "To the Understander," itself cast in the form of a resolve —longer, howbeit, than most of his.

Understander (for, to every Reader I write not) beholde this Booke with a gentle eye, and entertaine it with favour. It was penn'd by him who had rather say, *Est iudicium in nobis,* than *est furor in nobis.* Winke therefore at the want of witte thou shalt finde; since it is a worke of judgement onely. As for the Asses of the Age, I care as little for their censures, as their companies. Though they can pick out good sense, yet they will not; contrarie to the equity of a Reader; who, in a place doubtful, should strive to understand, before he cry out *Non* sense. They little knowe, that hee, who writes in every thing properly, shall never write anie thing pleasingly. If I were disposed to carpe I doe not thinke there are ten lines in any booke extant, out of which I would not pick somthing to cavill at. My greatest comfort is, I never yet saw any carper that had any judgement. Which whosoever wants, lacks the very salt of wit: without which, whatsoever is read, lies rawe, and undigested. But, that which makes mee most merrie, is, that some of our printed puppies thinke themselves worthy to bee compared with the most authenticke, auncient Authours: whose wittes they come as short of, as of their workes. I have heard some of them censure Authours, whome they doe as little understand, as they doe themselves. If they had but some small deale of matter with their manie wordes, they might (I confesse) rubbe-out reasonably well, amongst coxcombes, that are capable of no higher matters than themselves. But, as they are, I would intreate them to content themselves with their Jigge-learning: in which when they have knowne all they can, they then knowe just nothing; and, as *Seneca* saith, *operosè nihil agunt.* I write not this out of Spleene, for the wrong they have done mee: for, my spirite is pearcht so farre above them, that they cannot fling so high, as to hit it. Doe not I knowe, that these Times let-loose *literatores,* to set upon *literatiores?* Yes, yes: I knowe it; and have put-on a resolution to beare both with the iniquity, and the stoliditie of the Times. Farewell, Understander, and use mee wel. (Sigs. A8 recto–A10 recto)

MEDITATIONS AND RESOLUTIONS
MORAL, DIVINE, POLITICALL

I

When I consider in what estate man was created, I cannot but thinke of his folly; who, through a false hope of knowing good and evill, lost the enough of good hee had and found too much evill.[1] This makes mee call to minde the vaine ambition of those who seeke to prie into that unrevealed (and therefore inscrutable) knowledge of the Deity: uppon whom God looking down, saies in a pitifull derision (as hee did to Adam) *Beholde, the men are become as one of us*.[2] This meditation stretcheth-out it selfe, and biddes mee also consider the arrogancie of those who scorne to erre, or to bee reprehended for their errours, not-withstanding that they see man to have erred in the state of innocencie. I will therefore seeke to know my selfe (the next and surest way to knowe God) and by an humble confession, begge remission of my faults. I say, I will confesse them unto God; not boast of them to man.

IV

When a man is borne, hee beginnes to die; but when the just man dies, hee then but beginnes to live.[3] I will therefore in my beginning thinke of my end; that in my end, I may rejoyce in my better and never-ending beginning.

VIII

The first murtherer of all mankinde was also the first lyer;[4] two horrible vices, and alike bloudy. For, a man had better bee murthered, then belyed; have his person slaine, then his fame. I will therefore flie from a lyer as from an aspe, the poyson of whose tongue is mortall.[5]

XIII[6]

Laughing is onely proper to[7] man, amongst all living creatures. Whereas indeede he ought ever to be weeping, in that he ever sinnes; and the beasts ever laughing, to see man so much abuse his so much reason. O! if a man knew before hee came into the world

what hee should endure in the world, hee would feare his first day
more than his last. I will therfore weepe at mine owne misery,
and never laugh but at mine owne folly; and since my Master was
Vir dolorum,[8] a man of griefes, it shall not be said that I am *Vir
voluptatum*, a man of mirth.

XVI

It is a woonder to see the childish whining we now-adayes use at
the funeralls of our friends. If we could houl them back againe,
our lamentations were to some purpose; but as they are, they are
vaine, and in vain. If therfore my friend be good, I will be glad
that he is rid of the world; if hee bee bad, I will not bee sorry that
the world is rid of him but that so wofull a world is like to receive
him. If I have a friend whose soule joyn'd with mine makes but
one minde;[9] and that at his death I see my teares must burst out, or
my heart within; I may then perhaps yeeld to the infirmity of the
flesh. Yet not so much that he hath left the world as that he hath
left mee in it.

XVIII

Now-a-dayes the clothes are spoken to, and not the men; and few
have regard to the riches of the breast, but of the backe. He who
in his fashions differs and degenerates most from his ancestours
is held the most generous gentleman. The world is grown so sensuall that the parts[10] of the body are preferr'd before those of the
mind; so that to say, *He is a man of good parts* is as much to say
as, He is a man of good members. Christ sayes that the body is more
worth then the raiment;[11] but some of our gallants make them
clothes more worth then their bodies. With me it shall not be a
good argument to say, I will weare this because it becomes me;
but, I will weare this because it becomes a man. And he that
speakes to my clothes, and not to me, shall bee answered by my
clothes, and not by me.

XXIII

He that strives to please the intoxicated multitude labours as
much in vaine as he that sought to put the winds in a bagge.[12] And
the reason is, because it is impossible to please the godly and un-

godly, the judicial and the unjudiciall, the sensible and the sense-lesse, both at once. Neyther Christ nor his fore-runner[13] could please them. For John came neyther eating nor drinking, and they said he had a divell.[14] The Sonne of Man came eating and drinking; and they said, *Behold a glutton, and a drinker of wine, a friend to Publicans and sinners.*[15] I will therefore take my Saviour's counsel and seeke to justifie my judgement to the children of Wisedome, of whom she is justified;[16] and not to fooles, by whom shee is daily crucified.

XXVI

I have often wonder'd with my selfe, to thinke that Schollars are the most poore of all others; notwithstanding that they have the best wits of all others. And my wonder never left mee, till I considered, that they car'd not for the things of this world, which the mothe and canker could corrupt, but laid up their treasures in the other world;[17] whereas they who knew nothing but the things of this world carkt and car'd most for the world. Some say that because Salomon us'd the riches hee had to ill, therfore God would never since blesse schollars with them. But that is false: for wee see kings philosophers,[18] and divines. I wil beseech God to give mee an estate equally distant from abundance and penury. So shall I never rise so high as presumption, nor fall so low as despaire. Yet of the two, I had rather have nothing than know nothing; that my body should want, than my soule.

XXXII

Nothing torments a man more then ambition. She is the only enemy to content and rebel against reason. Shee is borne with her eyes cast up; that is, comparing her selfe with those that are above her. If shee cast her eyes downe, it is but in scorne of those that are belowe her. If shee should bee pearcht upon the verie toppe of heaven, yet shee would desire to clime higher. That I may not be subject to this aspyring divell,[19] I will be contrary to her, and never compare my selfe but with my inferiours. And if I see no man more contemptible than my selfe, I will yet retaine the majestie of a Man and thinke that I am placed lord and king over the beasts.

XXXIV

Friends are threefold:[20] profitable, delightful, vertuous. The two former are imbraced in this world, the later cassierd.[21] The name of an honest man is growne odious, and the reputation to be such a one is a clogge to a man's rising.[22] And therefore as one saies,[23] That he had rather be rich, than be accounted so; so a man had better be honest, than be reputed so. In these gayish times, the outward appearance is more looked into then the inward essence; and that of Seneca[24] is verified: *Annulis magis quam animus creditur.* For my part, I will not make choice of a friend that hath not all those three accidents united in him: to wit, profit, pleasure, and vertue. But of what profession shall this my friend bee? A knowing, doing scholar. Hee is the true profitable friend, the onely delightfull, the most trulie vertuous. That he is profitable appears in this: that in exchanging with him a demand[25] for an answere, a man shall gaine a secret worth a signiory. That he is delightfull, no man will deny that hath his understanding but once tickled with his discourse. That hee is the truliest vertuous is easily prooved in that other men are in love with vertue onely by relation; wheras the scholar, with his understanding part, pries into her fairest partes and loves her for her selfe onely, without any other base respect. A merchant loveth a merchant, as hoping to gaine by him; a souldier loveth a souldier, as expecting to be rescued by him; but a schollar loveth a schollar, as desiring to be better instructed by him. I, I:[26] this is love indeed, and this is a friend indeed; and he that loves not such a friend hates himselfe.

XLI

Amongst the diverse complaints of men, there is none so ordinarie as that of age; but especially women are vext with this old unwelcom guest, and had rather cease to be than cease to be young. Hee that tells a woman shee hath a wrinkle in her face gives her a wound in the hart. If her complexion faile never so little, her spirit falls with it. Shee feares not death a-whit, but his ordinarie forerunner, age. Many men also become womanish and have hermaphroditicall minds. If a verdit[27] of women once pronounce them ill-favor'd, they streight[28] sequester themselves from the world as unworthy of the world. I care not if my corruptible part rot, so my fairer part fade not; nor passe[29] I so much for the beautie of the case, as for the glorious splendour of the inclosed image.

XLII

Many travell, but few deserve to be stiled travellers. To fetch-home apish gestures, queint fashions, new vices, is now becom the proposed end of a traveller. There is no better sport than to read some of their written observations. One sets downe what delicate wines and salats have been subject to the command of his palate. Another discovers strange stratagems in a gun-hole. A third writes out all superscriptions of hospitals, etc. Phy upon it that a man should goe from home, to goe from himselfe, and returne destitute of the little wit he caried out with him.[31] The wisest of Grecians esteemed him wise, who had seene many cities and the divers manners of men.[32] Every carrier[33] can see many citties and the different natures of nations; but to discern betwixt them, and pick wisdome out of them, that requires the man;[34] and such a man did Homer require. The reason why wee travell is because all happy wits raigne not under one climate, and therfore are to be hunted out. Who would not wade a million of miles to enterchange discourse with a Scaliger, a Lipsius, or a Causabone?[35] My mind therefore shall travel more than my body; when the later rests, the former shall labour; and my care shal be greater to please my understanding, than my sense.

LIV

They say there is a kind of resemblance between sleepe and death.[36] As therefore hee that is wearied with the daye's toyle doth not grudge to goe to bed, as hoping to rise againe; so I, opprest with the excesse and cares of many dayes, wil gladly sleepe-out that long, slowe-pas't night. Neither will I think much to goe to my earthly bed, as knowing that I shall rise againe and put-on an incorruptible raiment.[37]

LVIII

It is a common speech that every man is either a foole or a physician;[38] that is, he knowes what does him good, and takes it;

and look what does him hurt, hee refuses it. It fares not so in matters of the soule. For in those most are fooles and few are physicians; like children, coveting that which harmes them and flying that which helps them. I care not if I be a foole in my bodily diet, so I be a physician for the health of my soule.

LX

Examples taken from great men hurt more than if they were taken from poore. The reason is, because adversitie makes a man know him selfe;[39] whereas prosperity makes him knowe himselfe too well. Now, it is more safe to follow him that knowes him selfe than him that does not. For, as a true knowledge of God, and of his truth, is the beginning of divine wisedome;[40] so a true knowledge of a man's selfe is the beginning of humane. I will therfore sooner imitate those whom misery hath tamed, than those whom joyes have made wilde.

LXIII

As the stomack if it be fedde a long time with one meate, at length loathes the same; so the soule despises ordinary and accustomed discourse. I will therefore feede my soule with varietie, but not with confusion.

LXVI

Nothing in this life is so unsavory as old-age. The sadnes of man's last dayes is sufficient to pay him for the folly of the first. The neerer age comes to her growth, the neerer beauty is to her bane.[41] For, in this pensive time every thing withers, and groweth old, but evill; and that retaines his full vigour. Lord, let my soule then flourish when my body fades; and let the concord of my minde fight against the discord of my body.

LXXII

The divell is never so busie[42] as when a man is idle. Hee hath no so fit instrument to worke by, as by sloth—which is, indeed, the mother of vice.[43] I will therefore abandon this mother, least in time she bring mee to that father.

LXXXI[44]

A great man's favor is hardly got and easily lost. Hee keeps a man to serve his turne, but not to observe his turnings. The greatest part of his followers are like his horses: they carry him, and hee guides them. That hors which offers to fling him, or that is not tender-mouth'd, hee puts off as a head-strong jade.[45] It is better therefore to serve God, who is voyd of all accidents and humors, than man, who by them is made voide of reason. And hee that is most unfit to observe man is the most fit to serve God.

LXXXV

It is an usuall speech, that nothing is saide which hath not beene said before.[46] If it be meant that no words are spoke, which have not beene spoke before, that is false; and if the meaning bee, that nothing is thought which hath not beene thought before, that is false too. For wee see that every day reveales[47] a new secret to the world; and that for never heard-of thinges wee are faine to faine never heard-of words. I wil rather think all braines are exhausted, than nature.

LXXXIX

A yong man is like a wilde horse; who, if hee want a curbe, will runne himselfe to death. Those parents, therefore, are wise, who joyne correction with direction and keepe those in who else would lash-out.

XCVII

Nothing should so neerely touch, nor so much move a prince, as a base report of his predecessour, though hee were his utter enemy. For though he himselfe lead the life of a blessed angell, yet from some mouthes (where in Calumny cloysters her selfe) as much imputation shall bee laied upon him, as can be cast upon the Divell; which his successour, in imitation of him, will winke-at. How many ministers of hell, now-adayes, not only revile gods on earth[48] with words, but with written wordes also? Historiographers may lightly touch the faults of princes, but if they raile at their persons, they cease to bee historians, and become malevolent oratours. Princes, therfore, should not imagine that their present fame wil be permanent, but should take this prescribed, or som other course: by which they may as well stoppe the mouthes of the revealers of their vices, and revilers of their persons, as let-loose the tongues that trumpet-out their vertues.

CI

If the miser did but looke into what he does, hee would never bee so miserable. He is ever solicitous, and hath scarce one happy houre in the course of his whole life. He hoords and layes-up, not knowing who shall enjoy it; and oftentimes they enjoy it who lay it out as fast, not caring what becomes of it. So that it plainly appears the whole life of an usurer is nothing but misery and vexation. O that a cormorant[49] did knowe how many beautiful bodies starve, and how many substantiall soules faint, for want of his cash! Hee would not onely willingly part with all his pelfe, but sel his owne body to solace their soules. But, indeed, he is not so much to be blamed; because, whereas charity begins at home in others, crueltie beginnes at home in him: and he almost starves himself that others, whom hee suffers to starve, may not take exception. Everyone is not guilty of this vice. The prodigall hath such use for his mony at home that he can put none to use abroad. Some get[50] by the use of their mony: he loseth by the use of his.

NOTES

1. *knowing good . . . too much evil:* Adam's fall through eating of the tree of the knowledge of good and evil is told succinctly in Genesis 3:1–7—and at large in Milton, *Paradise Lost*, Book IX. 2. *Beholde . . . one of us:* Genesis 3:22. 3. *hee beginnes to live:* The common Christian position that this life is mere prelude to the immortal life hereafter is intimated in many passages of the New Testament. See the motto of Mary, Queen of Scots: "In my end is my beginning." 4. *The first murtherer . . . lyer:* Cain; see Genesis 4:1–10. *Murther* is a common early spelling for *murder.* 5. *aspe . . . tongue is mortall:* The asp proved fatal ("mortall") to Cleopatra, but we may doubt that the poison lay in its *tongue.* 6. Resolve XIII: Behind this contrast of weeping-laughing lies the legend of the Greek philosophers, Heraclitus (the weeper) and Democritus (the laugher). Stafford's contemporary, Robert Burton,

called himself Democritus Junior because he could laugh at follies, his own and those of his fellowmen. 7. *proper to:* belonging exclusively to. 8. *Master was Vir dolorum:* In Isaiah 53:3 the coming Savior is prophetically styled "A man of sorrows, and acquainted with grief." 9. *soule joyn'd . . . one minde:* Classical (and later) theory of friendship; compare Laurens J. Mills, *One Soul in Bodies Twain* (Bloomington, Ind., 1937). 10. *parts:* gifts, graces.

11. *Christ sayes . . . raiment:* Luke 12:23. 12. *He that strives . . . bagge:* As Stafford was to find in his own experience upon the publication of his *Life and Death of the Holy Virgin Mary*. The would-be windbagger was a symbol of futility; compare Tilley, *Proverbs,* W416, who quotes Erasmus, *Adagia:* "Reti ventos venaris." 13. *his fore-runner:* John the Baptist, sent into the wilderness to preach the coming of Christ; compare Matthew 3:1–12. 14. *John came . . . divell:* Matthew 11:18. 15. *Behold a glutton . . . sinners:* Matthew 11:19. 16. *children of Wisedome . . . justified:* The deeds ("children") of the wise are their own justification; compare Matthew 11:19. 17. *they car'd not . . . other world:* Slightly modified reading of Matthew 6:19–20. 18. *wee see kings philosophers:* A piece of flattery aimed at James I, who fancied himself both a philosopher and a "divine." Perhaps Stafford was also recalling Plato, *Republic,* 5.473C-D. 19. *If shee should bee . . . divell:* An allusion to the pride and ambition of Lucifer and to his fall. Note that *pearcht* is a favorite word with Stafford. 20. *Friends are threefold:* Compare Bacon's triad of "fruits" in his essay "Of Friendship."

21. *cassierd:* cashiered, cast off. 22. *The name . . . a man's rising:* This is the general import of a work nearly contemporary with Stafford's, Barnaby Rich's *The Honestie of This Age* (1614). 23. *as one saies:* Compare Rich's motto "Malui me divitem esse quam vocari"—punning on his name. ("I would rather be rich than be called Rich.") 24. *that of Seneca:* I have not traced this reference. 25. *a demand:* a question (Ital., *domanda*). 26. *I, I:* I.e., Aye, aye. 27. *verdit:* verdict; here used in the sense of "jury." 28. *streight:* straightway, immediately. 29. *passe:* care. 30. Resolve XLII: This resolve contains the essence of many sixteenth- and seventeenth-century essays and discourses on travel.

31. *Phy [Fie] upon it . . . with him:* A work contemporary with Stafford's, Randle Cotgrave's French-English *Dictionarie* (1611), comments to the point: "Let no foole hope to become wise by travelling (at least as we use to say of some of our giddie Travellers) he is come home as verie a foole as he went"; cited by Tilley, *Proverbs,* F460. 32. *wisest of Grecians . . . manners of men:* Homer, describing Odysseus. 33. *Every carrier:* Except Milton's old Hobson, who knew only Cambridge and London. 34. *pick wisdome out . . . man:* Perhaps Stafford is recalling

Proverbs 20:5, "The purpose in a man's mind is like deep water, but a man of understanding will draw it out" (RSV). 35. *a Scaliger . . . Lipsius . . . Causabone:* Famous scholars, only one of whom was living when Stafford published his resolves: Julius Caesar Scaliger (1484–1558), Joseph Justus Scaliger (1540–1609), Justus Lipsius (1547–1606), Isaac Casaubon (1559–1614). 36. *They say . . . sleepe and death:* Proverbial and poetic commonplace; compare Tilley, *Proverbs,* S526, S527. 37. *an incorruptible raiment:* Compare 1 Corinthians 15:51–52. 38. *a common speech . . . physician:* I have traced no other instance of this "common speech." 39. *adversitie . . . know him selfe:* Compare Tilley, *Proverbs,* A42. See also Rous's resolve XXVI, "The benefite of Adversitie"; and Bacon's (later) essay, "Of Adversity." 40. *knowledge of God . . . wisedome:* Rephrased from Proverbs 1:7.

   41. *bane:* evil, downfall. 42. *never so busie:* Proverbial, "Satan finds work for idle hands"; compare Tilley, *Proverbs,* I13. 43. *sloth . . . mother of vice:* Compare Tilley, *Proverbs,* I13. 44. Resolve LXXXI: A resolve notable for its wordplay and balanced constructions. 45. *jade:* a vicious or worthless horse. 46. *nothing is saide . . . before:* The eternal refrain of the Preacher; see Ecclesiastes 1:10, "There is nothing new under the sun." 47. *every day reveales:* As the saying is, "Ex Africa semper aliquid novi"; or as Spenser says (*Faerie Queene,* II, proem, st. 2):

> But let that man with better sense advize,
> That of the world least part to us is red;
> And daily how through hardy enterprize
> Many great regions are discovered,
> Which to late age were never mentioned.
> Who ever heard of th' Indian Peru?
> Or who in venturous vessell measured
> The Amazons huge river, now found true?
> Or fruitfullest Virginia who did ever vew?

48. *gods on earth:* Princes, who, ruling by divine right (as the prevailing idea then was), were regarded as God's terrestrial vicegerents. Compare Psalm 82:6–7. 49. *a cormorant:* The usurer (or miser) thought of as a bird of prey. The cormorant was also an emblem of gluttony. 50. *get:* make profit.

Thomas Tuke

᠁

d. 1657

TEXT: *New Essayes: Meditations and Vowes: Including in them the Chiefe Duties of a Christian, both for Faith, and Manners. By Thomas Tuke, Minister of Gods Word, at S. Giles in the Fields* (London, 1614); *STC* 24312. I have used a copyflow reproduction, supplied by University Microfilms, of the original in the Bodleian Library. The work is dedicated to "the Right Vertuous and Honourable Lady, the Lady Alicia Dudley."

Thomas Tuke (d. 1657) was B.A. and M.A. of Christ's College, Cambridge. A supporter of King Charles in the Civil War, he suffered sequestration and imprisonment for his loyalty. As the title-page statement of the *New Essayes* reads, he was "Minister of Gods Word, at S. Giles in the Fields" in 1614 and for several years longer before being given the living of Saint Olave in the Old Jewry, where he was incumbent from 1617 to 1643. Besides the *New Essayes*, Tuke was author of a dozen or so other pious works, the latest, *The Israelites Promise* being published as late as 1651. Best known among them is his amusing and scathing *A Treatise against Painting and Tincturing of Men and Women . . . Whereunto is added The Picture of a Picture, or, the Character of a Painted Woman* (London, 1616). "Of painting the face," included among the resolves presented here, is a sort of abstract of the serious *Treatise* but lacks the wit and bite of the "character" which ends the 1616 volume.

In the dedication of the *New Essayes*, Tuke says, "I know not well how to call them"; and he is right in being puzzled for a proper label. Essays they are not, and of the total number of pieces in the book (58), not more than a bare half dozen clearly fit the pattern of the resolve. We will do well to follow the advice Tuke gives in his epistle "To the Courteous Reader": "Quarrell not with the name, if thou dislike not the nature. As children, so bookes, which are the birth of mens braines, have not ever the fittest names. It is oftentimes as Godfathers please. If thou dislike the name, call it what thou wilt." Shakespeare was not above allowing us a similar choice for his *Twelfth Night*.

In form—and not infrequently in length—these compositions most nearly resemble brief, unelaborated sermons; and in substance they are unrelieved, direct, plain-spoken expositions of nearly the whole range of Christian theology. The preacherly tediousness of Tuke, with his rhetorical questions, his plethora of scriptural and lay commonplaces, his prim (not to say puritan) religiosity, will soon wear upon the most patient of modern readers. But what seems to us defects were no doubt counted to him as virtues in his own more pious age. If one's ear is attuned to the voice of the earnest Protestant preacher rather than to that of the turtle, he will find nothing offensive in Tuke's palpable efforts to "improve" him.

NEW ESSAYES: MEDITATIONS AND VOWES

Of the Law

The law saith: Doe this, and thou shalt live. It rests not in faith, but exacteth action; and promiseth life to them which keepe it. It allowes not infirmities, but requireth all perfections; and if a man faile but in one point thereof, it denounceth a curse unto him. Alas then what are wee, what shall become of us, who are grievous and continuall sinners? Our very justice being strictly sifted by the law, which is the rule of justice, would bee found injustice;[1] and that would be contemned in the strict judgement of the judge, which is commended in the judgement of the worker. But could not this law have beene exactly kept? Surely Adam might have kept it, if hee would. But as the case now standeth, wee cannot but trangresse it. Neither yet is there injustice in God; for by commanding things impossible Hee makes not men sinners, but humble, that every mouth should bee stopped, and that all the world should bee made subject unto God; because by the workes of the law no flesh shal be justified in his sight. For when wee have received a commandement, and perceive what is wanting in us, wee are put in minde to send up our cries into heaven, and God will have mercy upon us; and that so wee may know that wee are not saved by the workes of righteousnesse, which wee have done, but by His owne free mercy.[2] For indeed therefore was the law given, and is yet urged, to shewe, not what wee can doe, but what wee should doe, and that the proude might see his weakenesse, and seeing it might bee humbled, and being humbled might confesse it, and confessing it might bee saved;[3] not resting upon his owne dignity, but on God's dignation;[4] not in his owne justice, but in the righteousnesse of Jesus Christ. Being therefore terrified by the law, let us seeke for comfort in the gospell; and seeing all hope in our selves is cut off by the law, let us flie to Christ Jesus, who is the fulfilling of the law, and in whom, whosoever beleeveth hath the perfection of the law. They say, the elephant[5] (as knowing his owne deformity) loves not to looke into cleere water. Foule faces would have false glasses; and such as would vent their copper[6] love not the touchstone; and they that have deceiptfull wares like not the light. But I doe desire to understand the law exactly, that I may see all my deformities and foulenesse, mine hypocrisies and falsedealings, that so I might bee brought to a loathing of them, and finding mine imperfections towards the law, I might bee provoked to seeke for the perfection revealed in the gospell. I will indevour to keep the law exactly, but when I faile, I will flie to the grace of the gospell speedily; as knowing that not by mine owne justice, but by the justice of Christ I must bee justified, and that I am not saved for any graces in mee, but by the grace of God in Christ unto mee.[7]

Of Justifying Faith

Justifying faith is that gracious gift whereby we beleeve in the justice of Christ for our justification and looke upon him with confidence, who was lifted up upon the Crosse for the cure of our soules, as the brazen serpent[8] was for the cure of the Israelites, being stinged with serpents; that as they by looking to the brazen serpent were cured of their bodily hurts, so we by beholding or fixing our beleefe on Jesus Christ crucified should not perish but have eternall life[9] by Him, being by the grace of God in Him delivered from all our sinnes. By Faith then a man goes out[10] of himselfe and goes into Christ Jesus; by faith he forsakes himselfe and cleaves unto Christ Jesus; by faith hee stands not upon his owne righteousnesse, which is required by the law, but desires to be found in the righteousnesse of Christ, which is revealed in the gospell. By faith hee puts off his owne ragges, his owne wisedome, holinesse, justice, and puts on[11] Christ Jesus, and applies him, or

at the least would faine apply Him to himselfe, as some rich robe,
or glorious garment; that being cloathed in his wisedome, holinesse, and justice, hee might appeare in the presence of God his
heavenly Father (as Jacob did to Isaac in Esau's cloathes)[12] and so
obtaine His everlasting blessing. This Saving Faith is a most precious jewell of the soule, full of comfort and content. Thou canst
not see God, but thou maist behold His Workes: this is His Worke,
that a man beleeveth in His sonne Jesus Christ. If then thou dost
truely beleeve, thou maist be sure that God is in thee, and hath
taken possession of thee. Wouldst thou know how the sunne goes
in the heavens? Then looke unto some true sunne dyall: in it the
motion of the sunne above appeareth. So, wouldst thou see how the
Son of Righteousness Christ Jesus is affected towards thee? Ascend
not on high, scale not the heavens; but descend into thy selfe, and
examine thine heart for thy faith; for thy faith apprehends Him,
followes Him up and downe, and lookes wishly[13] upon Him. Thy
Faith eyes Him, touches Him, holds Him, and will not let Him go.
And marke, even as thou by thy faith dost apprehend Him, so Hee
by His favour doth comprehend thee; as thou dost acknowledge
Him, so Hee doth acknowledge thee; as thou dost enter into Him,
so Hee doth inviron thee; as thou dost content thy selfe with Him,
so [doth] Hee delight Himselfe in thee; as thou dost rest and leane
thy selfe on Him, so Hee doth offer Himselfe as a prop to stay and
hold thee up. Not that wee beginne, and Hee followes; but Hee
beginnes, and wee follow; even as the diall followes[14] the sun, and
not it the diall; or, as the motion and turning of a boate at anchor
followes the motion and turning of the water, and not it the
boate: or, as the drynesse of the wayes,[15] follow[s] the drynesse of
the weather, and [not?] this that: or, finally, as the sea followes
the moone, and not it the sea. By this faith we heare with profite,
we walke with comfort, wee worke by charity, wee hope for
glory, we enjoy tranquillity, and though wee bee not justified
for the merite of it, yet are wee justified by it, as by that onely
meane whereby wee behold and hold, beleeve and place, our confidence in Jesus Christ, who was made unto us, of God, wisedome,
righteousnesse, sanctification, and redemption. So Saint Paul,
knowing that a man is not justified by the workes, but by the faith
of Jesus Christ: *Wee also* (Paul and Peter) *have beleeved in Jesus*

*Christ, that wee might bee justified by the faith of Christ, and not
by the workes of the Law: Because by the workes of the Law no
flesh shall bee justified.*[16] Epiphanius saith, justice is by faith,
without the workes of the law. Chrysostome saith, Hee hath saved
us by faith alone. Theodoret saith, by bringing onely faith we have
received pardon of sinnes. We judge, saith Ambrose, according to
the Apostle, that a man is justifyed by faith, without the workes
of the Law. Jerome[17] saith, thou knowest that thou, as the Gen-
tiles, hast found life in Christ, not by the workes of the Law, but by
faith alone. To omit many, heare onely now Saint Austen[18] a word,
or two: When the Apostle saith, a man is justified freely, without
the workes of the Law, by faith, it is not his drift, that when faith
is received and professed, the workes of justice should bee contemned; but that every man may know it is possible for him to bee
justified, although the workes of the Law have not gone before;
for they follow him that is justified and go not before him that is
to bee justified. So then, wee for our parts are justified before God
onely by faith. But wee, and our faith also, are justified before men
by good workes, as the goodnesse of a tree is shewed by the fruite,
the goodnesse of a rose by her sweete odors, the cunning of a workeman by his workes. And though faith bee not alone, but very well
attended, yet it justifies alone: as the eye sees alone, the eare heares
alone, the mouth tastes alone, the legges go alone, but yet are not
alone, but are coupled to other parts of the body. Hee that hath
this faith, hath all the vertues of a Christian; hee that wants it,
wants all. With it a man is something, without it a man is worse
then nothing. A man hath all that hath himselfe; he hath nothing
that wants himselfe; but hee hath himselfe that hath his Saviour,
and hee hath his Saviour, that beleeveth in Him, and by the vertue
of his faith doth seeke and serve Him. It is not faith, but faithless-
nesse; not trust but distrust, for a man to put affiance[19] in himselfe.
I will therefore distrust in my selfe, that I may beleeve in Christ; I
will despaire of my selfe, that I may have hope in Him; and I will
loose my selfe in my selfe, that I may finde my selfe in Him. I will
not distrust in His might, because Hee is Almighty; nor in His good
will, because Hee is most mercifull, and cryeth *Come unto me* (not
yee that are worthy, but) *yee that are weary, and heavy laden, and
I will refresh you.*

Of Good-deeds

Such are good workes, as are, and are done according to the will
of God revealed. For the rule of wel-doing is not our wils, who are
but servants; but the will of God, who is our Maister, whose will is
just, and the rule of justice, God being able to will nothing but
right and good, seeing Hee is wisedome, truth, and goodnesse it
selfe. And a thing may be according to His will, and yet not be
done of him that does it, according to it. A good deed is ill done, if
it bee not done for maner as well as for matter, according to the
will of God. For if a man do that that is good and thinke it is evill,
that man doth sinne; not onely because hee thinkes that evill which
is not evill, but also because he judging it to bee evill, yet doth it.
Even as a man may lye when he speakes the truth, if he thinke that
is a lye which hee speaketh, when hee speakes it. Againe, if a man
do that whereof he doubteth, and is not perswaded of the lawful-
nesse thereof, hee sinnes; for whatsoever is not of faith is sinne.[20]
And finally, though a man do a thing that is good, yet if hee do it
not to God's glory, but for his owne, or for base respects, and not
in way of obedience to God's Commandements, hee questionlesse
commits a sinne. A good man onely can do a good deed; for an
evill tree cannot bring forth good fruite, and a corrupt fountaine
can send forth no wholesome water.[21] Good deeds are necessary to
salvation, as the way to the kingdome, but not as the cause of
reigning. They are not the causes of salvation, but the workes and
testimonies of them that are to bee saved. And they are not the
matter nor forme of faith, but they are true effects, undoubted
tokens, and unseparable companions of true faith and of true
charity,[22] if well performed. For faith and charity are not idle
and unfruitfull, but laborious and full of goodnesse. And though
our wel-doing be no cause of our blessednesse, yet it shall not want
a reward, but as wee doe abound therein in this world, so shall we
exceed in glory in the world to come.[23] The more wee flourish in
fruit in this life, the more wee shall flourish in felicity in the life
to come. But some have beene heard to say, they can do no good
deeds, they have no riches, they are but poore. These are deceived;
thou hast not a penny,[24] hast thou a prayer? Thou hast no goods to
give, hast thou good counsell? Thou canst do no deeds of comfort,
hast thou any words of comfort? Thou hast no bread, hast thou a

blessing? Thy legs are lame, thou canst not go well; thy hands are lame, thou canst not worke well; hast thou a good tongue, canst thou speake well? There is no man so poore, but he may benefite his neighbour one way, or an other: if any way it is a good deed, if hee do it well. And God accepts any thing, a cup of cold water, if there be no better, the widdowe's mite, even any thing, haire to the building of the Tabernacle,[25] a pin to the dressing of his Bride. And suppose a man do a good deed to a wicked man, yet if hee do it not for his wickednesse, but either because he is a man, or that hee may win him unto goodnesse, or shew himselfe a follower of God, who is kind unto His enemies, and doth good even to the wicked,[26] surely hee doth a good, and shall not loose his reward. And say that a man should bee kinde unto some hypocrite, thinking him to bee a Saint, because hee could not discerne his simulations, being so cunningly carried, yet shall the benefactor bee rewarded of God, who regards his affection, and seeth his heart, and will recompense him according to his love, and not according to the condition of the party, which did not deserve it. If a man's beneficence proceeds of benevolence, and bee performed in the name of Christ to the glory of God, it shall never want a recompence. For God is not injust to forget the labour of our love; and as men sow,[27] so shall they reape; as they brue,[28] so shall they drinke. Our gifts shall be recompensed with glory, our paines with pleasures, our labours with life. Do well, and have well; live well, and die well.[29] Hee that doth well to the servant for the maister's sake, shall be sure to receive a reward from the maister himselfe. It shall never be said that hee that was kind and loving to the childe is unkindly and hardly dealt with of the father.[30] Let us not therefore bee weary of wel-doing; for in due season wee shall reape, if wee faint not.[31]

Of Ignorance[32]

It is better to bee ignorant, then to erre: simple ignorance is better then undiscreete knowledge. Ignorance, a bad mother,[33] hath two as bad daughters, Falsehood, and Doubting; that is the more miserable, but this the more to be pittied; that is the more dangerous, but this the more dolorous. Affected ignorance of that which a man should know doth double the sinne. For it is one to bee ignorant

and another, and that worse, to affect it, and to bee pleased with it.
It is no small matter for a man to know that hee doth not know;
for it is the way to get knowledge, to know that a man doth want
knowledge.[34] None prove ranker fooles, then they that thinke they
have all wisedome.[35] Many things worthy to be knowne are not
knowne, either because men care not to know them, or else because they thinke they know them, when they know them not. Hee
that is the best, and knowes the most, will ingenuously acknowledge
that hee knowes not many things which hee ought to know,
and that there are many things worthy to be learned, which yet hee
hath not learned. A wise scholar will not so much content himselfe
with what hee doth know, as enquire after those things which hee
doth not know; not blessing himselfe with what hee hath learned,
but endevouring to learne what hee hath not learned. Hee that
sees the light knowes how to judge of darkenesse, but hee that is
blind cannot judge of colours. A blinde man (they say) swallows
many a flye.[36] Ignorance is the mother of superstition; but true
devotion affecteth knowledge.[37] It is as evill[38] not to know what
is lawfull to bee done, as to doe that which a man knowes should
not bee done. When a man knowes not God, hee knowes not how
to worship Him; and when hee knowes not himselfe, hee knowes
not how to behave himselfe. From the ignorance of God comes
despaire; from ignorance of one's selfe ariseth pride and foollish
philauty.[39] The ignorance of our selves is the beginning of sinne,
the ignorance of God is the consummation of sinne. Hee commonly knowes most that knowes hee is ignorant of much; hee
knowes but little that thinkes hee is ignorant but of little; but hee
knowes just nothing that imagines hee knowes all and is ignorant
of nothing.[40] It is an easier punishment not to bee able to live,
then living not to bee able to know things needfull to bee knowne.
It were better to die being furnished with knowledge, then to live
being fraught with ignorance; it were better to have knowledge,
and to die like a man, then to be an ignorant sot, and to live like a
beast.

Of painting the face

If that which is most ancient be best, then the face that one is
borne with is better then it that is borrowed. Nature is more ancient
then art, and art is allowed to helpe nature, but not to hurt it;

to mend it, but not to marre it; for perfection, but not for perdition. But this artificiall facing doth corrupt the naturall colour of it. Indeed God hath given a man oile for his countenance, as Hee hath done wine for his heart, to refresh and cheere it;[41] but this is by refection, and not by plaister-worke;[42] by comforting and not by dawbing and covering; by mending and helping the naturall colour, and not by marring or hiding it with an artificial lit.[43] What a miserable vanity is it in a man or woman beholding in a glasse their borrowed face, their bought complexion, to please themselves with a face that is not their owne? And what is the cause they paint? Without doubt nothing but pride of heart, disdaining to bee behind their neighbour, discontentment with the worke of God, and vaine glory, or a foolish affectation of the praise of men. This kind of people are very hypocrites,[44] seeming one thing and being another, desiring to bee that in shew which they cannot bee in substance, and coveting to be judged that [which] they are not. They are very grosse deceivers; for they study to delude men with shewes, seeking hereby to bee counted more lovely creatures then they are, affecting that men should account that naturall, which is but artificiall. I may truely say they are deceivers of themselves; for if they thinke they doe well to paint, they are deceived; if they thinke it honest and just to beguile men, and to make them account them more delicate and amiable then they are in truth, they are deceived; if they thinke it meete that that should be counted God's worke, which is their owne, they are deceived. If they thinke that they shall not one day give account unto Christ of idle deeds, such as this is, as well as of idle words,[45] they are deceived; if they thinke that God regards not such trifles, but leaves them to their free election herein, they are deceivd. Now they that deceive themselves, who shall they be trusted with? A man that is taken of himself is in a worse taking then he that is caught of another. This selfe-deceiver is a double sinner; he sinnes in that hee is deceived; hee sinnes againe in that he doth deceive himselfe. To bee murdered of an other is not a sin in him that is murdered; but for a man to be deceived in what hee is forbidden is a sinne. It were better to bee murdered then so to bee deceived; for there the body is but killed, but here the soule her selfe is endangered. Now, how unhappy is the danger, how grievous is the sin, when a man is meerely[46] of himselfe indangered? It is a misery of miseries for a man to bee slaine with his owne sword, with his owne hand, and long of[47] his owne will. Besides, this painting is very scandalous and of ill report; for any man therefore to use it is to thwart the precept of the Holy Ghost in Saint Paul, who saith unto the Phillipians in this wise, *Whatsoever things[48] are true* (but a painted face is a false face) *Whatsoever things are venerable* (but who esteemes a painted face venerable? which is venereous[49] rather than venerable) *Whatsoever things are just* (but will any man of judgement say, that to paint the face is a point of justice?[)] Who dare say it is according to the will of God which is the rule of justice? Doth the law of God command it? Doth true reason teach it? Doth lawes of men enjoyne it? *Whatsoever things are* (chaste and) *pure:* (but is painting of the face a point of chastity, which is so commonly used amongst impure whoores and curtezans? Is that pure that proceeds out of the impurity of the soule, and which is of deceipt, and tends unto deceipt? Is that chaste, which is used to wooe men's eyes unto it?) *Whatsoever things are lovely* (but will any man out of a well informed judgement say that this kinde of painting is worthy love, or that a painted face is worthy to be fansied?) *Whatsoever things are of good report: If there bee any vertue, if there bee any praise, think of these things.* But I hope to paint the face, to weare an artificiall colour, or complexion, is no vertue; neither is it of good report amongst the vertuous. I read that Jezabel[50] did practise it, but I find not that any holy matrone or religious virgine ever used it. And it may perhaps of some be praised, but doubtlesse not of such as are judicious, but of them rather hated and discommended. A painted face is the devil's looking-glasse: there hee stands peering and toying (as an ape in a looking-glasse), joying to behold himselfe therein; for in it he may reade pride, vanity, and vaine-glory. Painting is an enemy to blushing, which is vertue's colour. And indeed how unworthy are they to bee credited in things of moment, that are so false in their haire, or colour, over which age and sicknesse and many accidents doe tyrannize; yea, and where their deceipt is easily discerned? And whereas the passions and conditions of a man, and his age, is something discovered by the face, this painting hindereth a man's judgement herein, so that if they were as well able to colour the eyes, as they are their haire and faces, a man could discerne little or nothing in such kind of people.[51] In briefe, these painters are sometimes injurious to those that are naturally faire and lovely, and no painters; partly, in that these are thought sometimes to bee painted, because of the common use of painting; and partly, in that these artificiall creatures steal away the praise from the naturall beauty by reason of their art, when it is not espyed; whereas were it not for their cunning, they would not bee deemed equall to the other. It is great pitty that this out-landish[52] vanity is in so much request and practise with us, as it is.

Of a King

Give unto Caesar the things that are Caesar's. Caesar is every free, full, and absolute monarch. The things of Caesar are love, hon-our, reverence, obedience, fidelity, tributes, subsidies, customes, and supreme authority under God over all his subjects in all tem-porall and secular things. A king is a certaine mixed creature, made of all the people in a kingdom. Man is a little world,[53] and a king is a little kingdome; there is not a man within his kingdome, but he is as a part and member of the king. Therefore, as every member of the body[54] serves in his place for the good of the whole body, and is obedient to the head, where wisedom, power, provi-dence, and government lyeth; so every subject should serve for the good of the state, and seek it in his place, and shold shew himselfe obedient to the king, who is his head. And as the head challengeth a right in every member, and therefore doth good unto them all, and is affected with compassion if even the smallest of them bee wronged, or ill affected; so a king hath a certaine right in all his subjects, hee should animate and rule them all with his authority, and by his lawes. Hee should study the welfare of them all, and should be affected truely with all their wrongs and miseries. The head will yeeld to the cutting off an ill-affected member, chusing rather that one should perish, then all; but it is not simply de-lighted in the death of any of the members. So a good king loves not to destroy any of his subjects, but had rather save a thousand, then kill one;[55] yet hee doth, as it were, enforce himselfe to draw his sword, as knowing that it is better to cut off one,[56] then disturbe or loose all. But though the head may determine to cut away a member, yet doth it not by it selfe, but by some other member, or instrument; so though judgement and determination belongs unto

the king, yet executions thereof are fittest by farre to bee performed of others.[57] But al-be-it the head agree to the destruction
of a member, yet no member is seene to lift it selfe up against the
head with violence (as it were) to strike, or hurt it. So it is altogether savage and unnaturall for subjects to lay violent hands[58]
upon the sacred bodies of their king, who is as Mount Sinai,[59]
which was not to bee touched under paine of death. Mercy and
justice are two save-gards of a king, and most comely for him. If
nothing can be safe from him, there can be no safety for him:
his safety and security stands in the safety and security of his subjects, of whom it is safer for him to be loved,[60] then to be feared.
It is surer for him to tye them to him by princely humanity, then
to exasperate and awe them with tyrannicall severity. The king of
the bees[61] himselfe is alone without a sting; nature would not
that he should be cruell, and hath left his anger without a weapon.
Doubtlesse clemency is a princely vertue.[62] Herein a king may
shew himselfe like the King of Kings, who though able easily to
be revenged of all that doe offend him, yet is he so indulgent that
he pardons many, and sometimes deferres the punishments of His
veriest enemies, and strikes not alwaies when[63] cause is given Him.
Every king should remember to serve the King of Kings, Christ
Jesus, to whom all kings are vassals. It is just that they should be
punisht with rebellious, treacherous, unfaithfull, and wicked subjects, that themselves neglect the lawes of their Soveraigne, and
are unfaithfull to their God. And herein a king doth most of all
serve Christ, to wit, in doing that good, and hindring that evill,
which hee could neither do, nor hinder, but as he is a king. Some
think a woman may not raigne.[64] What did Debora[65] among the
Israelites? If woemen (as many virgines, and widdowes) may be
ladies and mistresses of servants, even males, why may they not be
queenes, if the providence of heaven bring them to it[?] The regall
power is neither masculine nor foeminine, but divine. Sonnes are
tyed to honour their naturall mothers, and surely without staine
unto their sexe; and what blemish or indignity can it bee to men
to honour their politicall mother? Hee that honours an absolute
potentate aright, whether king or queene, honours the power and
authority, which is divine and not humane, and honours the person for the power, and not the power for the person. Bee the per-

son good or bad, the power is good, it is of God; and it may fall
out that an evill man may bee a good monarch. But whatsoever
the monarch is, the monarchy, the Monarche's power is ever good,
and never bad.[66] For there is no power, but of God;[67] and the
powers that be are ordained of God. Whosoever therefore resisteth
the power, resisteth the ordinance of God. And they that resist
shall receive to themselves condemnation. Let every soule therefore bee subject unto the higher powers, and not because of wrath
onely, but even for conscience' sake.[68]

NOTES

1. *Our very justice . . . injustice:* A rigid enforcement of the letter
of the law may produce injustice. Compare the legal maxim "summa
jus, summa injuria." 2. *by the workes . . . free mercy:* Compare Galatians 3:10–13. 3. *seeing it . . . bee saved:* This has a rhythm and con-
ciseness suggesting Hall. 4. *dignation:* Obsolete noun meaning "the
action of . . . treating one as worthy" (*OED*). 5. *They say, the elephant:*
Compare Hall, Book Two, resolve IV. 6. *vent their copper:* I.e., dispose
of their debased copper-alloyed coinage. The "touchstone" was used for
testing the precious metal (gold or silver) content. 7. *not by mine
owne . . . unto mee:* Compare Acts 15:11 and Romans 3:23–25. 8. *brazen
serpent:* See Numbers 21:9. 9. *fixing our beleefe . . . eternall life:* John
3:15–17—containing also the Moses-Christ comparison of the preceding
lines in Tuke's resolve. 10. *a man goes out:* Original reads "a mans goes
out."
11. *puts off . . . puts on:* Tuke seems here to have conflated the ideas
of several New Testament passages; compare Romans 13:14, Galatians
3:27, and Ephesians 4:22–24. 12. *Jacob . . . in Esau's cloathes:* For this
not very commendable action, see Genesis 27:15. 13. *lookes wishly:*
An old adverbial form meaning "fixedly" or, occasionally, "longingly."
14. *the diall followes:* I.e., the "true sunne dyall" mentioned in the resolve. 15. *wayes:* roads. 16. *So Saint Paul . . . shall be justified:* Compare Romans 3:19–28 and Galatians 2:16. 17. *Epiphanius . . . Jerome:*
These various Church Fathers are only saying what Paul (and Tuke)
have already said. But Tuke, like others of his time, and since, believed
that if one authority was good, half-a-dozen were better. 18. *heare . . .
Saint Austen:* Augustine (Austen) can be heard on this subject in his
De fide et operibus, chapt. 14. 19. *affiance:* trust, faith. 20. *againe . . .
is sinne:* Romans 14:22–23.

21. *A good man onely* . . . *water:* All three of these statements smack of the proverbial; compare Tilley, *Proverbs,* F777. See also Milton, *An Apology against a Pamphlet* (Columbia *Milton,* 3:287): "how he shall be truly eloquent who is not withall a good man, I see not." 22. *true effects* . . . *of true charity:* The greatly eloquent New Testament praise of faith and charity occurs in 1 Corinthians 13. 23. *our wel-doing* . . . *world to come:* This doctrine of good works is best set forth in James 2:14-26. 24. *no good deeds* . . . *penny:* Tuke has in mind Jesus' parable of the widow's mite; see Mark 12:42-44 and Luke 2:2-4. 25. *haire to the* . . . *Tabernacle:* God's instructions to Moses concerning acceptable gifts for the building of the Tabernacle included goat's hair. See Exodus 25:4. 26. *kind* . . . *even to the wicked:* Adapted from Luke 6:27. 27. *as men sow:* Galatians 6:7; also proverbial (with variations), Tilley, *Proverbs,* S687. 28. *as they brue:* Compare Tilley, *Proverbs,* B654. 29. *Do well* . . . *die well:* Both these statements are proverbial; see Tilley, *Proverbs,* D398, L391. 30. *It shall never* . . . *father:* Baby-kissing politicians are well acquainted with this idea.

31. *Let us not* . . . *faint not:* Galatians 6:9. 32. *"Of Ignorance":* This is perhaps the most heavily sententious of Tuke's resolves. 33. *Ignorance a bad mother:* The daughters of this bad mother, are proverbially, devotion and impudence; Tuke has given her a different set of twins. 34. *no small matter* . . . *want knowledge:* This was Plato's commendation of Socrates; compare Diogenes Laertius, "Socrates," *Lives of Eminent Philosophers,* II, 32. 35. *None prove* . . . *wisedome:* The drift of much of the "wisdom" literature in the book of Proverbs. Compare especially Proverbs 26:12: "Do you see a man who is wise in his own eyes? There is more hope for a fool than for him" (*RSV*). 36. *A blinde man* . . . *flye:* Proverbial; compare Tilley, *Proverbs,* B451. 37. *Ignorance* . . . *knowledge:* See these mother-daughter relations in note 33. Tilley, *Proverbs,* I17, quoting Bishop John Jewel, records: "Ignorantia enim, inquit, mater est verae pietatis, quam ille appellavit devotionem." 38. *It is as evill:* The original reads "It is an evill," but the rest of the comparison obviously calls for the change to *as.* 39. *philauty:* self-love. 40. *Hee commonly* . . . *of nothing:* This clutch of sententiae merely plays a verbal variation on what Tuke has already said in this resolve.

41. *Indeed God* . . . *cheere it:* Psalm 104:15. 42. *plaister-worke:* One of Tuke's better efforts at wit. 43. *artificiall lit:* artificial color or dye (*obs.*). 44. *very hypocrites:* true hypocrites (Fr., *vrai*). 45. *idle deeds* . . . *idle words:* Compare Matthew 12:36. 46. *meerely:* entirely, wholly. 47. *long of:* because of, in accordance with. 48. *Whatsoever things, etc.:* Philippians 4:8. 49. *venereous:* provoking to venery or libidinousness,

50. *I read that Jezabel:* In 2 Kings 9:30 Jezebel is said to have painted her eyes.

51. *And whereas the passions . . . people:* Contrary to Duncan's assertion (*Macbeth*, I, iv, 7) that "There's no art To find the mind's construction in the face," the men of the sixteenth and seventeenth centuries (and Lombroso afterwards) were thoroughly convinced that there was such an art (physiognomy), which was intimately involved with the theory of the humors. The transformation of Satan on Mount Niphates (*Paradise Lost*, Book IV, 114–130) is Milton's vivid assertion of the theory. 52. *outlandish:* foreign. 53. *Man is a little world:* See Hall, note 9. 54. *every member of the body:* The well-worn fable-analogy of Menenius Agrippa; compare Shakespeare, *Coriolanus*, I, i, 95 ff. The ultimate source is Plutarch's *Parallel Lives.* 55. *a good king . . . kill one:* So Spenser's ideal ruler, Mercilla, would rather "save than spill" (*Faerie Queene,* V, ix). 56. *better to cut off one:* Compare Matthew 18:8–9. 57. *the head may determine . . . others:* There is nothing amiss with this arrangement—indeed, it is most practical; but it happens to be precisely the teaching of Machiavelli (*Prince*, chapt. 7)—which would probably have scandalized Tuke had he recognized it as such. 58. *to lay violent hands:* Various passages of the Old Testament lay down the injunction not to touch the Lord's "anointed"; compare 1 Chronicles 16:22, 1 Samuel 26:23, and Psalm 105:15. 59. *as Mount Sinai:* Exodus 19:23. 60. *safer . . . to be loved:* This, too, is a point discussed by Machiavelli (*Prince,* chapt. 17), who comes to the opposite conclusion.

61. *king of the bees:* The queen bee, *hors concours*, has no use for a sting; but if a honeybee (worker) uses her sting it costs her her life, stinger and vital organs being inseparable. The "king" bee (a drone and stingless, as are the other males), is like other kings, a generally worthless fellow; his sole function is the fecundation of the real ruler, the queen bee. 62. *clemency . . . vertue:* The classic statement of this idea is Seneca's *De clementia*—addressed to the Emperor Nero! 63. *strikes not alwaies when:* But still strikes: God (the gods) may defer merited punishment, but it comes eventually. One of Feltham's resolves, not included in this anthology, is entitled "That no man always sins unpunished." 64. *Some think . . . not raigne:* Illustrated in the "Salic Law" of the French; and, for the English, in the notorious tract by John Knox, *The First Blast of the Trumpet against the Monstrous Regiment of Women* (1558). Spenser, condemning the Amazon Radigund, nevertheless hedges a bit where Elizabeth I is concerned: compare *Faerie Queene*, V, v, 25. 65. *What did Debora:* The story of Deborah is told

in Judges 4–5. 66. *Hee that honours . . . never bad:* Standard theory of kingship when Tuke was writing; but it had been severely tested in Elizabeth's execution of Mary, Queen of Scots, and it was to come upon almost total collapse with the execution of Tuke's own sovereign, Charles I. 67. *no power, but of God:* Compare Romans 13:1 (the passage quoted) and Proverbs 8:15–16. 68. *not because . . . conscience' sake:* Romans 13:5. Tuke has cleverly allowed Paul to phrase his resolve for him.

Nicholas Breton

ca. 1552-1626?

TEXT: *The Works in Verse and Prose of Nicholas Breton.* Ed. Alexander B. Grosart. 2 vols. Printed for Private Circulation (Chertsey Worthies' Library), 1879. "I Would and Would Not" (1614) consists of 154 six-line stanzas (*STC* 3664). Several of Breton's works went into numerous later editions; this one seems not to have been reprinted before Grosart included it in the *Works.* I reprint Grosart's text without attempting to make it conform to the practices otherwise observed in this volume, changing only *i, j, u,* and *v* to read as in modern texts.

Nicholas Breton (ca. 1552–1626?) was descended from an old, respectable, and moderately wealthy family. As with many other Elizabethans well known in their own time, definite facts in his career, including the dates of his birth and death, are hard to establish. His father died while Breton was still a youth, and his mother not long after was remarried—to the poet George Gascoigne. From various references scattered among his publications it appears that the young Breton was educated at Oxford. A prolific and not altogether contemptible poet and author of numerous satiric and fantastic works in prose, Breton remains one of the most engaging of the wits who adorned the reigns of Elizabeth and James I.

The ultimate formulation of "I Would and Would Not" allies the work closely to the "resolve" pattern. Since this was already an established form—though still lacking its name—by 1614, and since Breton was notorious as a follower of the times, it is perhaps not too unreasonable to offer it here, though in verse, as a modification of that form. The advance-and-retreat of Breton's characteristic witty pirouetting with language is well illustrated in the dedicatory epistle, "To the Reader":

You that reade, what you would be, I know not; what you would not be, you know your selfe: But what you should be, God knowes: But for my selfe, I have founde what is best to be, and so wishe other, except they neither knowe what they should be; nor well what they would, or would not be: Scorne it not, because it is in verse, or rime, for if you will reade it, you maie perhaps finde more pleasure and profit in it, then in a worse piece of prose: not to perswade you to any thing, further then your liking; I leave the censure of it, to your discretion, and my better Labours as they fall out, to your further content. And so, loath to make you beleeve more, then perhaps you shall finde, hoping, that no man will be angry with his owne shadowe, nor saie (meaning me) when hee comes to a foole point: But take the best and leave the worst, and break none of the pale; as kinde hearts doe in the Countrey: I rest, as you may see in my Discourse, what I would, and would not bee: and without would not, would be as I should be.

Some of the stanzas in "I Would and Would Not" are a bit livelier than the ones I quote, though Breton's ideas are not in the least startling or original. Nor are his diction and metrics: of the 924 lines in the poem, 349 begin with coordinating conjunctions —251 with *And.*

I WOULD AND WOULD NOT

I

I would I had, as much as might be had,
    Of wealthy wishes, to the worldes content;
That I might live, all like a lusty Ladde,
    And scorne the world, and care not how it went:
But eate, and drinke, and sleepe, and sing, and play,
    And so in pleasures, passe my time away.[1]

II

And yet I would not: for too wealthy then,
    I should be troubled with a world of toyes:
Kinred,[2] Companions, Troups of Serving-men;
    Fashion-Devisers, Fooles, and Guirles, and Boyes:
Fiddlers, and Jesters, Monkeys, Apes, Babounes,
    Drunckards, and Swaggerers, and such trouble-townes.[3]

III

Besides I should forget to finde the way,
    That leades the Soule to her Eternall blisse;

And then my state were at a wofull stay,
    No, I would wish, a better world then this.
And in Afflictions, here on Earth to dwell,
    Rather then seeke my Heav'n on earth, and run to hell.

IV

I would I were a man of such deepe wit,
    As might discerne the depth of every cause:
That wheresoere I did in Judgement sit,
    I might be held a Note-booke, in the Lawes.
My braine might seeme a kinde of miracle:
    And every word I spake an Oracle.

V

And yet I would not: for then, woe were me,
    I should be troubled with a world of Cases:
Both rich and poore, would then my Clients be,
    Some, with their pleasing, some with piteous faces:
And when the Rich had left their briberie,
    I should not rest for *Forma pauperie.*[4]

VI

I would I were a man of greatest power,
    That swaies a Scepter, on this worlds great Masse,
That I might sit on Toppe of pleasures Tower,
    And make my will, my way, where ere I passe,
That Lawe might have her being from my breath,
    My smile might be a life, my frowne a death.

VII

And yet I would not: for then, doe I feare,
    Envyy or Malice would betray my trust:
And some vile spirit, though against the haire,[5]
    Would seeke to lay mine honor in the dust.
Treason, or Murther,[6] would beset me so:
    I should not knowe, who were my friend, or foe.

VIII

No, I do rather wish the Lowe estate,
  And be an honest Man, of meane degree:
Be lov'd for good, and give no cause of hate,
  And clime no higher, then a Haw-thorne tree;[7]
Pay every man his owne, give Reason, right:
  And worke all day, and take my rest at night.

IX

For sure in Courtes, are worlds of costly Cares,
  That comber Reason, in his course of rest:
Let me but learne, how thrift both spends and spares,
  And make enough as good as any feast.[8]
And fast, and pray, my daies may have good end,
  And welcome all, that pleaseth God to send.

[Breton runs merrily along in this vein through many states and
professions, mainly secular, until he arrives at Stanza 113. There,
a change occurs and the thought becomes principally religious
through Stanza 119, after which a series of stanzas is given to things
the poet would not want to do or be, emerging in Stanzas 133-34
into something of a pious resolution.]

CXXXIII

This would I be, and would none other be,
  But a Religious servant of my God:
And knowe there is none other God[9] but he,
  And willingly to suffer mercies Rod.[10]
Joy in his Grace, and live but in his Love,
  And seeke my blisse but in the heaven above.

CXXXIV

And I would frame a kinde of faithfull praier,
  For all estates within the state of Grace:
That carefull love might never know despaire,
  Nor servile feare might faithfull love deface.
And this would I both day and night devise,
  To make my humble Spirits Exercise.

[The ensuing stanzas, 135–52, offer a set of model prayers and pious exhortations based on these *exercitia spiritualia;* and the poem ends in the positive spirit of the typical "resolve."]

CLIII

Thus would I spend in service of my God,
    The lingring howres of these fewe daies of mine,
To shew how sinne and death are overtrod,
    But by the vertue of the power divine.
Our thoughts but vaine, our substance slime and dust,
    And onely Christ, for our Eternall trust.

CLIV

This would I be, and say, would not, no more,
    But only not, be otherwise then this:
All in effect, but as I said before,
    The life in that life's kingdomes love of his,
My glorious God, whose grace all comfort gives.
    Then be on Earth, the greatest man that lives.[11]

NOTES

1. *But eate . . . time away:* Breton, "lusty Ladde" though he may have aspired to be, was apparently thinking of (and deterred by) the somber words in Luke 12:19–20. 2. *kinred:* old form of kindred. 3. *trouble-townes:* The OED, though listing the combined form (*trouble, v.,* III.6.), does not notice Breton's early use of this word. 4. *Forma pauperie:* A legal term for cases pleaded "in forma pauperis," i.e., under the character or form of a poor person. 5. *against the haire:* We should now say "against the grain." 6. *Murther:* old form of murder. 7. *clime no higher . . . Haw-thorne tree:* This has the sound of a proverbial saying, but I find no instance of its use elsewhere. 8. *enough as good . . . feast:* This is in the proverbial mode: compare Tilley, *Proverbs,* E158. 9. *none other God:* Exodus 20:3. 10. *mercies Rod:* Exodus 20:6.

11. Compare this stanza with the ending of Hall's Book One, resolve XXV.

Francis Rous, *the elder*

1579-1659

TEXT: *Meditations of Instruction* (London, 1616); *STC* 21342. The full title is useful for explaining the peculiar form of these resolves: *Meditations of Instruction, of Exhortation, of Reproofe: indeavouring the edification and reparation of the house of God.* This is a pudgy duodecimo volume containing eighty-seven numbered meditations, several of them in multiple parts. No author's name appears on the title page; the dedicatory epistle is signed only "F. R." The compound meditations are numbers 57 (eight parts), 59 (two parts), and 73 (ten parts; the longest one). Number 67, undivided, is also long. I have preserved Rous's numberings and have supplied headings drawn from his alphabetical "Table of all the Meditations" which appears at the end of the little volume. In his collective folio volume, *Treatises and Meditations* (London, 1657), the present collection of resolves is reprinted (pp. 488–608) and their number increased to 113.

Rous was an Oxford B.A., a seriously learned and pious man of puritan persuasion, strongly anti-Catholic. He was also an important member of Parliament (1625–1657) and the author of numerous other books. (See the long and important entry in the *Dictionary of National Biography.*) With Rous, whether the meditation—or resolve—be long or short, it commonly closes in a sermonlike exhortation to a course of action consonant with the conclusions suggested by the first part. His formula is not "The situation is thus-and-so . . . *I will* therefore . . . " but "The situation is . . . *let us* therefore . . . ." Though not differing perceptibly in length, form, or piety, the resolves of Rous offer a greater maturity of style and more vigor of imagery than most.

MEDITATIONS OF INSTRUCTION, OF EXHORTATION, OF REPROOFE

XXVI. *The benefite of Adversitie*[1]

If every thing bee desirable according to the benefit thereof, then either prosperitie or adversity may be loved, and neither determinately hated or condemned. For either is very profitable to a man, and most commonly, adversitie. Let us therefore cease to despise it in others, or impatiently to beare it in our selves, since adversitie hath whipt many to heaven, when prosperity hath coached[2] more to hell. Let us leave off, with children onely to desire pleasant things, and growne into men in Christ, let us desire wholesome things.[3] It is better in good sadnesse to be saved, then in good fellowship to be damned.[4]

XLVII. *Man is to learn of Beasts*[5]

The obedience of insensible and brute creatures unto the will of God is a great checke and reproofe unto the disobedience of man. Man is the chiefest of creatures, and they the lowest, yet doe they as farre exceede him in obedience, as he doth them in naturall eminence. The will of God is a straight and fixed line, to which all things created by the same will should so fit and fashion themselves that they should not bowe from it in any degree. This doe the baser things, steadfastly following the imprinted light and law[6] of their first creation. So the storke and swallow know[7] their appointed times, the oxe knowes his owner, and the asse his master's crib;[8] the sea moveth in a setled and unmooving course; the starres fit their many changes to a steadie rule, answerable to the will of him that never changeth. But man that had a burning lampe,[9] even a fountaine of light in his soule (whereas brute beasts have but a light determined and certaine; and livelesse things have no light of reason, but an orderly influence and mooving power fixed into them) this reasonable man is wholly gone astray from his rule, and not onely runneth from it but against it. Thus is he farre worse then things worse then himself, and openly shewes that he hath fallen and not they. What now remaines, but that as this abased lord of creatures hath beene checked and reprooved by the creatures his vassals, so he should also bee instructed by them? Therefore O thou man goe willingly hereafter to the oxe and asse to learne thy duty. There is in them, as in the asse of Balaam, that which may instruct thee. Be ashamed of thy corruption and fall, but bee not ashamed by any thing not falne to bring thy selfe back to the place from whence thou fellest: when thou seest creatures obedient to thee, thence know that obedience is also due to God from thee, who is infinitely more above thee, then thou above them. When thou seest mutuall love betweene creatures of one kinde, learne thence charitie to thy owne kind. In sum, when thou seest any creature continuing the steady and appointed course of his kinde, call thereby to minde that there is a certaine and appointed course to thee also, wherein thou shouldest as certainly satisfie the will of thy Creator, who requireth a conformitie of all things in their place and order, and the chiefest of the chiefest.

LVI. *How to use the world*

A main cause of much of the griefe and folly of men is this: that men resolve to make something of this world. They raise great plots upon it, and intend to bring it into a method;[10] and out of things so ordered to draw some great happines and contentment. But God hath resolved the contrary: to make nothing of the world, but to turne it into vanity of vanities. He hath set it forth as a thing to be shaken, to be remooved, to resolve with the lost fire,[11] and only to be a schole and nurcery[12] for the next world. Therefore doth hee suffer things in this world of vanity to run without difference, yea often without present justice, and often to perish, to be overthrowne and to undergoe great desolations. Now man's mind being prepared to receive comfort from the world fitted unto it selfe, and God's minde beeing to let the world run into many changes, destructions, and finally unto vanity it self, it must needs bee that men oftentimes have their purposes crossed by the purpose of God, and their courses overthrowen by the overruling destiny of God.[13] One hath gotten him a good wife, a good house, and a good demeanes,[14] and is, as they call it, well setled to live; he taketh comfort in the course which hee is entring into, and he hath bespoken his heart to bee merry and rejoyce. But behold, suddenly the disease of the world layes hold on his estate, on him or his wife; and then the plot is mard, the joy is lost, for the foundation therof is overthrowne.[15] Then what weeping, what wayling, what sorrow and breaking of hearts? Hope is turned into griefe, and the more the hope was, the more is the griefe. But the only way to prevent this is that the purpose of man agree to the purpose of God, and accordingly that man expect no more from the world then God alloweth the world to give. Therefore let him perswade himselfe, that whatsoever part of this world he hath gotten into his use, that part is subject to the law of the whole, which is bound under change, perishing, and vanity. And consequently let him expect no other certainty from it, then such as may be from a state of uncertainty. If he have a house well fitted, a wife well conditioned, a large demeanes, beautifull and towardly children; let him know his house may burne, his wife may die, his land may bee taken from him by publike or private enemies; his children may by sicknesse put on ashes for beautie[16] and become the children of death, yea of Belial.[17] Let him therefore build his hopes on these things, as men use to build scaffolds for spectacles, even with a certaine expectation of taking downe when the spectacle is ended. Let him use the world as if he used it not, or as readie not to use it, because the forme of the world passeth away. When God's providence calles, we must looke for their departure; and if thus expected to depart, they fall from us ripe, and are not pulled from us as greene; but if not expected, they depart as things glewde to the hart, which teares away some of the heart at parting. Thus not using this world as a place of certainty and rest (which it is not) yet let us use it as a nurcery and schoole for heaven, which it is. Let us learne here of the Spirit, of the word, of the sacraments, of affliction, and even of the generall condition of the world it selfe. For since the world is so full of miserie, incertainty, and vanity, it teacheth us to set our affections on another world, even that continuing citie[18] which is above, heavenly Jerusalem, where is stability, perpetuity, and glory incomprehensible. Let us pray, let us strive in this world to be fitted, to be trimmed, for that world, as a bride[19] for the wedding-chamber, though through a thousand changes, a thousand crosses; for if wee become inwardly faire, the King of heaven will have pleasure in our beauty; we shall be crowned with a crowne of joy immarcessible,[20] we shall be filled with the glory of God, and the blessednesse of his presence, which is perfit[21] happinesse.

LXIII. *The Divel in the last times most to be resisted*

The divel usually raiseth temptations out of the state which is present, and therefore though wee bee past one danger, into a calme and quietnesse, yet even then looke that out of that calme also some tentation will arise. He is more cunningly and industriously mischievous, then his schooler the Papist:[22] one treason being past[23] wee may not thinke it the last, but one among the rest, and so looke for his fellowes; if we have scaped, we must pray, hope, and endeavour to scape againe. Our life is a warfare,[24] which is not a single battaile, but a continuance of many. If the devil have lost, he is the more angrie for loosing, and surely in this last time of the world as hee is more cholericke and fierce then ever, so is he more cunning. He hath man at his fingers' ends, and this his increased knowledge, hee sets on worke by an increased malice, desiring because his time is short,[25] to get in breadth what he cannot in length. It concernes us therefore proportionably to increase our resistance; and if wee meane to overcome, by prayer, watchfulnesse, and industry, so to advance our selves in the power of Christ, that we may overmatch the power of Satan; that the house of David growing stronger, and the house of Saul weaker, the kingdome of Christ the sonne of David may bee throughly and firmely established in us, and we in it.

LXX. *The use of the Gospell*

The divel's preaching is cleare contrary to God's. God beginneth with the Law, and endeth with the Gospell; but the divell begins with the Gospel, and ends in the Law. God saith, When ye eate ye shall die; yet to man being dead giveth Christ to restore him. The divel saith, ye shall not die at all; yet when man (by his temptation being become mortall) should be restored by Christ, he goes about to kill that Christ which was to be the life of them, whom he had promised that they should not die at all. So continually before we sinne he saith to every one of us, God is mercifull, and Christ is a reconciliation for all our sinnes; but after wee have sinned, he saith, whosoever sinneth[26] is not borne of God; the soule that sinnes[27] shall die. And to them that sinne after grace received: there remaines no more sacrifice for sinne, but a fearefull looking for of judgement.[28] But we must cure our selves by contraries.[29] Therefore let us[30] still use God's kinde of preaching to our selves; which is contrary to Satan's. Before we sinne let us set the whole Law, even the terror of God before us, to affright us from sinne; and having sinned, let us carry the yoke of the Law untill we be truly humbled for our sinnes. But after due humiliation, let us take hold on the Gospell; which to all penitent Christians, is the true and rightfull successour of the Law.

LXXV: *Against spirituall pride*

Silly and foolish is the pride that any man takes in his service toward God. For first, the whole man being from God, wee can give him out of man nothing but his own. Againe, the whole man being due to God, there can returne no good thing from man to God, but what is his due. Thirdly, it is God's free choise, that vouchsafeth to use thy service, who refuseth the imploiment of many men, excellent in naturall abilities. Certainly, we have seene many such of great hope turned into earth, before any, or small use of them. God Al-sufficient, who can raise up servants of stones, thus often sheweth that men have need of God and his choise, to doe him any good service; but hee needeth not them. Therefore let us rather thanke God, then boast before him, if he imploy us in his service. Let us with humilitie readily performe it, as to that great Lord, who hath refused infinite better, to be served by us; and whom therefore to serve is a happines and priviledge of ours from him, not a benefit of ours to him.

NOTES

1. Resolve XXVI: With this resolve, compare Stafford, note 39. 2. *coached:* carried in a comfortable vehicle, a coach. 3. *with children . . . wholesome things:* Behind this lie Paul's words, 1 Corinthians 13:11: "When I was a child, I spoke like a child, I thought like a child, I reasoned like a child; when I became a man, I gave up childish ways" (*RSV*). 4. *in good fellowship . . . damned:* "To go to hell in good company" was proverbial; compare Tilley, *Proverbs,* H409. 5. Resolve XLVII: Rous takes his cue from various passages of the Scriptures; compare Numbers 22:30 or Proverbs 6:6. 6. *imprinted light and law:* instinct. 7. *storke and swallow know:* Which is why the swallows return to Capistrano—on schedule. Rous is speaking, of course, of the regular seasonal flights of migratory birds at large. 8. *oxe knowes . . . crib:* Isaiah 1:3. 9. *a burning lampe:* I.e., reason. 10. *bring it into a method:* regulate it according to their own desires.

11. *the lost fire:* I have preserved the reading of the original, though I

suspect that the word should be *last.*   12. *schole and nurcery:* The theory
that this life is a mere trying-ground or testing-place for a life hereafter
is fundamental to Christian doctrine. See below, note 22.   13. *their
purposes . . . destiny of God:* Compare the familiar saying of Thomas à
Kempis, "Man proposes, but God disposes" (*Imitatio Christi,* chapt. 1,
sect. xix).   14. *a good demeanes:* demesne (collectively, estate).   15. *he
taketh comfort . . . overthrowne:* Back of this passage lies the lesson taught
in Jesus' parable, Luke 12:15–20   16. *ashes for beautie:* This reverses
the order of Isaiah 61:3.   17. *children of . . . Belial:* I.e., wicked ones.
The calamities described recall those of Job.   18. *that continuing citie:*
Compare Hebrews 13:14.   19. *as a bride:* Compare John's vision of the
heavenly Jerusalem, Revelation 21:2.   20. *joy immarcessible:* I.e., im-
marcescible (Latin, *immarcescibilis*), immortal, imperishable; compare
1 Peter 1:4.

21. *perfit:* perfect.   22. *his schooler the Papist:* Rous's anti-Ro-
manism is showing here.   23. *One treason being past:* Probably a reference (which zealous Protestants never ceased to make) to the allegedly
Jesuit-inspired Gunpowder Plot of 1605.   24. *Our life is a warfare:* It
would be difficult to guess the origin of this venerable metaphor; but let
Paul speak for all when he tells us to "fight the good fight of the faith"
(1 Timothy 6:12), or, in 1 Corinthians 16:13, "Watch you, stand fast
in the faith, quit you like men: be strong" (KJV).   25. *his time is short:*
Compare Revelation 20.7.   26. *whosoever sinneth: Compare* 1 John
3:9–10.   27. *the soule that sinnes:* Ezekiel 18:20.   28. *And to them . . .
judgement:* Compare Ezekiel 18:24.   29. *So continually . . . by contraries:* Compare Tuvill, resolve XXIX.   30. *Let us:* Rous's hortatory
plural endings lift his resolve pattern from the merely personal resolution to the level of an envisaged communal procedure.

Richard Brathwait

⁕

1588-1673

TEXT: *Essaies upon the five senses, with a pithie one upon Detraction. Continued with sundry Christian Resolves, full of passion and devotion, purposely composed for the zealously-disposed* (London, 1620); *STC* 3566. Characteristically, both for Brathwait and, for the time, this small octavo (144 pp.) contains essays (pp. 1–85), resolves (pp. 87–114), and characters (pp. 119–42). A second edition of the work appeared in 1635, in which the "essays" are augmented by half a dozen pieces. This second edition was reprinted in *Archaica* (London, 1815) by Sir Samuel Egerton Brydges. The most complete study of Brathwait, unfortunately containing but small attention to *Essaies upon the Five Senses*, remains that by Matthew W. Black, *Richard Brathwait: An Account of His Life and Works* (Philadelphia, 1928).

The long-lived Richard Brathwait (1588–1673), a voluminous general and popularizing author and country gentleman, left untouched few of the literary genres popular in his time. He was educated at Oxford, Cambridge, and Gray's Inn—the last providing him with the legal knowledge which made him, in his later years, an able administrator and public official in his native Westmorland. Although he wrote under a number of pseudonyms, an adequate record of his publications can be traced in the *STC* (Nos. 3553–3591) and in Wing (B4256–4278A). As a literary jack-of-all-trades, it was perhaps inevitable that he should try his hand at resolves; and it should be noted to his credit that even before Feltham had fixed that label upon this kind of writing, Brathwait was already calling his exercises by the name that has come down to posterity.

Brathwait's resolves begin in a sort of formless brevity which lacks the epigrammatic turn of those in Joseph Hall's collection, by which he was probably influenced; but as he continues to write, the average length grows, and a number of his resolves clearly fit into the standard pattern. If they do not quite meet the title-page promise of "passion and devotion," they are at least conventionally pious. Wordplay, alliteration, repetition, balanced and parallel

constructions are tediously abundant. The individual resolves
are neither numbered nor given titles. For such of the longer and
firmer ones as are here included, I have supplied headings.

ESSAIES UPON THE FIVE SENSES

[Confiteor]

I offered before the sacrifice of my teares; now remaines the prose-
cution of my resolves: that as the first were symbols and signalls
of my conversion and contrition, so the latter might be persuasive
motives of my firmer resolution. Dry be those teares of repentance, which are not seconded by a zealous continuance; sith the
perfection of vertue is perseverance;[1] and fruitlesse is that zeale,
which like the seede in the parable, is either by the thornie cares of
the world choaked, by the heat of persecution parched, or by the
stonie impenitencie and obduracie withered: I will therefore by
the power of him that made me, so forme my resolution, that I
may finde a comfortable friend in the day of my dissolution; so
shall the howre of my death be my convoy to life, my exit a conduct to a more glorious *intrat*,[2] my farewell on earth to my welfare in heaven; reaping for what I sowed in teares, in a plenteous
harvest of joyes.[3] Thus therefore I addresse my resolves, which I
wish may be with like fervor received, as they were composed, min-
istring no lesse matter of consolation to the devout reader, then
they did of mortification to the penitent author.

[Brevities]

I resolve to fix mine eye (more intentively) upon my image,
that my forme may put me in minde of my former.[4]

I have conversed too long with the world: I will fall from
discourse to contemplation; from talking with the world, to con-
template him that made the world.

I will no longer put my candle under a bushell, shrowding
my soule's lustre with my bodie's cover, but will display the eminence of the one, by the baseness of the other.

The most precious things have ever the most pernicious keepers; which I found too true, when I made my bodie my soule's guardian: I will henceforth esteeme more highly of such a treasure, than to commit it to the trust of a traytor.

[Reckonings][5]

I have wondred at the strict accounts betwixt man and man, while man the image of his Creator,[6] forgets his accounts due to God by man: I resolve therefore to make the evening the summer up of the day and morning; that my daily memorandums may direct me in my reckoning, when I shall come to be accomptant for my dispensing.

[The Repentant Sinner]

It grieves mee when I call to minde, how those many howres of vanitie, which did once delight me, shall be produced as so many witnesses, to condemne me; yet am I cheered[7] with this resolve, that He, who moved me to this remorce for my sin, will not suffer me to make relapse into sin, nor will pronounce the judgement of death on me for my former sin.

[Deeds, Not Words]

I have heard many call this life a pilgrimage;[8] yet did they live in it, as if it had bin the sole hope of their inheritance: I resolve therefore to take in hand the active part, and leave the discursive; doe before I speake, practise mortification before I prattle of it: so shall my discourse be powerfull, subsisting in the worke not word, not externall or for fashion, but in essence and operation.

[Wise and Foolish Virgins]

I have oftentimes entred into discourse with my selfe, making the scope thereof *venite et abite:*[9] I contemplated withall, the happinesse of those five virgins received,[10] the miserie of those five rejected: reasoning with my selfe what this should meane; and I found that no entry was admitted, where the oyle of grace was not infused, and that the heavenly bridegroome will be by us watchfully attended, ere we be by him gloriously received. I resolved, therefore, to prepare a wedding garment to adorne me, a lampe full of oyle to lighten me, and a trustie friend to direct me; the garment of humilitie, the oyle of charitie, and my friendly conscience within me.

[The Sun Also Rises]

I have collected that there is a reward for the good, as revenge for the wicked, after this life; because the "Sunne shineth aswell on the wicked as the good in this life."[11] I have resolved, therefore, that as the temporary sunne cheeres mee with his heate, so to dispose of my actions, that by his operation which workes in mee, I may bee exalted by the Sunne of righteousnesse, being made pertaker of his glory.

[The Workman's Hire]

Making ech day an abstract of my life, I finde by bitter experience (yet hopefull repentance) that I have spent my morning in wantonnesse; now my resolve is, to redeme my morning idling with my mid-dayes labouring, that I may receive my penny[12] in the evening.

[*Respice finem*]

Hee that seeks to prevent that which cannot be avoyded, flies into Adam's grove to sconce himselfe from God's judgment:[13] I finde this approved, when I labour to be exempted from the stroke of death, which can by no meanes be prevented, whose doome as it is certaine, so is his date uncertaine; knocke he will, but at what time I know not: I will therefore so set all things in order before he come, that he may finde me provided when he comes. I would be loth to be taken napping, I will therefore so addresse my selfe every houre, that I may cheerfully embrace death in my last houre; receiving him not with feare, as a guest that will be of necessitie harboured, but with a friendly wellcome, as one, by whom I shall be to a secure harbour conducted. Death, as he is importunate, so is he imminent; fearefull to the rich, but cheerefull to the poore: for affliction breeds a loathing in living, an accomplished content in dying; knowing that there is an end of miserie[14] apportioned by death, which was not granted to man during life. I wish so to live, that my life may be an argument that I did live; sith life without employment [15] (the essence of man's life) hath more affinitie with death than life.

NOTES

1. *perfection of vertue is perseverance:* Compare Joseph Hall, *Works* (1625), p. 670: "Perfection is the child of Time." 2. *intrat:* entrance; literally, "he enters." Note the "witty" wordplay in "farewell . . . welfare." 3. *sowed in teares . . . joyes:* Compare Psalm 126: 5–6. 4. *image . . . forme . . . former:* Brathwait has in mind Genesis 1:27. 5. [*Reckonings*]: This brief resolve is a veritable farrago of bookkeeper's language. 6. *image of his Creator:* Genesis 1:27. 7. *yet am I cheered:* On the repentant sinner, see Ezekiel 18:20–24; also Rous, note 27. 8. *life a pilgrimage:* A popular metaphor from antiquity onward; compare Erasmus, *Adagia,* "Peregrinatio quaedam est vita." It is the essence of Homer's *Odyssey;* has its medieval great exemplar in Guillaume de Deguilleville's *Pèlerinage de vie humaine;* and a more recent representative in Bunyan's *Pilgrim's Progress.* 9. *venite et abite:* commands, "come and go." 10. *virgins received:* Jesus' parable of the wise (prepared) and foolish (unprepared) virgins invited to a wedding feast; see Matthew 25:7–12.

11. *"sunne shineth . . . in this life":* Compare Ecclesiastes 9:2; Matthew 5:45. 12. *receive my penny:* Compare Matthew 20:8. The reference is to one of the parables of Jesus. 13. *Adam's grove . . . judgment:* Compare Genesis 3:9. *Sconce* means to "shelter" or "protect." 14. *an end of miserie:* Compare *Faerie Queene,* I, ix, 47: "Death is the end of woes." 15. *life without employment:* This sounds proverbial but I have not traced it.

Owen Feltham

1604?-1668

TEXT: *Resolves. A Duple Century. Y^e 3^d Edition* (London, 1628/29); *STC* 10758. The first form of this work was entered in the Stationers' Register 26 May 1623, and the first edition, undated, (*STC* 10755) has been customarily assigned to that year. A second part, or "century," was printed in 1628 (*STC* 10757.8); and in 1628/29, in the third edition (our text; *STC* 10758) and thereafter the two parts were issued together as "A Duple Century"—with the order of the parts, however, reversed. In this third edition the original second "century" occupies pages 1–315; the original first "century," pages 323–448. The earlier resolves, in other words, are considerably shorter than the ones written later. The first edition (first "century" only) was in duodecimo; the "Duple Century" editions of 1628, 1629, 1631, 1634, 1636, 1647 were all in quarto; and there were folio editions, with a reprint of Feltham's *Brief Character of the Low Countries* and with added poems and letters, in 1661, 1670, 1677, 1696. The Resolves had reached a twelfth (?) edition by 1709, and there have been various reprints since. The book is thus easily the most popularly successful representative of its genre.

Owen Feltham (Owin Felltham on the engraved title page of the first edition), 1604?–1668, is the prince of resolve writers; and his *Resolves,* as a minor masterpiece of seventeenth-century English literature, is the only representative of the form to be remembered and treasured today. The date and place of his birth are not certainly known, though there seems more reason for placing the former at 1604 (?) than at 1602(?), as was formerly done (e.g., by the writer of the *DNB* article). It has been conjectured that he was born at Mutford, Suffolk. If he received all, or part, of his education at either university, no record remains. Probably during the mid- or later 1620s he visited the Netherlands on a three-weeks' tour, a visit which supplied him with the lively observations in his *Brief Character of the Low Countries.* This work, after circulating for some years in manuscript and in pirated editions, was not published with the author's blessing until 1652. At some time during mid-life he became chaplain-secretary-steward to the Earls of Thomond, overseeing their estate in Northamptonshire and continuing in their service until his death. Other incidental facts concerning his life and family—neither particularly interesting or important—can be read in the unpublished dissertation of Donald Cornu, *A Biography and Bibliography of Owen Feltham* (Seattle, Wash., 1928), which, though now supplemented by a few scattered details, is still the prime authority on the subject.

In his epistle "To the Reader" (sig. A4) Feltham excuses himself, as being no scholar, for not citing his sources. These, he says, should be brought in occasionally, casually, not sought out and laboriously searched for—"especially in Essay, which of all writing, is the nearest to a running Discourse." He continues: "What you finde heere, if you please, like: But remember alwaies, to censure a Resolve in the middle, is to give your Judgement a possibility of erring. If you ask why I writ them? 'Twas because I lov'd my Study. If, why I publish them? Know, that having no other meanes to shew myselfe to the World, so well, I chose this, not to boast, but because I would not deceive." Elsewhere, in a prefatory "To the Peruser," Feltham plays a slightly different tune concerning his reasons for writing and publishing his book: "I writ it without incouragement from another; and as I writ it, I send it abroad. Rare, I know it is not: *Honest,* I am sure it is: Though thou findest not to admire, thou maist to like. What I aime at in it, I confesse hath most respect to my selfe; That I might out of my owne Schoole take a lesson, and should serve mee for my whole *Pilgrimage.* . . . Reade all, and use thy mindes libertie; how thy suffrage falls, I weigh not: For it was not so much to please others, as to profit my selfe" (sig. Y).

Feltham's title page was not the first to carry the term *resolve* to describe this class of writings, though he first made it popular But even he was not wholly satisfied with it. In the separate title page to the first edition (1628) of the second "century" the pieces are called "Resolves or, Excogitations." We have already seen him referring to his productions as "Essays." And the reader will observe that in the first selection, a sort of model for the genre, Feltham writes not "Of Resolves" but "Of Resolution." This hesitancy over the proper designation was not resolved in his century.

James Cumming, who published in 1806 a jumbled edition of

the *Resolves,* saw in Feltham's "matter" his most valuable element, declaring that his language was "a consideration of inferior importance." Times and tastes change, however; and a modern reader might very well find the "matter" less attractive than some of the fascinating neologisms and word-manipulations of the *Resolves,* particularly the Latinizings, several of which the *OED* cites as the earliest (or only) occurrence. This aspect of the *Resolves* deserves a full study.

Feltham's tone is essentially ethical and religious. In this third edition, the first "century" (which, remember, was written second) ends with the motto *Omnia Deo;* the second "century" here (which was the original publication) ends with a two-page prayer, *Deo Authoris votum.* Feltham himself considered his early resolves, written when he was but eighteen, less satisfactory than his later ones. And indeed they are a veritable Dead Sea of piety, unrelieved by the humane touches and vigorous language of the later resolves. From the likeness of themes, correspondence of illustrations, style, and manner of presentation, there is much to suggest that Feltham could have been "inspired" to write his *Resolves* by reading Tuvill's *Essays* (1608; 1609) and *Christian Purposes and Resolutions* (1611, 1622); for it is here, in the early attempts, that Feltham's resolves most nearly resemble the *Christian Purposes* in theme, in length of statement, and in their wholly "divine" tone. Certainly there is little to suggest Bacon as his model. Classical, or even secular, allusions are few. In his critique of the elaborate rhetoric of some preachers—Was he thinking of such baroque practitioners as Andrewes and Donne?—Feltham plumps for the curt and clear period. But when that topic is not foremost in his attention, he can be guilty of some pretty long-winded and complicated concoctions of his own. Though his later resolves are not devoid of religious feeling and teaching, they are at the same time more secular in tone than those of the other resolvers. In him the resolve comes nearest to the familiar essay, as Bush observes; and this may be the reason for posterity's remembering him while the rest are forgotten.

R. B. Daniels says of him, "In general his remarks are practical and not without Christian charity, his style straightforward and sententious." C. V. Wedgewood calls the *Resolves* "an unusually charming collection of personal thoughts, easily and gracefully ex-

pressed." And Bush, again, speaks of his "clipped, pointed sen-
tentiousness." Even so, posterity has not been overgenerous with
him. *The Cambridge History of English Literature* gives him only
passing notice among the essayists. Chambers's *Cyclopedia of
English Literature* (1: 578–79) has a brief entry for Feltham, the
only resolves writer quoted; and the same situation prevails in
almost all the leading modern histories and anthologies of seventeenth-century prose. Exception should here be made for Douglas Bush, whose *English Literature in the Earlier Seventeenth
Century, 1600–1660* (Oxford; 2d ed., 1962) gives a few pages of
notice and provides the fullest current bibliography. There is also
a brief essay, "Resolves of a Royalist," in R. B. Daniels's *Some
Seventeenth-Century Worthies* (Chapel Hill, N. C., 1940); and a
study by Jean Robertson in *Modern Language Review,* 39 (April
1944): 108–15, points out the extent to which the *Resolves* were
plagiarized by other writers during Feltham's century. *The Poems
of Owen Felltham* (University Park, Pa., 1973) have been edited
by Ted-Larry Pebworth and Claude J. Summers. But among all
the various discussions, one looks in vain for any consideration of
the resolve as a separate literary genre.

RESOLVES: A DUPLE CENTURY

from the FIRST CENTURIE
II. *Of Resolution*

What a skeyne of ruffled silke is the uncomposed man? Every
thing that but offers to even him intangles him more, as if, while
you unbend him one way, he warpeth worse the other. He cannot
but meet with variety of occasions, and every one of these in-
twine him in a deeper trouble. His waies are strew'd with briers,
and he bustles himselfe into his owne confusion. Like a partridge
in the net, he maskes[1] himselfe the more by the anger of his fluttering wing. Certainely, a good resolution is the most fortifying ar-
mour that a discreete man can weare. That can defend him against
all the unwelcome shuffles[2] that the poore rude world puts on him.
Without this, like hot iron, hee hisses at every drop that finds him.
With this, he can be a servant as well as a lord, and have the same

inward pleasantnesse in the quakes and shakes of Fortune that he carries in her softest smiles. I confesse, biting penury has too strong talons for mud-wall'd man to graspe withall. Nature is importunate for necessities and will try all the engines of her wit and power, rather then suffer her owne destruction. But where she hath so much as shee may live, resolution is the onely marshall that can keepe her in a decent order. That which puts the loose woven minde into a whirling tempest is by the resolute seene, slighted, laughed at—with as much honour, more quiet, more safety. The world has nothing in it worthy a man's serious anger. The best way to perish discontentments is either not to see them or convert them to a dimpling mirth. How endlesse will be the quarrels of a chollericke man and the contentments of him that is resolved to turne indignities into things to make sport withall? 'Tis, sure, nothing but experience and collected judgement can make a man doe this; but when he has brought himself unto it, how infinite shall he finde his case? It was Zantippe's observation,[3] that she ever found Socrates returne with the same countenance that hee went abroad withall. Lucan can tell us,[4]

> *Fortunaque perdat*
> *Opposita virtute, minas.*

> All Fortune's threats be lost,
> Where vertue does oppose.

I wish no man so spiritlesse as to let all abuses presse the dulnesse of a willing shoulder; but I wish him an able discretion to discerne which are fit to be stirred in, and those to prosecute for no other end but to shew the injury was more to vertue and deare Nature's justice then to himselfe. Every man should be equitie's champion, because it is that eternall pillar wheron the world is founded. In high and mountain'd fortunes resolution is necessary to insafe us[5] from the thefts and wyles of prosperity, which steale us away, not only from our selves, but vertue; and for the most part, like a long peace, softly delivers us into impoverishing warre. In the wane of fortune, resolution is likewise necessary to guard us from the discontents that usually assaile the poore, dejected man. For all the world will beat the man whom fortune buffets. And unlesse by this he can turne off the blowes, he shall be sure

to feele the greatest burthen in his owne sad minde. A wise man
makes a trouble lesse by fortitude; but to a foole, 'tis heavier by his
stooping too't. I would faine bring my selfe to that passe that I
might not make my happinesse depend on another's judgement.
But as I would never doe any thing unhonestly, so I would never
feare the immateriall winde of censure when it is done. He that
steeres by that gale is ever in danger of wracke. Honesty is a warrant of farre more safety then fame.[6] I will never be asham'd of
that which beares her seale, as knowing 'tis onely pride's being in
fashion that hath put honest humility out of countenance. As for
the crackers of the braine, and tongue-squibs,[7] they will dye alone
if I shall not revive them. The best way to have them forgotten
by others is first to forget them my selfe. This will keepe my selfe
in quiet, and, by a noble not-caring, arrow[8] the intender's bosome,
who will ever fret most when he finds his designes most frustrate.
Yet, in all these, I will something respect custome, because she
is magnified in that world wherein I am one. But when she parts
from just reason, I shall rather displease her by parting then offend in her company. I would have all men set up their rest[9] for
all things that this world can yeeld, yet so as they build upon a
surer foundation then themselves; otherwise, that which should
have been their foundation will surely crosse them; and that is,
God.

XX. *Of Preaching*

The excesse which is in the defect of preaching ha's made the
pulpit slighted: I meane, the much bad oratory we finde it guilty
of. 'Tis a wonder to me, how men can preach so little and so long
—so long a time, and so little matter—as if they thought to please
by the inculcation of their vaine tautologies.[10] I see no reason that
so high a princesse as divinity is should be presented to the people
in the sordid rags of the tongue; nor that he which speakes from
the Father of Languages should deliver his embassage in an ill
one. A man can never speake too well, where he speakes not too
obscure.[11] Long and distended clauses are both tedious to the eare
and difficult for their retaining. A sentence wel couch'd takes both
the sense and the understanding. I love not those cart-rope speeches
that are longer then the memorie of man can fathome. I see not
but that divinity, put into apt significants, might ravish as well

as poetry. The waighty lines men finde upon the stage, I am per-swaded, have beene the lures to draw away the pulpit's followers. We complaine of drowzinesse at a sermon, when a play of a doubled length leades us on still with alacrity. But the fault is not all in our selves. If wee saw divinitie acted, the gesture and varietie would as much invigilate.[12] But it is too high to bee personated by humanity. The stage feeds both the eare and the eye; and through his latter sense, the soule drinks deeper draughts. Things acted possesse us more and are, too, more retaineable then the passable[13] tones of the tongue. Besides, heere we meete with more composed language—the *Dulcia sermonis*[14] moulded into curious phrase. Though 'tis to bee lamented such wits are not set to the right tune and consorted to divinitie; who, without doubt, well deckt, will cast a farre more radient lustre then those obscene scrurrilities that the stage presents us with, though oe'd and spangled[15] in their gawdiest tyre. At a sermon well dress'd, what understander can have a motion to sleepe? Divinitie well ordered casts forth a baite which angles the soule into the eare; and how can that cloze when such a guest sits in it? There are sermons but of baser mettall which leadd the eyes[16] to slumber. And should we heare a contin-ued oration upon such a subject as the stage treates on in such words as wee heare some sermons, I am confident it would not only be farre more tedious, but nauseous and contemptfull. The most advantage they have of other places is in their good lives and actions.[17] For 'tis certaine Cicero and Roscius[18] are most com-pleate when they both make but one man. He answered well that, after often asking, said still that action was the chiefest part of an orator.[19] Surely, the oration is most powerfull where the tongue is diffusive and speakes in a native decencie, even in every limme. A good orator should pierce the eare, allure the eye, and invade the minde of his hearer. And this is Seneca's opinion:[20] fit words are better than fine ones. I like not those that are in-judiciously made; but such as be expressively significant, that leade the minde to something beside the naked terme. And he that speakes thus must not looke to speake thus every day. A kemb'd oration[21] will cost both sweate and the rubbing of the braine. And kemb'd I wish it—not frizzled, nor curl'd: divinite should not lasciviate. Un-wormewooded jests[22] I like well; but they are fitter for the taverne then the majestie of a temple. Christ taught the people with authoritie. Gravitie becomes the pulpit. Demosthenes confest[23] he became an orator by spending more oyle then wine. This is too fluid an element to beget substantials. Wit procur'd by wine is, for the most part, like the sparklings in the cup when 'tis filling: they briske it[24] for a moment, but dye immediately. I admire the valour of some men that before their studies dare ascend the pulpit; and do there take more paines then they have done in their library. But having done this, I wonder not that they there spend sometimes three houres but to weary the people into sleepe. And this makes some such fugitive divines that, like cowards, they run away from their text. Words are not all, nor matter is not all, nor gesture; yet, together, they are. 'Tis much moving in an orator when the soule seemes to speake, as well as the tongue. Saint Augustine sayes Tully was admired more for his tongue then his minde; Aristotle more for his minde then his tongue; but Plato for both.[25] And surely nothing deckes an oration more then a judgement able well to conceive and utter. I know, God hath chosen by weak things, to confound the wise;[26] yet I see not but in all times a washed language hath much prevailed. And even the Scriptures, though I know not the Hebrew yet I beleeve they are penn'd in a tongue of deepe expression, wherein almost every word hath a metaphoricall sense, which does illustrate by some allusion. How politicall is Moses in his Pentateuch? How philosophicall Job? How massie and sententious is Salomon in his Proverbs? how quaint and flamingly-amorous in the Canticles? how grave and solemne in his Ecclesiastes? that in the world, there is not such another dissection of the world as it. How were the Jewes astonied at Christ's doctrine? How eloquent a pleader is Paul at the bar? in disputation how subtile? And he that reads the Fathers, shall finde them as if written with a crisped pen. Nor is it such a fault as some would make it, now and then, to let a philosopher or a poet come in and waite and give a trencher[27] at this banquet. Saint Paul is president[28] for it. I wish no man to bee too darke and full of shaddow. There is a way to be pleasingly-plaine, and some have found it. Nor wish I any man to a totall neglect of his hearers. Some stomackes rise at sweet-meates. Hee prodigals a mine of excellencie that lavishes a terse oration to an apron'd auditory.[29] Mercury himselfe may move his tongue in vaine if hee has none to heare him but a non-intelligent. They that speake to

children assume a pretty lisping. Birds are caught by the counterfeit of their owne shrill notes. There is a magicke in the tongue
can charme the wilde man's motions. Eloquence is a bridle wherewith a wise man rides the monster of the world, the People. Hee
that heares ha's onely those affections that thy tongue will give
him.

> Thou maist give smiles, or teares, which joies do blot:
> Or wrath to judges, which themselves have not.[30]

You may see it in Lucan's words:[31]

> *Flet, si flere jubes, gaudet, gaudere coactus:*
> *Et te dante, capit judex quum non habet iram.*

I grieve that any thing so excellent as divinitie is should fall
into a sluttish handling. Sure, though other interposures[32] doe
eclipse her, yet this is a principall. I never yet knew a good tongue
that wanted eares to heare it. I will honour her, in her plaine
trimme: but I will wish to meete her in her gracefull jewels:
not that they give addition to her goodnesse, but that shee is
more perswasive in working on the soule it meetes with. When
I meet with worth which I cannot over-love, I can well endure
that art which is a meanes to heighten liking. Confections that are
cordiall are not the worse but the better for being guilded.

XXVII. *Of curiositie in knowledge*[33]

Nothing wraps a man in such a myst of errors as his owne curi-
ositie in searching things beyond him.[34] How happily doe they
live that know nothing but what is necessary? Our knowledge doth
but shew us our ignorance. Our most studious scrutiny is but
a discovery of what we cannot know. We see the effect but cannot
guesse at the cause. Learning is like a river whose head, being farre
in the land, is at first rising little and easily viewed; but, still as
you go, it gapeth with a wider banke, not without pleasure and
delightfull winding; while it is on both sides set with trees, and the
beauties of various flowres. But still the further you follow it,
the deeper and the broader 'tis; till at last it inwaves it selfe in the

unfathom'd ocean. There you see more water; but no shore, no end of that liquid, fluid vastnesse. In many things we may sound[35] nature in the shallowes of her revelations. We may trace her to her second causes; but beyond them, we meete with nothing but the puzzle of the soule and the dazle of the mind's dim eyes. While we speake of things that are, that we may dissect and have power and meanes to finde the causes, there is some pleasure, some certaintie. But, when we come to metaphisicks, to long buried antiquity, and to unreveal'd divinity, we are in a sea which is deeper then the short reach of the line of man.[36] Much may be gained by studious inquisition; but more will ever rest, which man cannot discover. I wonder at those that will assume a knowledge of all; they are unwisely ashamed of an ignorance which is not disgracive; 'tis no shame for man not to know that, which is not in his possibility. We fill the world with cruell brawles in the obstinate defence of that whereof we might with more honour confesse our selves to be ignorant. One will tell[37] us our Saviour's disputations among the doctors. Another, what became of Moses' body. A third, in what place Paradise stood: and where is locall hell. Some will know heaven as perfectly as if they had been hurried about in every spheare—and I thinke they may. Former writers would have the zones inhabitable;[38] we finde them by experience temperate. Saint Augustine would by no meanes indure the Antipodes;[39] we are now of nothing more certaine. Every age both confutes old errors and begets new. Yet still are we more intangled, and the further we goe, the neerer we approach a sunne that blindes us. He that went furthest[40] in these things, we finde ending with a censure of their vanity, their vexation. 'Tis questionable, whether the progresse of learning hath done more hurt or good, whether the schooles have not made more questions then they have decided. Where have we such peaceable and flourishing common-wealths[41] as we have found among those which have not so much as had the knowledge of letters? Surely, these fruitlesse and aenigmatique questions are bones the Divell hath cast among us, that while we strive for a vaine conquest in these toyes we forget the prize we should run for. The husbandman that looks not[42] beyond the plough and the sythe is in much more quiet then the divided braine of the statist or the scholler. Who will not approove the judgement of our moderne epigrammatists![43]

Iudice me, soli semperque perinde beati,
Sunt, quicunque sciunt omnia, quique nihil.

If I may judge, they onely happy show,
Which doe or nothing, or else all things know.

In things whereof I may be certaine I will labour to be instructed.
But when I come where reason loseth her selfe, I will be content
with retiring admiration. Why should I racke my braines for unprofitable impossibilities? Though I cannot know how much is
hid, I may soone judge what may be discovered.

XXXV. *That Sinne is more craftie then violent*

Before wee sinne, the Devill shewes his policie; when we have
sinned, his baseness. Hee makes us first revile our Father, and
then steps up to witnesse how we have blasphem'd. He begs the
rod and the wand for faults which had not beene but for his owne
inticement. Hee was never such a souldier as he is a politician:
hee blowes up more by one mine then he can kill by tenne assaults.
He prevailes most by treaty and facetious[44] wayes. Presents and
parlies winne him more then the cruell wound or the dragge of
the compulsive hand. All sinne is rather subtill then valiant. The
Devill is a coward and will, with thy resisting, fly thee; nor dare
hee shew himselfe in a noted good man's company; if he does, he
comes in seeming-vertues and the garments of belyed truth. Vice
stands abash't at the glorious majestie of a good confirmed soule.
Cato's presence stopt the practices of the Romans' brutish Floralia's.[45] Satan beganne first with hesitations and his sly-couch'd
oratorie;[46] and ever since hee continues in wiles, in stratagems,
and the fetches of a toyling braine, rather perswading us to sinne
then urging us. And when we have done it, he seldome lets us
see our folly til we be plunged in some deepe extremity; then he
writes it in capitall letters, and carries it as a pageant[47] at a show,
before us. What could have made David so heartlesse when Absalom rose against him but the guilt of his then presented sinnes?
when he fled, and wept, and fled againe? It appeares a wonder that
Shimei should raile[48] a king to his face; and, unpunisht, brave
him and his host of souldiers, casting stones and spitting taunts,
while he stood incompassed with his Nobles. Surely, it had beene

impossible but that David was full of the horror of his sinnes and knew he repeated truth; though in that hee acted but the Devil's part, ignobly to insult over a man in misery. Calamity, in the sight of worthinesse, prompts the hand and opens the purse to relieve. 'Tis a Hellish disposition that watcheth how to give a blow to the man that is already reeling. When wee are in danger hee galls us with what we have done; and on our sicke beds shewes us all our sinnes in multiplying glasses. He first drawes us into hated treason; and when we are taken and brought to the barre he is both our accuser[49] and condemning witnesse. His close policy[50] is now turn'd to declared basenesse. Nor is it a wonder, for unworthinesse is ever the end of unhonest deceit; yet sure this coozenage is the more condemned, for that it is so ruinous and so easie. Who is it but may coozen, if he minds[51] to be a villaine? How poore and inhumane was the craft of Cleomines[52] that, concluding a league for seven daies, in the night assaulted the secure enemy, alledging the nights were not excluded from slaughter. Nothing is so like to Satan as a knave furnisht with dishonest fraud: the best way to avoid him is to disdaine the league. I will rather labour for valour, at the first, to resist him then after yeelding, to endevour a flight. Nor can I well tell which I should most hate, the Devill or his Machiavill.[53] For though the Devill bee the more secret enemie, yet the base politician is the more familiar and is, indeed, but a Devill in hose and doublet, fram'd so, in an acquainted shape, to advantage his deceit the more.

XXIII. *Of Truth, and bitternesse in jests*

It is not good for a man to be too tart in his jests. Bitternesse is for serious potions, not for healths of merriment and the jollities of a mirthfull feast. An offensive man is the Devil's bellowes, wherewith hee blowes up contentions and jarres. But among all passages of this nature, I finde none more galling then an offensive truth. For thereby we runne into two great errors. One is, wee childe that in a loose laughter which should be grave and savour both of love and pitty. So we rub him with a poyson'd oyle, which spreads the more for being put in such a fleeting supplenesse. The other is, wee descend to particulars and by that meanes draw the whole company to witnesse his disgrace we break it on. The souldier is not noble, that makes himselfe sport with the wounds of his owne companion. Whosoever will jest should be like him that flourishes at a show: hee may turne his weapon any way but not aime more at one then at another. In this case, things like truth are better then truth it selfe. Nor is it lesse ill then unsafe to fling about this wormewood of the braine: some noses are too tender to endure the strength of the smell. And though there be many, like tyled houses, that can admit a falling sparke, unwarm'd; yet some, againe, are cover'd with such light, dry straw that with the least touch they will kindle and flame about your troubled eares. And when the house is on fire, it is no disputing with how small a matter it came; it will quickly proceede to mischiefe. *Exitus irae, furor:*[54] anger is but a step from rage; and that is wilde fire which will not be extinguished. I know wise men are not too nimble at an injury. For, as with fire, the light stuffe and rubbish kindles sooner then the solid and more compacted; so anger sooner inflames a foole,[55] then a man composed in his resolutions. But we are not sure alwaies to meete discreet ones; nor can we hope it, while wee our selves are otherwise in giving the occasion. Fooles are the greater number; wise men are like timber-trees in a wood, heere and there one. And though they bee most acceptable to men wise like themselves, yet have they never more need of wisedome then when they converse with the ringing elboes;[56] who, like corrupt ayre, require many antidotes to keepe us from being infected. But when wee grow bitter to a wise man, wee are then worst; for hee sees further into the disgrace, and is able to harme us more. Laughter should dimple the cheeke, not furrow the brow into ruggednesse. The birth is then prodigious[57] when mischiefe is the childe of mirth. All should have libertie to laugh at a jest; but if it throwes a disgrace upon one, like the cracke of a string it makes a stop in the musicke. Flouts we may see proceed from an inward contempt; and there is nothing cuts deeper in a generous mind then scorne. Nature at first makes us all equall; wee are differenc'd but by accident, and outwards. And I thinke 'tis a jealousie that shee hath infus'd in man for the maintaining of her owne honour against external causes. And though all have not wit to reject the arrow; yet most have memorie to retaine the offence; which they will be content to owe a while, that they may repay it both with more advantage and ease. 'Tis but an unhappy wit that stirs up enemies against the owner. A man may spit out his friend from his tongue;[58] or laugh him into an enemie. Gall in mirth is an ill mixture; and sometimes truth is bitternesse. I would wish any man to bee pleasingly merry; but let him beware he bring not truth on the stage, like a wanton, with an edged weapon.[59]

XLVII. *Of Death* [60]

There is no spectacle more profitable, or more terrible, then the sight of a dying man, when he lyes expiring his soule on his death-bed: to see how the ancient society of the body and the soule is divelled; and yet to see how they struggle at the parting, being in some doubt what shal become of them after. The spirits shrink inward and retire to the anguisht heart as if, like sons prest from an indulgent father, they would come for a sad *Vale*[61] from that which was their life's maintainer; while that in the meane time pants with afrighting pangs, and the hands and feet, being the most remote from it, are by degrees encoldned to a fashionable clay, as if death crept in at the nailes and by an insensible surprize suffocated the inviron'd heart. To see how the mind would faine utter it selfe, when the organes of the voyce are so debillitated that it cannot. To see how the eye settles to a fixed dimnesse, which a little before was swift as the shootes of lightning, nimbler then the thought, and bright as the polisht diamond; and in which this miracle was more eminent then in any of the other parts: that it, being a materiall earthly body, should yet be conveyed with quicker motion then the revolutions of an indefinite soule, so suddenly bringing the object to conceits that one would thinke the apprehension of the heart were seated in the eye it selfe. To see all his friends, like conduts,[62] dropping teares about him, while hee neither knowes his wants, nor they his cure. Nay, even the physician, whose whole life is nothing but a study and practice to continue the lives of others and who is the anatomist of generall nature, is now as one that gazes at a comet, which he can reach with nothing but his eye alone. To see the countenance (through which there shin'd a lovely majesty, even to the captiving of admiring soules) now altered to a frightfull palenesse and the terrours of a gastly looke. To thinke how that which commanded a family, nay perhaps a kingdome, and kept all in awe with the moving of

a spongie tongue, is now become a thing so full of horrour that
children feare to see it and must now therefore bee transmitted
from all these inchanting blandishments to the darke and hideous
grave; where, in stead of shaking of the golden Scepter, it now
lyes imprison'd but in five foot of lead and is become a nest of
wormes, a lumpe of filth, a box of pallid putrefaction. There is
even the difference of two severall worlds, betwixt a king enamel'd
with his robes and jewels, sitting in his chaire of adored state,[63]
and his condition in his bed of earth, which hath made him but a
case of crawlers; and yet all this change without the losse of any
visible substantiall, since all the limbes remaine as they were,
without the least signe either of dislocation or diminution. From
hence 'tis, I thinke, Scaliger defines death[64] to bee the cessation
of the soule's functions: as if it were rather a restraint, then a
missive ill.[65] And if any thing at all bee wanting, 'tis onely colour,
motion, heate, and emptie ayre. Though indeed, if wee consider
this dissolution, man by death is absolutely divided and disman'd.
That grosse object which is left to the spectators' eyes is now
onely a composure but of the two baser elements, water and earth;
and now it is these two only that seeme to make the body, while
the two purer, fire and ayre, are wing'd away, as being more fit for
the compact of an elementall and ascentive soule.[66] When thou
shalt see all these things happen to one whose conversation had
indeared him to thee; when thou shalt see the body put on death's
sad and ashy countenance in the dead age of night, when silent
darknesse does incompasse the dimme light of thy glimmering
taper, and thou hearest a solemne bell toled to tell the world of it;
which now, as it were, with this sound, is struck into a dumbe
attention—tell me if thou canst then find a thought of thine de-
voting thee to pleasure and the fugitable[67] toyes of life? O what a
bubble,[68] what a puffe, what but a winke of life is man! And with
what a general swallow death still gapes upon the generall world!
When Hadrian askt Secundus[69] what death was hee answered in
these severall truths: *It is a sleepe eternall; the bodie's dissolution;*
the rich man's feare; the poore man's wish; an event inevitable;
an uncertaine journey; a thiefe that steales away man; sleepe's
father; life's flight; the departure of the living; and the resolution
of all. Who may not from such sights and thoughts as these learne,

if he will, both humility and loftinesse? the one, to vilifie the body, which must once perish in a stenchfull nastinesse; the other to advance the soule, which lives heere but for a higher and more heavenly ascension? As I would not care for too much indulgiating[70] of the flesh, which I must one day yeeld to the wormes, so I would ever bee studious for such actions as may appeare the issues of a noble and diviner soule.

LV. *Of Logicke*

Nothing hath spoyl'd truth more then the invention of logicke. It hath found out so many distinctions that it inwraps reason in a mist of doubts. 'Tis reason drawne into too fine a thread, tying up truth in a twist of words which, being hard to unloose, carry her away as a prisoner. 'Tis a net to intangle her, or an art instructing you how to tell a reasonable lye. When Diogenes heard Zeno, with subtle arguments, proving that there was no motion, he suddenly starts up and walkes. Zeno askes the cause? Sayes he againe, *I but confute your reasons.*[71] Like an overcurious workeman, it hath sought to make truth so excellent that it hath marr'd it. Vives sayes hee doubts not but the Devill did invent it;[72] it teaches to oppose the truth and to be falsely obstinate, so cunningly delighting to put her to the worse by deceit. As a conceitist,[73] it hath laide on so many colours that the counterfeit is more various then the patterne. It gives us so many "likes" that we know not which is the same. Truth in logicall arguments is like a prince in a masque, where are so many other presented in the same attire that wee know not which is hee. And as wee know there is but one prince, so wee know there is but one truth; yet by reason of the masque, judgement is distracted and deceived. There might be a double reason why the Areopagitae banish't Stilpo[74] for proving by his sophistry Minerva was no goddesse. One, to shew their dislike to the art; another, that it was not fit to suffer one to wanton with the gods. Sure, howsoever men might first invent it for the helpe of truth, it hath prov'd but a helpe to wrangle, and a thing to set the minde at jarre in it selfe; and doing nothing but confound conceit, it growes a toy to laugh at. Let me give you but one of our owne:[75]

Nascitur in tenebras animal, puer, inscius, infans
Conferat Oxonium se, cito fiet homo.

A thing borne blinde, a child, and foolish too,
Shall be made man, if it to Oxford goe.

Aristarchus his quip[76] may fall upon our times: Heretofore (sayes
he) there were but seven wise men; and now it is hard to find the
number of fooles. For every man will be a sophister, and then hee
thinkes hee's wise; though I doubt some will never be so but by
the helpe of logicke. Nature her selfe makes every man a logician;
they that brought in the art have presented us with one that hath
over-acted her, and something strain'd her beyond her genuine
plainenesse. But I speake this of logicke at large, for the pure art
is an excellency. Since all is in use, 'tis good to retaine it, that we
may make it defend us against it selfe. There is no way to secure
a mine but to countermine;[77] otherwise, like the art of memory, I
thinke it spoyles the naturall. How can it bee otherwise, when the
invention of man shall strive with the investigation of supreme
nature? In matters of religion, I will make faith my meanes to as-
certaine, though not comprehend them; for other matters, I will
thinke simple nature the best reason and naked reason the best
logicke. It may helpe me to strip off doubts, but I would not have
it helpe to make them.

LIX. *Of Opinion*[78]

Not any earthly pleasure is so essentially full in it selfe, but that
even bare conceit may returne it much distastfull. The world is
wholly set upon the gad and waving: meere opinion is the genius
and, as it were, the foundation of all temporall happinesse. How
often doe wee see men pleased with contraries? as if they parted
the fights and frayes of nature, every one maintaining the faction
which he liketh. One delighteth in mirth and the friskings of an
ayery soule; another findeth something amiable in the saddest
looke of melancholy.[79] This man loves the free and open-handed;
that, the grasped fist and frugall sparing. I go to the market and see
one buying, another selling; both are exercised in things different,
yet either pleas'd with his owne; when I, standing by, thinke it my
happinesse that I doe not either of these. And in all these, nothing

frames content so much as imagination. Opinion is the shop of pleasures, where all humane felicities are forged and receive their birth. Nor is their end unlike their beginning; for, as they are begot out of an ayerie phantasme, so they dye in a fume and disperse into nothing. Even those things which in them carry a shew of reason, and wherein (if truth bee judge) wee may discerne solidity, are made placide[20] or disgustfull, as fond opinion catches them. Opinion guides all our passions and affections, or at least begets them. It makes us love, and hate, and hope, and feare, and vary; for, every thing wee light upon is as we apprehend[81] it. And though we know it bee nothing but an uncertaine prejudgement of the minde, mis-informed by the outward sences, yet wee see it can worke wonders. It hath untongued some on the sudden, and from some hath snatcht their naturall abilities. Like lightening, it can strike the childe in the wombe and kill it ere 'tis worlded; when the mother shall remaine unhurt. It can cast a man into speedy diseases and can as soone recure him. I have knowne some but conceiting they have taken a potion have found the operation, as if they had taken it indeed. If we believe Plinie,[82] it can change the sex: who reports himselfe to have seene it; and the running Montaigne[83] speakes of such another. Nor is it onely thus powerfull when the object of the minde is at home in our selves, but also when it lights on things abroad, and apart. Opinion makes women faire and men lovely. Opinion makes men wise, valiant, rich, nay any thing. And whatsoever it can doe on one side to please and flatter us, it can doe the same on the other side to molest and grieve us. As if every man had a severall seeming truth in his soule which, if hee followes, can for a time render him either happy or miserable. Heere lies all the difference: if wee light on things but seeming, our felicitie fades; if on things certaine and eternall, it continues. 'Tis sure, we should bring all opinions to reason and true judgement, there to receive their doome of admittance or ejection; but even that, by the former is often seduced, and the grounds that wee follow are erronious and false. I will never therefore wonder much at any man that I see swayed with particular affections, to things sublunary. There are not more objects of the minde, then dispositions.[84] Many things I may love, that I can yeeld no reason for; or if I doe, perhaps opinion makes me coine that for a reason which another will not assent unto. How vaine then are those that, assuming a liberty to themselves, would yet tie all men to their tenents?[85] Conjuring all men to the trace of their steps; when, it may be, what is truth to them is error to another as wise. I like not men that will be gods and have their judgements absolute. If I have liberty to hold things as my minde informes me, let me never desire to take away the like from another. If faire arguments may perswade, I shall with quiet shew what grounds doe leade me. If those cannot satisfie, I thinke I may wish any man to satisfie his owne conscience. For that, I suppose, will beare him out in the things that it justly approves.[86] Why should any man be violent for that which is more diverse then the wandring judgements of the hurrying vulgar, more changing then the love of inconstant women, more multivarious then the sports and playes of nature, which are every minute fluctuous[87] and returning in their new varieties? The best guide that I would chuse is the reason of an honest man, which I take to be a right-informed conscience. And as for bookes, which many rely on, they shall be to me as discourses but of private men, that must bee judged by religion and reason; so not to tie me, unlesse these and my conscience joyne in the consent[88] with them.

LXXI. *Of Poets and Poetrie*[89]

Surely he was a little wanton with his leisure that first invented poetrie. 'Tis but a play which makes words dance in the evennesse of a cadencie;[90] yet without doubt, being a harmonie, it is neerer to the minde then prose, for that it selfe is a harmonie in height. But the words being rather the drossy part, conceit I take to be the principall. And here though it disgresseth from truth it flies above her, making her more rare by giving curious rayment to her nakednesse.[91] The name the Grecians gave the men that wrote thus shew'd how much they honour'd it: they coll'd them *makers*.[92] And had some of them had power to put their conceits in act, how neere would they have come to Deitie? And for the vertues of men, they rest not on the bare demeanour, but slide into imagination; so, proposing things above us, they kindle the reader to wonder and imitation. And certainly poets that write thus Plato never meant to banish.[93] His owne practice shewes, hee excluded

not all. He was content to heare Antimachus[94] recite his poem,
when all the Herd had left him; and hee himselfe wrote both
tragaedies and other pieces.[95] Perhaps he found them a little too
busie with his gods; and he, being the first that made philosophie
divine and rationall, was modest in his owne beginnings. Another
name they had of honour, too, and that was *vates*. Nor know I
how to distinguish betweene the prophets and poets of Israel.
What is Jeremie's Lamentation, but a kinde of Saphicke elegie?
David's Psalmes are not onely poems but songs, snatches, and raptures of a flaming spirit. And this indeed I observe to the honour of
poets: I never found them covetous or scrapingly-base. The Jewes
had not two such kings in all their catalogue as Salomon and his
father,[96] poets both. There is a largenesse in their soules beyond
the narrownesse of other men; and why may we not then thinke
this may imbrace more, both of heaven and God? I cannot but
conjecture this to bee the reason that they, most of them, are
poore: they finde their mindes so solaced with their owne flights
that they neglect the studie of growing rich; and this, I confesse
againe, I thinke, turnes them to vice and unmanly courses. Besides,
they are for the most part mighty lovers of their pallates; and this
is knowne an impoverisher. Antigonus, in the tented field, found
Antagoras cooking of a conger[97] himselfe. And they all are friends
to the grape and liquor—though I think many more out of a ductible[98] nature, and their love to pleasant companie, then their
affection to the juice alone. They are all of free natures; and are
the truest definition of that philosopher's man, which gives him
animall risibile.[99] Their grossest fault is that you may conclude
them sensuall; yet this does not touch them all. I know there be
some riming fooles; but what have they to doe with poetrie?
When Salust would tell us[100] that Sempronia's wit was not ill,
sayes hee, "Potuit versus facere, et jocum movere:" shee could
make a verse and breake a jest. Something there is in it more then
ordinarie, in that it is all in such measured language as may bee
marr'd by reading. I laugh heartily at Philoxenus his jest,[101] who,
passing by and hearing some masons mis-sensing his lines (with
their ignorant sawing of them), falls to breaking their bricks
amaine. They aske the cause, and hee replyes, they spoile his
worke, and he theirs. Certainely, a worthy poet is so farre from

beeing a foole, that there is some wit required in him that shall
bee able to reade him well; and without the true accent, numbred
poetrie[102] does lose of the glosse. It was a speech becomming an able
poet[103] of our owne, when a lord read his verses crookedly, and
he beseecht his lordship not to murder him in his owne lines. He
that speakes false Latine breakes Priscian's head;[104] but he that
repeates a verse ill puts Homer out of joynt. One thing commends
it beyond oratorie: it ever complieth to the sharpest judgements.[105]
Hee is the best orator that pleaseth all, even the crowd and
clownes. But poetrie would bee poore that they should all approve
of. If the learned and judicious like it, let the throng bray.
These, when 'tis best, will like it the least. So, they contemne what
they understand not; and the neglected poet falls by want. Calphurnius makes one complaine the misfortune.

> *Frange puer calamos, et inanes desere Musas:*
> *Et potius glandes, rubicundaque collige corna.*
> *Duc ad mulctra greges, et lac venale per urbem*
> *Non tacitus porta: Quid enim tibi fistula reddet,*
> *Quo tutere famem? certe, mea carmina nemo*
> *Praeter ab his scopulis ventosa remurmurat Eccho.*[106]

> Boy, breake thy pipes, leave, leave thy fruitlesse Muse:
> Rather the mast, and blood-red cornill[107] chuse.
> Goe leade thy flockes to milking; sell and cry
> Milke through the citie; what can learning buy,
> To keepe backe hunger? None my verses minde,
> But Eccho babbling from these rockes and winde.

Two things are commonly blamed in poetrie: nay, you take away
that, if them: and these are lyes and flatterie. But I have told them
in the worst words, for 'tis onely to the shallow insight that they
appeare thus. Truth may dwell more cleerely in an allegorie, or a
moral'd fable, than in a bare narration. And for flatterie, no man
will take poetrie litterall; since, in commendations, it rather
shewes what men should bee[108] then what they are. If this were not,
it would appeare uncomely. But we all know hyperbole's in poetrie
doe beare a decency—nay, a grace—along with them. The greatest
danger that I finde in it is that it wantons the blood[109] and im-

agination; as carrying a man in too high a delight. To prevent
these, let the wise poet strive to bee modest in his lines. First, that
hee dash not the gods; next, that hee injure not chastity, nor corrupt the eare with lasciviousnesse. When these are declined, I
thinke a grave poem the deepest kinde of writing.[110] It wings the
soule up higher then the slacked pace of prose. Flashes that doe
follow the cup, I feare me, are too spritely to be solid: they run
smartly upon the loose for a distance or two; but then being foule,
they give in and tyre. I confesse, I love the sober muse, and fasting;
from the other, matter cannot come so cleere but that it will bee
misted with the fumes of wine. Long poetry some cannot bee
friends withall; and, indeed, it palles upon the reading. The wit-
tiest poets have beene all short, and changing soone their subject;
as Horace, Martiall, Juvenall, Seneca, and the two comaedians.[111]
Poetry should be rather like a coranto[112]—short and nimbly-loftie
—than a dull lesson, of a day long. Nor can it but bee deadish, if
distended: for, when 'tis right, it centers conceit and takes but
the spirit of things; and therefore foolish poesie is of all writing
the most ridiculous. When a goose dances, and a foole versifies,
there is sport alike. Hee is twice an asse that is a riming one. He is
something the lesse unwise that is unwise but in prose. If the
subject bee historie, or contexted fable,[113] then I hold it better put
in prose or blanks;[114] for ordinarie discourse never shewes so well
in meeter as in the straine that it may seeme to be spoken in: the
commendation is, to doe it to the life; nor is this any other then
poetry in prose. Surely, though the world thinke not so, hee is
happy to himselfe that can play the Poet. Hee shall vent his passions by his pen and ease his heart of their weight; and hee shall
often raise himselfe a joy in his raptures which no man can perceive but he. Sure, Ovid found a pleasure in't, even when hee
writ his *Tristia*.[115] It gently delivers the mind of distempers and
workes the thoughts to a sweetnesse in their searching conceit. I
would not love it for a profession, and I would not want it for a
recreation. I can make my selfe harmelesse, nay, amending mirth
with it; while I should perhaps be trying of a worse pastime. And
this I beleeve in it further: unlesse conversation corrupts his easi-
nesse, it lifts a man to noblenesse; and is never in any rightly, but
it makes him of a royall and capacious soule.

from the SECOND CENTURIE

IV. *Of Lyes and Untruths*

I finde, to him that the tale is told, beliefe onely makes the difference betwixt a truth and lyes; for a lye beleeved is true, and truth
uncredited, a lye—unlesse he can carry his probation in's pocket, or
more readily at his tongue's end. For as he that tels a smooth lye
is judged to speake truth, till some step forth to contradict his
utterance; so hee that tels an unlikely truth is thought to broach
a lye, unlesse he can produce convincing reason to prove it; onely
the guilt or justice of the thing rests in the knowing conscience
of the relator. In the hearer I cannot account it a fault: 'tis easie
to be deceived in miracles, in probabilities; albeit the judgement
that passeth on them bee both honest, wise, apprehensive,[116] and
cleere. In the teller, justly; if it be a lye, there needs no text to
confute it; if it seeme so, and he cannot purge it, discretion were
better silent. I will tell no lies, lest I be false to my selfe; no improb-
able truths, lest I seeme so to others. If I heare any man report
wonders, what I know I may haply speake; what I but thinke shall
rest with my selfe; I may as well bee too suspicious as over-
credulous.

XV. *How to establish a troubled Government*

A man that would establish[117] a troubled government must first
vanquish all his foes. Factious heads must be higher by a pole
then their bodies.[118] For how will the folds be quiet while yet
among them there be some wolves? Hee that would rule over many
must fight with many, and conquer; and be sure either to cut off
those that raise up tumults, or by a majesticke awe to keepe them
in a strict subjection. Slacknesse and connivence are the ruines
of unsettled kingdomes. My passions and affections are the chief
disturbers of my civill state: what peace can I expect within mee
while these rebels rest unovercome? If they get a head, my kingdome is divided so it cannot stand.[119] Separations are the wounds
of a crowne, whereby (neglected) it will bleed to death. Them will
I strive to subdue. If I cut them not off, I will yet restraine them.
'Tis no cruelty to deny a traytor liberty. I will have them be my
subjects, not my prince; they shall serve me, and I will sway them.
If it cannot be without much striving, I am content with a hard

combate, that I may have a happy raigne. 'Tis better I endure a short skirmish then a long siege;[120] having once wonne the field, I will hope to keepe it.

XX. *Of Reputation: Or, A good Name*

To have every man speake well of mee is impossible; because, howsoever I carry my selfe, some cynicke will bark at my course. Who can scape the lash of censure? If I should be vicious and profuse,[121] I should be loved of some—but not the best, not the good. If I should, camelion-like, change my selfe to every object, if I were not extraordinarie wearie[122] I might soone counterfet some man's humour false, and that would bane my drift. For both to vertue and to vice, is flatterie a false glasse, making the one seeme greater, the other lesse then it is; and if it lights on a noble discretion, it is ever so unhappy as to beget the ruine of it selfe. But imagine I could doe it with such exactnesse that even the eye of Lyncaeus[123] could not espy it; yet when one should commend me for one thing and another for the contrarie, what would the world thinke of mee that could thus in one bee hot and cold? Should I not be censured as a tymorist?[124] Yes surely, and that justly; neither could it but bee just with God, at last, to unmaske my flatterie and unrippe my folly in the view of the multitude. Private sinnes are punisht with a publike shame. A supposed honest man found lewd is hated as a growne monster discovered by the blabbe of time. Sinne is a concealed fire, that even in darknesse will so worke as to bewray it selfe. If I live vertuously and with pietie, the world will hate mee as a separatist,[125] and my reputation will be traduced by the ignominious aspersion of malevolent tongues. To bee good is now thought too neere a way to contempt:[126] that which the Ancients admired, we laugh at. A good honest man is a foole. What then? shall I to please a man displease a Christian, I had rather live hated for goodnesse then be loved for vice. He does better that pleaseth one good man then hee that contents a thousand bad ones. I would, if it could bee, please all; yet I would win their loves with honesty: otherwise, let their hate wound me rather then their love embrace. What care I for his friendship that affects not vertue? Having his hate, hee may hurt me outwardly; but enjoying his love, I will justly suspect my soule of some ill.[127] For if his affection be toward me, 'tis sure because hee sees something in me that pleaseth himselfe; but while he sees every thing unlike him, how is't possible I should be beloved of him? since diversities breed nothing but dis-union, and sweet congruity is the mother of love.

XXVII. *A Rule in reading Authors* [128]

Some men reade authors as our gentlemen use flowers, onely for delight and smell, to please their fancie, and refine their tongue. Others like the bee extract onely the honey, the wholesome precepts; and this alone they beare away, leaving the rest, as little worth, of small value. In reading I will care for both, though for the last, most. The one serves to instruct the minde, and other fits her to tell what she hath learned; pitty it is they should be divided. He that hath worth in him and cannot expresse it is a chest keeping a rich jewell, and the key lost. Concealing goodnesse is vice; vertue is better by being communicated. A good stile with wholesome matter is a faire woman with a vertuous soule, which attracts the eyes of all; the good man thinkes chastly, and loves her beauty for her vertue, which he still thinkes more faire for dwelling in so faire an out-side. The vicious man hath lustfull thoughts, and he would for her beauty faine destroy her vertue; but comming to sollicite his purpose, findes such divine lectures from her angel's tongue, and those deliver'd with so sweet a pleasing modesty, that he thinkes vertue is dissecting her soule to him, to ravish man with a beauty which he dream'd not of. So he could now curse himselfe for desiring that lewdly, which he hath learn'd since onely to admire and reverence; thus he goes away better that came with an intent to be worse. Quaint phrases on a good subject are baits to make an ill man vertuous; how many vile men, seeking these, have found themselves convertites? I may refine my speech without harme, but I will indevour more to reforme my life. 'Tis a good grace both of oratory or the penne to speake or write proper; but that is the best worke, where the Graces and the Muses meet.[129]

XXXVIII. *The Misery of being Old and Ignorant* [130]

'Tis a capitall misery for a man to be at once both old and ignorant. If he were onely old, and had some knowledge, he might abate the tediousnesse of decrepit age by the divine raptures of contemplation. If he were young, though he knew nothing yet his yeeres would serve him to labour and learne, whereby in the winter of his time hee might beguile the wearinesse of his pillow and chaire. But now his body being withered by the stealing length of his dayes, and his limbes wholly disabled for either motion or exercise, these together with a minde unfurnished of those contenting speculations of admired science cannot but delineate the portraicture of a man wretched. A gray head with a wise minde is a treasurie of grave precepts, experience, and judgement; but foolish old age is a barren vine in autumne or an universitie to study folly in. Every action is a patterne of infirmitie; while his body sits still, he knowes not how to find his minde action; and tell me, if there be any life more irkesome then idlenesse. I have numbered yet but a few dayes, and those I know I have neglected; I am not sure they shall bee more, nor can I promise my head it shall have a snowie haire. What then? Knowledge is not hurtfull, but helpes a good minde; any thing that is laudable, I desire to learne. If I dye to morrow, my life to day shall bee somewhat the sweeter for knowledge; and if my day proove a summer one, it shall not be amisse to have provided something that in the evening of my age may make my mind my companion. Notable was the answer that Antisthenes gave[131] when hee was asked what fruit hee had reaped of all his studies? By them, saith he, I have learned both to live and to talke with my selfe.

C. *Though Resolutions change, yet Vowes should know no Varietie*

Resolutions may often change, sometimes for the better; and the last ever stands firmest. But vowes well made should know no variance; for the first should bee sure without alteration. Hee that violates their performance failes of his dutie, and every breach is a wound to the soule. I will resolve oft, before I vow once; never resolve to vow, but what I may keepe; never vow, but what I both can and will keepe.

NOTES

Oliphant Smeaton, in his Temple Classics edition (1904) of Feltham's *Resolves*, supplies a few notes. Where these are relevant to the present selections, I have occasionally used them, indicating my borrowings by a parenthesized initial (S) at th end of the cited note.
1. *maskes:* I.e., entangles. The *OED* cites this passage from Feltham.
2. *shuffles:* The *OED*, citing this passage, defines *shuffle* as "evasive trick, evasion, subterfuge." 3. *Zantippe's observation:* Xanthippe, the shrewish wife of Socrates; there are numerous references to her in Plutarch and Diogenes Laertius, but I do not find this particular one. Seneca, however, had seen it: see *Moral Essays*, 3 vols. (Loeb), "De Ira," I, 179.
4. *Lucan can tell us:* The lines quoted are from the *Pharsalia*, IX, 569–70.
5. *to insafe us:* to insure, protect; the *OED* cites only this instance from Feltham. 6. *Honesty is a warrant . . . fame:* Feltham's version of "Honesty is the best policy." *Warrant* is a guarantee. 7. *crackers . . . tongue-squibs:* fireworks, noise-makers. 8. *arrow:* Note the force of Feltham's verbal invention. *OED* cites Feltham here as the only instance of this usage. 9. *set up their rest:* A military phrase meaning "to place (and make firm) the support for a firearm." 10. *vaine tautologies:* empty repetitions.

11. *A man . . . to obscure:* Perhaps Feltham is recalling Horace, *Ars poetica*, 25–26, "brevis esse laboro, obscurus fio." 12. *invigilate:* keep awake. 13. *passable:* fleeting, passing. 14. *Dulcia sermonis:* sweets of speech. 15. *oe'd and spangled:* decorated with sequins and other glittering ornaments. 16. *leadd the eyes:* put, as it were, lead upon the eyelids. 17. *good lives and actions:* I preserve the reading of the original, but *lives* should probably be *lines*. 18. *Cicero and Roscius:* The first an orator, the second an actor; their combined functions, Feltham is saying, would have made a "compleate" man. 19. *He answered well . . . orator:* The saying of Demosthenes; compare Cicero *De oratore*, III, lvi, 213; Valerius Maximus, *Dictorum factorumque memorabilium exempla,* VIII, x. 20. *Seneca's opinion:* I have not found this in Seneca.

21. *a kemb'd oration:* "combed," that is, polished and well ordered. 22. *Un-wormewooded jests:* I.e., jests without bitterness. According to Bacon, *Apophthegms,* Number 6, "Pace the fool was not suffered to come at Queen Elizabeth, because of his bitter humour." 23. *Demosthenes confest:* Plutarch, *Parallel Lives,* "Demosthenes," tr. Dryden (Modern Library ed.), p. 1026. 24. *they briske it:* Note again Feltham's innovation in verb-forms; *OED* cites Feltham (but not this passage). 25. *Saint Augustine sayes . . . both:* I have not traced this saying in Augustine's

works. 26. *I know . . . the wise:* 1 Corinthians 1:27. 27. *waite and give a trencher:* I.e., serve up a tray of goodies. 28. *president:* precedent. 29. *terse oration to an apron'd audience:* A finely composed speech to an inappropriate audience, "pearls before swine." 30. *Thou maist give . . . have not:* This translates, loosely, the Latin passage that follows. 31. *Lucan's words:* Not Lucan, but C. Calphurnius Siculus; see J. W. Duff, *A Literary History of Rome* (1960), p. 269. Translate: "If you command weeping, he weeps; constrained to rejoice, he rejoices. And you giving, the judge who had it not shows wrath." 32. *interposures:* interpositions; *OED* cites this passage of Feltham's as the first occurrence of this word in English. 33. Resolve XXVII: Compare Bacon, *Meditationes Sacrae, De Haeresibus* (S). 34. *Nothing wraps . . . beyond him:* Feltham's thought springs from the two classic maxims: "altum non sapere" and "quae supra nos, nihil ad nos." 35. *we may sound:* take soundings, probe. 36. *short reach . . . line of man:* continuing the figure of the seaman's sounding line. 37. *One will tell:* With these silly concerns of quibbling disputants, compare Tuvill, *Essays,* p. 79. 38. *inhabitable:* I.e., not habitable—an obsolete meaning of the word. 39. *Saint Augustine . . . Antipodes:* "St. Augustine considered that such an idea as that the Antipodes could exist was only fit for fools and madmen" (S). Smeaton, however, gives no indication of source (*City of God,* Book XVI, chapt. 9). 40. *He that went furthest:* Solomon, presumably; certainly "vanity" and "vexation" are the burden of his(?) song in Ecclesiastes.

41. *flourishing common-wealths:* I do not know what illiterate commonwealths Feltham has in mind. Not even the Spartans were without letters. 42. *husbandman that looks not:* The age-old contrast between the innocent pleasures of the country, supposedly, and the sophisticated worries of the town—Horace's country mouse and city mouse (*Satires,* II, vi). Or, as expressed in Virgil (*Georgics,* II, 458), "O fortunatos nimium, sua si bona norint Agricolas!" 43. *our moderne epigrammatists:* The lines quoted are from the *Epigrammatum* of John Owen, 4th ed. (London, 1612), Book III, 134. 44. *facetious:* pleasant, urbane (Lat., *facetus*). 45. *Cato's presence . . . Floralia's:* This effect of the austere Cato's presence is recorded in Valerius Maximus, *Dict. fact. memorab.,* II, v; compare also Tuvill, *Essays,* p. 100. 46. *Satan beganne . . . oratorie:* "Cf. Genesis iii.1; also Milton, *Par. Lost,* B. IX, *ll.* 518–576" (S). 47. *pageant:* Here, something represented by blazoning, as a scene in painted cloth or tapestry, perhaps to be carried as a banner might be. 48. *that Shimei should raile:* For Shimei's cursing of David and throwing stones at him, see 2 Samuel 16:5–14. 49. *our accuser:* See Tuvill, note 35. 50. *close policy:* secret policy.

51. *minds:* intends. 52. *the craft of Cleomines:* This double-dealing

of Cleomenes, however, failed of its objective; compare Plutarch, *Moralia* (tr. Philemon Holland, 1603), p. 459. 53. *the Devill or his Machiavill:* "Nothing is more curious than the horror wherewith the name of Machiavelli was regarded by Englishmen. It was the synonym for every kind of treason and traitorous dealing" (S). 54. *Exitus irae, furor:* "The extremity of wrath is fury (madness)." Compare Horace, *Epistles*, I, ii, 62: "ira furor brevis est." 55. *anger sooner inflames a foole:* Ecclesiastes 7:9, "Be not quick to anger, for anger rests in the bosoms of fools." 56. *the ringing elboes:* A puzzling phrase. I take it to mean, here, "the vulgar many," probably because fools tend to "elbow" wiser men aside. 57. *prodigious:* monstrous. 58. *A man may spit out . . . tongue:* Feltham's animated version of the proverb "Better lose a jest than a friend"; compare Tilley, *Proverbs*, J40. 59. *like a wanton . . . edged weapon:* This adapts the proverbial "It is ill jesting with an edged tool"; compare Tilley, *Proverbs*, J45. 60. Resolve XLVII: With the disturbed and emotional tone of this resolve, contrast the calm, philosophic detachment of Bacon's essay on the same topic.

61. *a sad Vale:* a sad farewell. 62. *conduts:* conduits, pipes, or troughs for carrying flowing water. 63. *chaire of adored state:* throne. 64. *Scaliger defines death:* See Henry Montague, First Earl of Manchester, *Contemplatio Mortis, et immortalitatis* (1631), p. 11. 65. *missive ill:* one that is *sent* (for whatever purpose); *OED* quotes this passage from Feltham. 66. *ascentive soule:* Like fire, the soul was supposed to be inherently of an ascending (aspiring) nature. 67. *fugitable:* fleeting; *OED* records only this passage of Feltham's. 68. *O what a bubble:* Smeaton has a note—his only one for this resolve—referring the reader to "an analogous thought" in Johnson's *Winter:* "Life's a short summer —man a flower / He dies—alas, how soon he dies." With notes like these a man could develop a taste for unannotated texts. 69. *When Hadrian askt Secundus:* See Montague, *Contemplatio Mortis* (1631), p. 11. 70. *indulgiating:* pampering, indulging; passage again cited by *OED*.

71. *When Diogenes heard Zeno . . . reasons:* Compare Diogenes Laertius, *Lives of Eminent Philosophers*, VI, ii, 39 (Loeb). 72. *Vives sayes . . . invent it:* not found. 73. *As a conceitist:* Like an inventor of conceits (i.e., fanciful figures or comparisons); *OED* cites this passage only. 74. *the Areopagitae banish't Stilpo:* I omit Smeaton's unhelpful note on Stilpo—his solitary comment on this resolve. For the argument that led to the action of the Areopagus, see Diogenes Laertius, *Lives of Eminent Philosophers*, "Stilpo," II, 116 (Loeb). 75. *one of our own:* See John Owen, *Epigrammatum*, editio prima (London, 1612), Book III, epig. 45. 76. *Aristarchus his quip:* Two famous Greeks bore this name. I have been unable to find which, if either, is responsible for this quip. 77. *to secure*

a mine . . . countermine: In military tactics, to blow up a mine before it can harm. 78. Resolve LIX: A topic given larger treatment in Barnaby Rich's *Opinion Diefied* (1613). 79. *One delighteth in . . . melancholy:* The contrasting tastes of Milton's "L'Allegro" and "Il Penseroso." 80. *placide:* Used in the original Latin sense (*placidus*), "pleasing." For this usage the *OED* cites only this passage in Feltham.

81. *every thing . . . as we apprehend:* Compare Shakespeare, *Hamlet,* II, ii, 259: "There is nothing either good or bad, but thinking makes it so." 82. *If we beleeve Plinie:* Pliny, *Natural History,* vii, 4. 83. *the running Montaigne:* Montaigne, *Essays,* Book I, chapt. 20, "Of the Force of Imagination," does indeed mention Pliny on this odd subject; but his own account of the sex-change of "Marie/Germaine" is stranger still. 84. *There are not . . . then dispositions:* The Terentian "Quot homines, tot sententiae," "So many heads, so many opinions." 85. *How vaine . . . tenents:* "Cf. Dryden's *Absalom and Achitophel,* Pt. I, *l.* 545" (S). For *tenents* we would now say *tenets.* 86. *If those . . . approoves:* Compare "conscientia mille testes," "a good conscience is worth a thousand witnesses." 87. *multivarious . . . fluctuous:* "variegated" and "flowing" like waves of the sea; not Feltham's inventions but typical of his choice of words. 88. *consent:* consensus. 89. Resolve LXXI: Smeaton offers not a single note on this long and important resolve. 90. *evennesse of a cadencie:* regular rhythm, measure.

91. *disgresseth from truth . . . nakednesse:* Compare Bacon, *Essays,* "Of Truth." To the nakedness of truth, says Bacon, "A mixture of a *Lie* doth ever adde Pleasure." *Disgresseth:* digresses; the form is frequently used in these resolves. 92. *the Grecians . . . coll'd them makers:* Compare Sir Philip Sidney, *Defence of Poesie.* Feltham's discussion of *vates* which follows and of the Hebrew poets and prophets also reflects Sidney's views. 93. *Plato never meant to banish:* More Sidney; but the basic reference is to a famous passage in the *Republic,* X, iii–viii. 94. *content to heare Antimachus:* Plato is said to have sent Heraclides Ponticus to Colophon to collect the poems of Antimachus; compare *Oxford Classical Dictionary,* 2d ed., art. "Antimachus." 95. *tragaedies and other pieces:* Other "pieces" certainly Plato did write; but if he wrote tragedies, at least of the theatrical variety, they must have been youthful indiscretions and the world has yet to discover them. 96. *his father:* David. 97. *Antigonus . . . found Antagoras . . . conger:* Compare Plutarch, *Moralia* (tr. Holland), p. 419. 98. *ductible:* pliable, easily drawn. 99. *animall risibile:* "an animal capable of laughter"; traditional definition. 100. *When Salust would tell us:* See *The Conspiracy of Catiline,* tr. Heywood (1608), chapt. 8.

101. *Philoxenus his jest:* Diogenes Laertius, *Lives of Eminent Philoso-*

phers, "Arcesilaus," IV, 36. 102. *numbred poetrie:* classical (quantitative) verse. 103. *an able poet:* Not identified. 104. *breakes Priscian's head:* Priscianus was a sixth-century author of *Institutiones grammaticae,* an exhaustive and authoritative Latin grammar. "To break Priscian's head" was proverbial for speaking or writing false Latin. Compare Tilley, *Proverbs,* P595. 105. *complieth to the sharpest judgements:* I.e., it is directed to an audience capable of appreciating and judging it. 106. *Calphurnius . . . remurmurat Eccho:* C. Calphurnius Siculus, *Buccolica* (Paris, 1503), Eclogue IV, lines 23 ff. 107. *blood-red cornill:* one of several cherries or cherrylike fruits. 108. *what men should bee:* The standard justification of such outrageous flattery as was commonly to be found in epideictic poetry. 109. *wantons the blood:* Again, notice Feltham's vigorous molding of language to his own purposes. In this instance, however, he had predecessors. 110. *First, that hee . . . writing:* Exceptions also taken by Plato, *Republic,* II.

111. *the two comaedians:* Plautus and Terence. 112. *coranto:* a lively French dance. 113. *contexted fable:* a tale woven together, well connected; *OED* cites this passage from Feltham. 114. *blanks:* blank verse. 115. *Ovid found . . . Tristia:* Ovid wrote his elegiac *Tristia* while in exile at Tomis on the Black Sea. 116. *apprehensive:* quickly perceptive. 117. *establish:* stabilize. 118. *Factious heads . . . bodies:* Feltham here perhaps refers to the custom of placing the heads of traitors atop poles (or pikes) on London Bridge. 119. *my kingdome . . . cannot stand:* One of the fairly numerous biblical references in this "century" of Feltham's resolves; compare Matthew 12:25. 120. *better . . . siege:* This has all the brevity and wit of proverbial wisdom but appears to be Feltham's own.

121. *profuse:* a liberal party-giver. 122. *wearie:* So in the original text, but probably meant for *wary.* 123. *the eye of Lyncaeus:* In Greek mythology, Lynceus, one of the Argonauts, was extremely keen-sighted. 124. *hot and cold . . . tymorist:* *OED* cites this passage as the only instance of *tymorist* and suggests, hesitantly, that it seems to mean "timist, timeserver." The hot-and-cold figure may refer to the satyr's distrust of the man who, out of the same mouth (symbolizing untrustworthiness), blew hot to warm his hands and cold to cool his broth; see Aesop, *Fables,* "The Man and the Satyr." 125. *as a separatist:* one withdrawn from the official (Anglican) church, a "puritan." 126. *To bee good . . . contempt:* For this Juvenalian sentiment, compare Tuvill, *Essays,* pp. 102–3 and the note to that passage. 127. *but enjoying . . . some ill:* Compare Diogenes Laertius, *Lives of Eminent Philosophers,* "Antisthenes," VI, i, 4: "Once, when he was applauded by rascals, he remarked, 'I am horribly afraid I have done something wrong'" (Loeb). 128. Resolve XXVII:

This resolve is a sort of gloss on the "prodesse aut delectare" of Horace (*Ars poetica*, 333). 129. *Graces and the Muses meet:* A marriage of beauty (delight) and substantial thought (profit). "Omne tulit punctum." 130. Resolve XXXVIII: A remarkable statement from an eighteen-year-old. The neatly managed sententiae sound proverbial without being so. 131. *the answer that Antisthenes gave:* Diogenes Laertius, *Lives of Eminent Philosophers,* "Antisthenes," VI, i, 6.

In John Chetwynd's *Anthologia Historica Containing Fourteen Centuries of Memorable Passages and Remarkable Occurrents* (London, 1674; Wing C3793), there occur some brief anecdotal excerpts from Feltham's *Resolves*—but nothing complete enough to illustrate the resolve pattern.

William Struther

❦

ca. 1578-1633

TEXT: *Christian Observations and Resolutions. Or, the daylie practise of the renewed man, turning all occurrents to spirituall uses,
and these uses to his union with God. I. Centurie. With a Resolution for Death, &c.* Newlie published by Mr William Struther,
Preacher of the Gospel at Edinburgh (Edinburgh, 1628); STC
23367. This is a small octavo in two (three) parts: *Christian Observations . . . I. Centurie,* 290 pp.; *Resolution for Death* (with
separate title page and separate pagination), 78 pp. Like the son-
neteers, the writers of resolves tended to write in "centuries"; the
Folger Library (Harmsworth) copy, which I have used, contains
only the first "centurie"; other copies, according to the *STC,* contain a second "centurie." These I have not seen. A second edition
of the *Christian Observations* appeared in 1629. All Struther's
other publications were sermons *(STC* 23369–23371) or learned
polemics.

William Struther (or Struther*s*), ca. 1578–1633, was in 1629–
1630 one of the Scottish ministers "at the center of the Kingdom"
who most vigorously opposed the introduction into Scotland of the
Anglican Church ceremonies. His career and only noteworthy ac-
tivity are sufficiently described in the title-page designation of
"Preacher of the Gospel at Edinburgh." He is said to have refused
a bishopric and was in the last year of his life named dean of
Edinburgh.

Struther's book is composed of random pious meditations
which only occasionally achieve a recognizable resolve form; all
are brief, sermonlike exhortations to a life of piety. It should be
noticed that a number of Struther's resolves end with the quotation of a verse of scripture. Transferred to the head of the observation, this would emphasize the pulpit connection of these
pieces. The Gospeler "at Edinburgh" is a murky thinker and a
murky writer, whose resolves (if that is what they are to be called
—and his title loudly bespeaks Tuvill) generally work toward
the quotation of a scriptural text or texts that will suggest the
desired course of action. He is included here rather for the

quaintness of his Scottish burr than for any more positive merit.

Struther's sentence pattern is too loose and repetitious, not curt enough to achieve the ideal effect of epigrammatic utterance which marks the style of the best among the resolve writers. With Struther, too much of the garrulous oratory of the extempore preacher still shows through. Though his resolves seldom employ the strict "I-will-therefore" conclusion of the elementary pattern, his own calling of them "Resolutions" and the drift of such argument as they observe would seem to warrant their inclusion in the genre.

CHRISTIAN OBSERVATIONS AND RESOLUTIONS

20. *Short care for a short life*

The workes of the most part of men tell that they thinke not of heaven, or that such a heaven as they minde is on earth: they seeke earthly thinges and compt their happinesse by their obtaining, and their miserie by their want. Riches, honour, fame, pleasure, etc., are the hight of their reach, and that not in a small measure as passengers for the way, but excessively as possessors of their end: no care of another life, because no minde of it. Or, if the thought of heaven bee forced upon them, it is soone banished by the strength of earth-delights.

Their desires are as base as the beasts', and worse, for the beast can doe no more and ought[1] no more; but men are reasonable and called to heaven. They may reckon on many branches with wormes:[2] they come of the earth, live on it, creepe on it, and in end creepe in it, and more wormish than they, being more affected with the dungue of the earth digged out of the bowels of it than with the heaven. What priviledge their body hath in beeing living earth, they loose it in seeking life-lesse earth for their happinesse.

Both doe heere agree: an earthly life, and an earthly spirit, spent in the cares of the earth. But a friend of the life of God lifteth up the renewed spirit to heavenlie things. It cannot be so basely abject as to mynde and glutte[3] the baggage of the earth; but as it is from above, so it is all sette on things above and turneth even the necessar[4] and moderate cares of this life to an heavenlie temper by that reference that it hath in their use to life eternall.

Occasionall errors come in at a side and wrest some part of our course, and, beeing discovered, are easilie remeeded.[5] But this is a fundamentall error, to place our happinesse in the earth and to seeke it therein. It perverteth all the course of their wayes, and the greatest conviction of it is when tyme of amendment is past; when that consuming fire at the last day destroyed[6] all which they have scraped together, they will then see their error.

I thinke it great wisedome to carve our cares according to the things themselves. If eternitie were heere, men's scraping and raking of the earth might seeme reasonable; but since our time in this life is but short at the longest, and shorter possiblie than I know, I will set all mine heart for heaven, and a short life shall have as short a care.

23. *Three faultes with the world, but not with God*

These three things are counted faults in the world, and yet no man needeth to repent him of them: the modest shifting of occasioned honour and riches,[7] the patient disgesting of great wrongs, and the not following of the fashions of the world. Who so are[8] disposed are counted dolts, but that sentence falleth on the judge. The first is counted basnesse of spirit; the second, an evill conscience (he swalloweth injuries so patiently that hee incurreth the suspition of senslesnesse and stupour); and the third, a saucie singularitie.

But such a spirit beareth out that censure upon better grounds: the first commeth of true contentment in God; the second, of a care to keepe himselfe in peace with God; and the third, of a just contemning of the world. True honour followeth the modest shifter of it, and the riches of true contentment are treasured in the heart that hungreth for no more. Hee is truelie content who hath fixed a period to his desires and doeth not so much as loose them to a racklesse wishing of further; and the best way to keepe peace in our soule is not to frette at injuries; and it is a token that hee who dwelleth in us is greater than the world, when we count the world's fashions a witlesse folie.

Hee who is so possessed in his choise securelie indureth that ignorant censure and hath indeede attained the trueth of that which they are seeking imaginarlie:[9] hee seeth that by time they will either applaude him in his course, or else fall short by the way to their greater losse.

If the world can shewe mee where I shall finde it, or what fixed paterne and exampler of good it followeth, with some reason it might exact of mee an imitation; but since it can neither tell, where to finde it selfe, neither hath any paterne but its owne new fangle vanitie, it is shamelesnesse for it to sute, and madnes in mee to give it obedience. It must bee a bad stuffe[10] that keepeth not the colour, and a bad colour that changeth every day. Stuffe and colour of so changeable a stampe agree well together; but the renewed man, dyed with the unchangeable colour of grace, contemneth them both.

I will not render my selfe to that schoole where posed soliditie[11] is counted a vice and newe fangled folies are counted perfection.

34. *Resolutions performed*

Resolution is a good precedent[12] to our actions, but is not the actions themselves. If we dwell on it, wee shall doe nothing commendable: that resolution is as a false conception, that is buried in the birth, and commeth not to execution. If the husbandman shall bee ever preparing his plough, and never teill,[13] he can neither sow nor reape. A weake and staggering resolution is broodie[14] of scruples and findeth matter of stay in it selfe, but so soone as the worke is well begun, then resolution endeth.

There is oft-times more difficultie in resolution than in doing; for in resolution the minde is on many thinges atonce, but in the action it is upon the worke alone. It is rent in diversities and contrarieties in resolving, but trussed up in doing. Many times wee are in torture resolving, but in the action wee finde peace. A solide and masculus[15] resolution giveth us no rest till it put us over in the hand of practise; yea, it resolveth for doing, and turneth all the resolving powers to execution.

These are twinnes of a rype spirit: both to resolve and doe; to doe without resolution is rashnesse, and to resolve without doing is faintnesse. He who doeth without resolution dreameth of none impediment; but hee who resolveth and delayeth execution waiteth upon impediments, and rather than hee lacke them, hee will faine a thousand in his owne fansie. Even fansied difficulties doe terrifie the lazie, as much as reall difficulties doe the wise and diligent. The sluggard sayeth, *There is a lyon in the way, I dare not goe foorth, least I bee killed.* Prov. 26. 13.

37. *A constant dyet of God's Worshippe*

Appetite is a good preparation for meate; so is a zealous affection for the worshippe of God. It is good to have our appointed tymes for spirituall exercises, and to keepe them; but, withall, to strive for the spirituall appetite.

How sweete is that exercise to the soule? wherein our necessitie wakeneth our desire; our desire sharpneth our appetite; and our appetite thrusteth our heart to God, and God pulleth both our heart and our selfe to him. In one instant it is both pressed with sense of miserie and burnt with a desire of God and sweetly allured and drawen by him to himselfe. These are wonderfull actions betweene God and us, and all wrought in us by his Spirit to carie us up to him. Though I tye mee not superstitiouslie to houres of holy exercise, yet religiouslie I will keepe them: these houres are sweete to mee, when God draweth my soul by strong desires and fayth to him. It is pleasant, when either these exercises doe tryst with[16] our desires, or God in them bringeth us to an holy disposition; and great is the fruite of these exercises: thereby our soules even at other times are keeped, if not under the sense, yet under the conscience, or at least under a fresh remembrance of God.

Such a disposition is both a virtuall supplie of feeling bygone, and a seale of our eternall fruition of him to come: God hath promised a blessing to his worship, and the neglect of it is punished with profannesse and hardnesse of heart.

It is good to keepe acquaintance with God: and there is none houre wherein wee have not an businesse to him, and hee never sent away an holy heart from him without some comfort. Hee needeth none exhortation to the worke, who findeth daylie fruite of it. *Seven times a day doe I praise thee Lord, because of thy righteous judgements.* Psal. 119. 164.

50. *God alone better than all*

Hee shifteth much needlesse labour, and provideth great content-ment, who closeth himselfe with God alone. To deale with man alone, beside God, is both an endlesse and fruitlesse labour. If we have counsel to aske, helpe or benefite to obtaine, or appro-bation to seek, there is none end with man; for every man we must have sundrie reasons, and motives, and what pleaseth one, will offend twentie; as many heads, as many wits[17] and fansies. No man can give contentment to all, or change himselfe in so many fash-ions as he shall encounter humours; and yet it is more easie to take sundrie fashions than to bee active in them.

Hee preasseth to lift water in a sife,[18] and sand in open fingers, who thinketh so to carrie himselfe as to please all. He is prodi-gall of the peace of his soule, and carelesse of good successe, who maketh man either his rule or his rewarder. That spirit must bee rent asunder, that applyeth it selfe to the contrarietie of men's opinions.

Man's bodilie senses both ruleth and overruleth[19] his reason; therefore, as hee seeth men and not God, so he preferreth seene man to an unseene God. But when hee shall see God in the clouds, at the last day, and all mankynd present, they shall all bee nothing in respect of God. The godly now see him more than man, and therefore preferre him to all men, and runne that course to offend and lose all men rather than him. This is a course whereof hee shall never neede to repent.

It is grievous indeede to loose our friendes or familiars, and he is foolish who loseth any that hee may brooke with God; but it is a great triumph of grace, when for conscientious and faithfull service to God wee lose them. They are not worth the keeping who cannot be brooked[20] with him; and he is not worthie of God, who will not forsake father and mother for him. All the hurt that these selfe-pleasing men bring to the God-pleasing[21] Sainctes is the greater increase of the fruites, the seales, and sense of God's love in them.

Since I cannot please all, I will take mee to please One, and that One who is better than all for counsell, approbation, and re-ward. So long as God draweth all my thoughts to him and calmeth them in him by sweete contentment, I will not buy a torture from foolish man. While hee answereth my desires, and communicateth himselfe more to me than I can conceive, I will not vex my selfe in courting of man. *Whom have I in heaven but thee, and there is none on the earth that I desire beside thee.* Psal. 73:25.

74. *The right use of observing of our neighbours' infirmities*

Observation is a commentarie of every occurrent, but that commentar is written in the heart of the observer. It is wisedome to observe at all times, but there is no necessitie to utter all our observations to other: there is as great wisedome in some cases to suppresse as to marke them.

If wee see God offended, wee ought not then to be silent; when wee see him dishonoured, it is our part as loving children to pleade zealouslie his cause, and to admonish the offender according to our calling. But if we observe our self injured by men, it is better to misken[22] that wrong and suppresse our owne observation.

Hee who travelleth through a rough forrest should not rubbe on everie thorne and brier; that will both rent his garments and flesh, and stoppe him in the way. Hee is more wise who draweth his garments hard to his body and shifteth the touch of thornes; and (if they fasten on him) softlie freeth himselfe off them.

It is a safe course through this thornie world to have no medling but necessar, and then not to provocke men's infirmities; or, if they will rubbe upon us, wisely to decline or passe them over.

Hee who carpeth at every thing breedeth much needlesse and endlesse labour; but he who passeth by tollerable things without challenge provydeth[23] great peace to himselfe. Observation is the eye that seeth these thornes; patience and prudence are the two hands, the one to decline them, the other to loose them, when they fasten in us.

This is not a politicke dissembling, but a Christian disgesting of wrongs. The first is a craftie smoothering of anger, which will arise to reveng at the owne occasion;[24] the second is a buriall of it, never to revive or bee remembred. The worke of observation in it selfe is a good degree of wisedome, but the right use of it is greater wisedome. If wee shall ever communicat all our remarkes to men, wee could not have peace in the world; men are not so sanctified as to suffer themselves to bee challenged of that whereof they are guiltie. Passions in their hearts, when they are touched by observation, are as lyons in the denne and serpents in their holes. To shew that wee see them provocketh a greater irritation. It is better to let a dogge sleepe than to waken him; it is sufficient to know hee is a dogge and wiselie to decline his barking and byting.

The particular directions of this point would bee many, but this is the summe of all; to make such use of observation, that God bee not dishonoured; our neighbour be not offended; our peace with God, our neighbour, and our selves bee not broken.

82. *Complementing is a windie fulnesse*

Complementing in speach is a verball idolatrie;[25] it is counted a perfection in talking, but is indeed the quintessence of pratling, and unworthie of a free and ingenuous minde. The giver and reciever are both deceived; the first speaketh that which hee meaneth not, and the other troweth that which he expecteth not: As tilting[26] men have armes and facts of hostilitie without wrath; they break their speares on other and intend none hurt; so complementing hath friendly words without love. As jesters breake their jests on other, so doe Polititians their smoakie wishes and praise.

They live by that smoake; but modest spirits are tormented with it. That mist fleeth moste among men of least true worth. Where that flatterie is mutuall, then two birds of one feather flee together, and two horse (of one itch) doe nippe other.[27]

It is a pitie to see men teach their tongs to speake lies, and to labour to be trusted more than understood. But they trow[28] not themselves; how shall other men trust them? No man can justly crave more credite to his speach of other, than himself giveth to it; or, if he doe, he must conceat[29] stronglie that hee dealeth with a foole.

Hee mindeth[30] one thing and speaketh, or rather soundeth, the contrare. Hee knoweth his heart thinketh not what hee speaketh, and therefore hee taketh the floorish of faire speech to supplie the want of trueth. His heart must fetch the reasons of his owne perswasion from his mouth; and, measuring others by himselfe, hee thinketh that many faire wordes shall beguile them as well as hee beguileth himselfe with them.

They are no more vexed to coyne their wordes than I am to keepe my countenance when I heare them.

Ingenuitie[31] of affection goeth plainly to worke. The more care to fill mine eares with officious offers, the lesse credite they finde in mine heart: thinke their spirit is so spent in that vapour that there is left neither spirit nor life in their affection.

This sort of lying is not vulgare,[32] but with a singular mode. Poets have libertie to lie, and for keeping their rythme, they are licenced to quite reason[33] ofttimes. There is none odde veine of poesie without some degree of abstractnes of spirit. The strictnesse of meeter looseth them from the strictnesse of veritie and secureth them from rigorous censure for that slippe; and their hyperbolees doe passe for good coyne. But the complementer[s] doe lie without either libertie or licence; and their hyperbolees are none other thing, in broad tearmes, than lyes in folio.[34]

Their speaches run usuallie on three thinges: 1. large praises of some excellent worth in them whom they idole;[35] 2. officious offers of service as due to it; 3. and large wishes of all happinesse to them. In the first, their idoles know they are speaking false, except they be as sensles of flatteries as there[36] flatterers are shamelesse. In the second, their owne heart giveth them the lie; for they think themselves more worthie of service than hee to whom they offer it. In the third, their conscience checketh them for mocking of God; for they pray for that which they desire not to bee granted: yea, they would bee grieved if it were granted.

They are equivocaters, minding one thing and speaking another. Many doe practise the Jesuits' mentall reservation[37] who know not their doctrine. (It must bee a cousening[38] religion that teacheth, practiseth, and alloweth such cousening.) I never suspect them more, than when they double their complements.[39]

Hee is short and shallow witted who is glosed[40] with these flowrishes: Let them paint out their speach and gesture, I wil give lesse credite to so onerous and insidious speach. I shall trow the heart and the person so affected as it deserveth: an honest meaning simplie expressed hath more weight than all these buskinges and fairdings.[41]

The heart that God made (but they abuse) hath the owne meaning: I trust that, but not the person[42] which they assume and laye downe as soone as they have spent their borrowed breath. The next moment, and the first man they meete with findeth them in another, if not a contrare, minde; it cannot byde in their heart which bred not in it, nor was never in it. Their wordes are but carcases of language, and let the credulous beleever looke for no more than carcase of offices.[43] Belike, they thinke their words either not to bee idle, or that they shall not give an accompt of them at the last day.[44]

The soule indeede must bee filled with something, but wee may soone choose better substance to fill it withall than that wind of frothie complementing. While they are feeding themselves with their fancies, let the children of Trueth speake the trueth from their heart.

Let complementing have the owne[45] due, without a complement. It is the birth of an emptie braine; the maske of hatred and envy; refined hypocrisie, with simulation and dissimulation, her twins ingraned; the breathing of an evill mind under hope of good deede. Hee who knoweth it can neither bee moved to offer it nor patientlie admitte it.

NOTES

1. *ought:* owes. 2. *reckon . . . with wormes:* Compare Job 17:14. 3. *to mynde and glutte:* to "have a mind to" and "greedily desire." 4. *necessar:* (Scottish) necessary. For identification and definition of Struther's Scotticisms I rely upon John Jamieson, *An Etymological Dictionary of the Scottish Language,* new edition, 4 vols. (Paisley, 1879). 5. *remeeded:* remedied (Scot., *remeid,* "to remedy"). 6. *destroyed:* The reading of the original, though the context calls for *destroys.* Possibly an auxiliary *has* may have been omitted before *destroyed.* 7. *modest shifting . . . riches:* disclaiming credit for unearned advantages. 8. *Who so are:* original reads *art.* 9. *imaginarlie:* for the form compare *necessar,* above. 10. *a bad stuffe:* poor quality of cloth.

11. *posed soliditie:* posed (Scot.), "amassed," "accumulated"; the text of the original reads *sodilitie*—surely a misprint. 12. *precedent:* forerunner, prelude. 13. *teill:* cultivate the soil, till (Scot.). 14. *broodie:* prolific, productive of (Scot.). 15. *masculus:* manly, virile. 16. *tryst with:* arrange to meet with (Scot.). 17. *as many heads, as many wits:*

Translating the Latin saying "Tot homines, quot sententiae" (Terence, *Phormio*, II, iv, 14). 18. *Hee preasseth . . . a sife:* "To carry water in a sieve" was proverbial for impossible tasks; compare Tilley, *Proverbs,* W111. 19. *ruleth and overruleth:* singular forms used for plurals. 20. *brooked:* put up with, tolerate.

21. *God-pleasing:* Original omits the necessary hyphen. 22. *to misken:* to ignore, take no notice of (Scot.). 23. *provydeth:* original reads *provided.* 24. *at the owne occasion:* in its own time. 25. *verball idolatrie:* original has comma after *verball.* 26. *As tilting:* Original reads At tilting. 27. *two horse . . . nippe other:* The reader will think—as perhaps Struther was thinking—of Holbein's satiric illustration of this theme in Erasmus's *Praise of Folly.* 28. *trow:* believe, trust in (Scot.). 29. *conceat:* imagine. 30. *mindeth:* means, intends. 31. *Ingenuitie:* innocence, genuineness. 32. *vulgare:* common. 33. *their rythme . . . to quite reason:* not *rhythm,* but *rhyme; to quite,* here: quit, abandon. 34. *lyes in folio:* whoppers. 35. *idole:* idolize, make an idol of. 36. *there:* their (probably reflecting Struther's pronunciation). 37. *the Jesuits' mentall reservation:* Often criticized by Protestants, who assumed that it gave the Jesuit liberty to swear to patent untruth so long as he added, sotto voce, "in a pig's eye"—or an equivalent negating formula. But the problems involved are, of course, much more subtle and vexatious. For better modern statements, see the articles by F. L. Cross, ed., *Oxford Dictionary of the Christian Church,* 2d ed., and by D. Hughes in the *New Catholic Encyclopedia.* As defined by the latter, "In the broad sense, mental reservation is the use of equivocation or ambiguity to conceal the truth." 38. *cousening:* cheating, deceiving. 39. *I never suspect . . . complements:* The Italians have a proverb to this effect: "Chi t'accarezza più di quel che suole / O t'ha engannato od ingannar ti vuole." 40. *glosed:* deceived.

41. *buskinges and fairdings:* "decorations, fancy dressings" and "paintings, disguisings"; both terms Scottish. 42. *person:* persona, mask (or role). 43. *offices:* services, performances. 44. *Belike, they thinke . . . day:* Compare Matthew 12:36. 45. *the owne:* its own.

Joseph Henshaw

✠

1603-1679

TEXT: *Horae Succisivae, or, Spare-houres of Meditations; upon our duty to God, Others, Our Selves. The fifth Edition, corrected and much enlarged* (London, 1640); *STC* 13170. Duodecimo, in two parts. The first and second editions were published in 1631; 3d ed., 1632; 4th ed., 1635. Henshaw neither numbers nor labels his resolves.

This eminent "worthy," though not noticed by Fuller, was educated at Sutton's new Charterhouse in London and at Oxford (B.A., 1624; B.D., 1635; D.D., 1639). He was a private chaplain to the Earl of Bristol and to the Duke of Buckingham. A Royalist during the Civil War, he was deprived upon the collapse of the king's cause. After the Restoration he enjoyed rapid ecclesiastical advancement and was made Bishop of Peterborough in 1663. In addition to the *Horae Succisivae* Henshaw also published another set of pious meditations, *Meditations Miscellaneous, Holy, and Humane* (1637). These latter, intermixed with some mediocre verses and much repetition of Henshaw's meager store of wit, are brief and direct moral maxims to be applied to the conduct of daily life. Both works, under slightly altered titles, were several times republished during the seventeenth century and later.

Of the two parts of the *Horae Succisivae,* the first is dedicated to "The Right Honourable Ladie, the Ladie Anne Cotington," wife of Francis, Baron Cottington, a notorious crypto-Catholic; the second, to "The Right Reverend Father in God, and Right Honourable, William [Laud], Lord Bishop of London, one of his Majesties most Honourable Privy Councell." Both contain expressions clearly indicating that Henshaw was consciously following the resolves pattern. In that to Lady Cottington he writes: "Your desire many times to heare others writing out of my mouth, made me to put this of my owne into your hands; a rapsodie of resolves and observations, some for contemplation, others for caution, the first divine, the other morall." To the second dedicatee he writes: "The matter is almost as divers as the pages *nugae miscellaneae* of Directions, Instructions, Resolutions; what wee should doe, what we should bee." In their general brevity, if not exactly in moral acuity, these resolves resemble those of Bishop Hall; in their phraseology and sentiment, those of Daniel Tuvill. The resolves of Part II are perhaps more consistently pious than those of Part I; certainly they are, on the average, longer. One can sympathize with Pepys, who found Henshaw's preaching dull (*Diary*, entry for May 19, 1669).

HORAE SUCCISIVAE, OR
SPARE-HOURES OF MEDITATIONS

from Part I

Sleepe is but death's elder brother,[1] and death is but a sleepe nicknam'd; why should I more feare to goe to my grave, than to my bed, since both tend to my rest? When I lye down to sleepe, I will thinke it my last, and when I rise againe, account my life not continued, but restor'd.

To doe any thing to thinke to bee talk'd of is the vainest thing in the world; to give almes, and aske who sees, loseth the prayse and the reward:[3] I may bee seene to give, I will not give to be seene. That others are witnesse to my piety is not my fault, nor my praise; I will never bee so ill a friend to my selfe, to sell heaven for vaine-glory.

In injuries it is better to take many, than give one, in benefits the contrary: I will requite the first with bearing them, the second with requiting them.

Evill communication corrupts good manners.[3] Peter denied[4] his Master among the Jewes, whom hee confessed among the Apostles: I may have a bad man of my family, I will never have a bad familiar; or if at any time of my court, never of my counsell.

Prosperity is like *vinum merum*, all wine. It makes drunke the soule, and therefore God mingles it, that He may keepe us sober; feeds His children with a bit and a knocke,[5] ever dishes his sweete meate with sowre sauce. If we did alwaies abound, wee would grow proud, and forget our selves, and if not sometimes, we would despaire and forget our God. I will pray with Salomon,[6] give me neither wealth nor poverty, but a meane; or if wealth, grace to imploy[7] it; if poverty, patience to endure it.

There was never good but was hard to get. The prison and the hatchet, sores and crums leade to Abraham's bosome,[8] and the way thither is by weeping-crosse.[9] If many tribulations will carry me to heaven, on [sic] God's name let me have them; welcome the poverty, which makes me heire to those riches that never shall have an end.

I will deale for my soule, as for my body: never refuse health because the physicke that should procure it is bitter. Let it distast me, so it heale me.

Therefore hath nature given us two eares, and but one mouth,[10] that we should heare twice as much as we should speake. With all thy secrets trust neither thy wife nor thy friend.[11] He that is thrifty of his owne tongue shall lesse feare another's.

There are that affect not so much to have true friends, as to have many, and whisper to that friend what they heare from this, and againe, to this, what from that: and glory to have it knowne, how much they are trusted, whereas they were therefore trusted that it might not be knowne. I have ever thought it a maxime in friendship,[12] that hee which will be intimate with many is entirely none's; let mee love and be lov'd of all, I will be inward[13] onely with a few. I had rather have one meane friend that I may call my own, than the most potent where I must share with others.

Let another praise thee, and not thine own mouth.[14] Either we are farre from neighbours or ill beloved among them, when wee are faine to be our owne trumpet and blaze our selves.[15] The Jewes, not the Centurian[16] say, Hee loved our Nation and hath, etc. It is both honourable and humble to heare of our praises and tell of our unworthinesse.

Many a little make a mickle;[17] every day a mite will increase our store. I will be ever adding to my heape of knowledge, of faith, etc., that when the Master returnes I may be able to say, Behold Lord, thy two talents have gained other two.[18]

Every thing almost we see borrowes its nature from its soile; thus the body and temper of men differ with the ayre; and the soule like the body commonly savours something of the company it keepes, and we grow familiar with their sins, together with their persons; at first winke at them, then imitate them, then defend them. I will not be more perspicuous[19] in the choyce of any thing than of this: hee can hardly have a good soule, that hath a bad companion.[20]

Contentation is a blessing, not wealth; true riches consist not so [much] in having much, as in not desiring more.[21] Why then doe we so labour to abound, and not rather to be content? If I have but a little, my account is the lesse; if I have much, and doe not more good, I shall adde to my condemnation, together with my store. I will ever study rather to use my little well, then to en-crease it.

To speake little is a note of a wise man; to speake well, of a good man. Goodnesse is not seen in the length or brevity of our speech, but in the matter. The streames of the tongue runs [sic] from the current of the heart and are like the fountaine; it is a signe wee have little goodnesse in us, when there comes little out of us. If God were more in our hearts, He would be often in our mouthes, and with more reverence. Though I will never affect to speake of my goodnesse, yet I will shew it in my speech.

Hee that will bee a criticke of others' actions had need look well to his owne: 'tis a foule shame to have that found in our selves, which we would take upon us to mend in others. In this I will ever follow my Saviour's rule, first get out mine owne beame, and I shall see better to helpe my brother out with his mote.

Great men's words are like dead men's shooes: he may go bare-foot, that waits for them.[22] I will ever bee a Didymus[23] in these:

beleeve onely what I see, so I shall neither be deceived with others' promises my selfe, nor deceive others with them.

from PART II

When I at first look out into the world and see many men (and those none of the best) in better case, I thinke my selfe forgotten and wish for more. But when I remember my account, I feare I have too much and forget those wishes. It may be if I had more wealth, I should be more riotous. Outward losses are sometimes gainefull, and it is good for us that we are afflicted. It would bee worse with us if it were not sometimes thus bad.[24] Many, if they were not kept short of these, would come short of heaven.[25] Hee knowes us that keeps us, and if He will have us Lazar's, and not Dive's,[26] bring us to heaven that way rather than another, His will bee done; let Him give my goods to the poore, and my body to bee burn'd,[27] and bring mee to heaven, though in a fiery chariot;[28] I cannot complaine of the foulenesse of that way that carries me to God.

Things which wee come easily by, wee easily part with: lightly come, lightly goe. True friendship, as it is hard to finde, so it is hardly lost, and therefore hardly lost, because hard to finde. I will put up many injuries, before I put off one friend; small faults I will swallow: others I will wink at; and if hee will not bee my other selfe,[29] I will bee his, and change my nature before my friend. Friends, like stones, get nothing by rolling.[30]

The best ornament of the body is the minde, and the best ornament of the minde is honesty. I will care rather how to live well, than how to goe fine. I may have an ill garment, and come to Heaven; I cannot, and have an ill soule. He who first bid[31] us cast our care upon Him did not so meane, as if wee should take no care our selves; it will not come to our share to sit still and cry, *God helpe us.* Salomon hath read his fortune, that will not worke in summer; therefore shall hee starve in winter.[32] It was the destiny sinne brought upon the world, *in the sweat of thy browes thou shalt eate thy meate,* and thanke God wee can have it so. Hee that made us without our selves will not keepe us without our selves; it is mercy enough for us, that we eate with sweating. I will never thinke much of my paines, where it is rewarded with a blessing.

It is appointed to all men once to dye.[33] Death is a punishment of sin, not sinne it selfe; yet sure it is the height of punishment when it is sudden;[34] I doe not desire not to dye at all, but not all at once. I know I must dye, and I thinke of my death, yet is it not alwaies in my thoughts; the best of us all may be taken napping. I will ever pray God when he doth fell mee, not to doe it at a blow, that I may see my selfe falling, and bethinke mee in the fall; and thus it is a comfortable thing to fall into the hands of the living God.[35]

This world is oft compar'd unto a sea: our life is the ship, wee are the passengers, the grave is the common haven, Heaven is the shore. And well is the grave commonly compar'd unto a haven, for there wee unload; the things of this world are neither borne with us, nor doe dye with us: wee goe out of this world as wee came into it, naked.[36] Why are wee so covetous of those things, which are so hard to get, and so certaine to be lost? If I enjoy them all, I shall not enjoy them long; or if [I] enjoy but some, I shall shortly have use of none. I will comfort my selfe against the want of them, with the assurance that I shall one day not have need of them.

Some there are that heare onely to tell, and many times make differences, where there were none meant. It is not good alwaies to tell all wee heare; many a man speakes that in his anger, which in coole bloud, hee would not owne; and wee doe a double wrong by relating that which the one is sorry to heare, and the other to have spoken, when hee is himselfe. I will heare all, and report onely the best; hee that makes debate betweene others, layes a bait for himself. It is safe and honest to compose discords, but sow none. I will labour what I can, to set others together, but not by the eares.[37]

The way to sweeten death is to think of it. Every day I live, I will remember I might dye; and I will not desire to live a day longer, than I grow some drammes better. What will it benefit mee that I have liv'd some hours which I cannot answere for?

No man is so provident for his owne good, as God is for every man's. Every sinner is an Absolom to Him, and He doth not onely wish, *Would God I had dyed for thee,*[38] etc., but dyed indeed. We doe not so desire our owne salvation, as He doth all ours, promiseth, perswadeth, begges our obedience. He leaves no way untried, that Hee may leave us inexcusable, wash His hands of us, and say, *perditio tua ex te,*[39] etc. Our destruction if it come is from our selves; if wee could but wish well to our owne soules, wee could not but doe well: and yet it is not wishing, but doing well that doth the deed. I will doe what I can, and I will desire to doe what I should and cannot. God accepts a willing minde, and if I am willing beyond my ability, He will either make me able, or accept my will. O God, thou that workest in mee both to will and to doe, worke my will to thine, and my power to my will, that I may not onely will or desire, but doe thy will.

Death is as hatefull to man, as old age to beauty; and we are ever complaining of the shortnesse of our time, unlesse calamity make it seeme long; which yet if they be never so little over, they are weary of that which before they wished for, death. As I will not bee in love with tribulations, so I will not love my life the worse for them, nor the better for wanting them. If prosperity make mee fond of living, or afraid of dying, it had beene better for mee, if it had not been so well; I shall pay deare for my ease.

NOTES

1. *Sleepe is but death's . . . brother:* This commonplace has already been encountered; see Stafford, note 36. 2. *to give almes . . . reward:* On Christian almsgiving, see Matthew 6:1-4. 3. *Evill communication . . . manners:* 1 Corinthians 15:33; and, with slight variations, also proverbial. Compare Tilley, *Proverbs,* C558. 4. *Peter denied:* Compare Matthew 26:69-75; see also Tuvill, Resolve XXI. 5. *feeds . . . with a bit and a knocke:* Proverbial; compare Tilley, *Proverbs,* B416. 6. *pray with Salomon:* Proverbs 30:8. 7. *grace to imploy:* This is the reading of the third edition (1632); 1640 reads *imply.* 8. *sores and crums . . . Abraham's bosome:* In reference to the beggar Lazarus; compare Luke

16:20–25; also Tuvill, note 40.   9. *weeping-crosse:* "To come home by
Weeping-Cross" was proverbial for meeting with sharp disappointment
or failure, or for performing some action which one later regrets; compare Tilley, *Proverbs,* W248. Weeping-Cross was also an English place-
name, the origin of which is not entirely clear. See the interesting
entry, *s.v.,* in the *OED.*   10. *two eares . . . one mouth:* The saying of one
of the Greek philosophers. Diogenes Laertius, *Lives of Eminent Philosophers,* "Zeno," VII, 23, attributes it to that philosopher.
      11. *trust neither . . . wife . . . friend:* Similar sentiments were pro-
verbial; compare Tilley, *Proverbs,* S196.   12. *a maxime in friendship:*
Compare Tilley, *Proverbs,* F698.   13. *inward:* intimate, familiar.   14.
Let another praise . . . mouth: With this compare the adage "Laus in ore
proprio sordet," "Praise in one's own mouth soils"; compare Tilley,
Proverbs, P547.   15. *Either . . . blaze our selves:* A widely used proverb;
compare Tilley, *Proverbs,* N117. *Blaze* means to "celebrate," "publish
abroad."   16. *The Jewes, not . . . Centurian:* Compare Luke 7:2–5. This
centurion was mentioned before; see Tuvill, note 47.   17. *Many . . .
make a mickle:* A Scots proverb; *mickle* (or *muckle*): "much," "a great
heap."   18. *Behold Lord . . . other two:* In reference to Jesus' parable of
the talents; compare Matthew 25:15–29.   19. *perspicuous:* cautiously
sharp-sighted; 3d ed. (1632) reads *scrupulous.*   20. *hee can . . . bad
companion:* With this sentiment compare Hall, resolve VIII.
      21. *true riches . . . desiring more:* This adapts the familiar Latin say-
ing "Non qui parvum habet, sed qui plus cupit pauper est."   22. *Great
. . . waits for them:* This sounds proverbial though I trace no other clear
instance. See, however, Hall, note 23.   23. *Didymus:* Another name (the
"Twin") for "doubting Thomas"; see John 20:24–28.   24. *Outward
losses . . . thus bad:* On the benefits of adversity, a favorite theme with
resolve writers, see Stafford, note 39.   25. *Many . . . short of heaven:*
The sentence appears not to say what Henshaw obviously means. Perhaps the first "short of" should be read "short by." (The antecedent of
"these" is "Outward losses").   26. *Lazar's . . . Dive's:* See Tuvill, note
40. Henshaw's punctuation (preserved) indicates that he considers these
words plurals, not possessives.   27. *give my goods . . . burn'd:* 1 Corinthians 13:3.   28. *to heaven . . . fiery chariot:* Referring to Elijah's supposed mode of ascension; compare 2 Kings 2:11.   29. *my other selfe:*
A friend was considered an alter ego; "alter ipse amicus."   30. *Friends
. . . by rolling:* Alluding to the proverb "A rolling stone gathers no moss";
compare Tilley, *Proverbs,* S885.
      31. *bid:* the reading of 3d ed. (1632); 1640 reads *bids.*   32. *Salomon
read . . . winter:* Compare Proverbs 6:6–8, 30:25—the industrious and
foresighted ant.   33. *It is appointed . . . dye:* Hebrews 9:27.   34. *when it*

is sudden: The horror of dying without adequate time to prepare one's soul was so strong that it remained as one of the evils for delivery from which a special prayer was included in the litany of the *Book of Common Prayer.* 35. *comfortable thing . . . living God:* More comfortable, certainly, than what Jonathan Edwards had in mind when he preached his sermon "Sinners in the Hands of an Angry God." 36. *this world . . . naked:* A medley of commonplaces, ending in a biblical chorus; compare Job 1:21. 37. *to set . . . together . . . by the eares:* Proverbial for stirring up contention. 38. *Would God . . . for thee:* David's celebrated lament for his errant son Absalom; compare 2 Samuel 18:33. 39. *perditio tua ex te:* Translated (with change of person) in the next sentence.

Arthur Warwick

❧

fl. 1632

TEXT: *Spare-Minutes; or, Resolved Meditations and Premeditated Resolutions. Written by A. W. . . . . The second Edition corrected and enlarged* (London, 1634); STC 25097. I use as copytext the duodecimo Harmsworth copy from the Huth Library, which is copy one (of two) in the Folger Library. Another "second" edition, also printed in 1634, is in quarto. No copy seems to have survived of any earlier edition. The work is divided into two parts. Part One contains sixty-one brief resolves and is dedicated by the author to "My much Honoured Friend, S^r. William Dodington Knight." Part Two, with thirty-five prose resolves and two in verse, has a separate title page but continuous signatures. It is signed by Arthur Warwick, father of the author. The son seems to have died in the interval between the printing of the two parts. The two verse meditations at the end of the second Part are followed by a longer set of verses headed "The last thing the Author wrote a few daies before his death." From the total number of resolves and the incomplete nature of the book it may be surmised that Warwick proposed to write the conventional "century" of resolves. The little work had reached a "seventh" edition by 1639; a London reprint of 1829 is called the "eighth" edition.

I transcribe the first ten resolves of Part One, the last ten of Part Two, with the addition of [No. 24, "Of Resolutions"] from the first part. The original neither numbers the resolves nor supplies titles.

Of Arthur Warwick (fl. 1632) virtually all that is known must be gleaned from this, his only known publication. It adds up only to this: that he was a studious and earnest young minister who died prematurely.

The resolves of the second part seem, on the whole, slightly longer than those of the first part, though all are brief. The very brief and wittily sententious contrapuntal dedicatory epistle of Part One reads much like any of the resolves:

I will not make an over-large gate to my little City: A short Epistle best suites with so small a volume, and both fitly resemble your knowledge of mee, and mine acquaintance with you, short, and small. But a mite freely given, makes a poor widow liberall: and in this Present, poore, like my habilities, is a thankefullnesse, infinite, like your deservings. To speake much, might be thought flattery; to say nothing would be knowne ingratitude: I must therfore be short, I may not bee silent. The happy fortune of my tongue hath incouraged my penne: and I humbly crave in the one, what I favourably found in the other, a courteous acceptance. Which if you please to add to your former favours, and my happinesse, I shall have just cause to rest

Your Worships truly devoted
ARTHUR WARWICK

Warwick's title, modeled after Henshaw's, indicates the difficulty the age experienced in arriving at a definitive label for the genre: even Feltham, though he has set it for ours, had not succeeded in fixing it for the seventeenth century. Although Warwick, like Struther, Trenchfield, Tuke, and other resolvers was a clergyman, it is something of a relief to escape from their excessive and long-winded piety into the brevity and comparative secularity of his resolves. He takes us, for the moment, back to the Senecan modulations of Hall; and if he has an overriding fault—as, in my opinion, he has—it is that he strives too hard to achieve an epigrammatic effect of witty contrast. We could wish, with Hamlet's mother, more matter, with less art. Warwick is somewhat old-fashioned in his toying with alliteration; but he was quite abreast of his more bizarre contemporaries (and some ill-advised modern writers) in his obsession with the idiocies of paradox.

The *Spare-Minutes* are the thoughts, not the mere mouthings, of a young man, and they show the precocious youth's attempt to emulate the wisdom of older men. They are indeed marked—sometimes marred—by an obvious striving for point and balance; and if they remind us of the Senecan brevity and epigrammatic finish of Bishop Hall, that is not always to Warwick's discredit. To paraphrase Webster, we may say of him, "Cover his face; mine eyes dazzle. He died young."

SPARE-MINUTES; OR, RESOLVED MEDITATIONS AND PREMEDITATED RESOLUTIONS

[1. Of Ambition]

It is the over curious ambition of many to be best or to be none:[1] if they may not doe so well as they would, they will not doe so well as they may. I will doe my best to doe the best, and what I want in power, supply in will. Thus whils I pay in part, I shall not bee a debtor for all. Hee owes most that payes nothing.

[2. Of Pride]

Pride is the greatest enemy to reason, and discretion the greatest opposite to pride. For whiles wisdome makes art the ape of nature, pride makes nature the ape of art. The wiseman shapes his apparell to his body, the proud man shapes his body by his apparell. 'Tis no marvell, than, if hee know not himselfe, when hee is not to day like him he was yesterday; and lesse marvell, if good men will not know him when hee forgets himselfe and all goodnesse. I should feare, whilest I thus change my shape, least my maker should change his opinion; and finding mee not like him hee made mee, reject mee as none of his making. I would any day put off the old cause of my apparell, but not every day put on a new fashioned apparell. I see great reason to bee ashamed of my pride, but no reason to bee proud of my shame.

[3. Unreasonable Desires]

The reason that many men want their desires is because their desires want reason.[2] Hee may doe what hee will that will doe but what he may.

[4. Of Covetousness]

I should marvell that the covetous man can still bee poore, when the rich man is still covetous, but that I see a poore man can bee content, when the contented man is onely rich: the one wanting in his store, whiles the other is stored in his wants.[3] I see, then, wee are not rich or poore by what wee possesse, but by what we desire.

For hee is not rich that hath much, but hee that hath enough; nor hee poore that hath but little, but he that wants more.[4] If God then make mee rich by store, I will not impoverish my selfe by covetousnesse; but if hee make mee poore by want, I will inrich my selfe by content.

[5. Of Seeming and Being[5]]

Hypocrisie desires to seeme good rather than to be so: honestie desires to bee good rather than seeme so. The worldlings purchase reputation by the sale of desert; wisemen buy desert with the hazard of reputation. I would do much to heare well, more to deserve well; and rather loose opinion then merit. It shall more joy mee that I know my selfe what I am, than it shall grieve me to heare what others report mee. I had rather deserve well without praise, than doe ill with commendation.

[6. Of Confessing One's Faith]

A coward in the field is like the Wiseman's foole: his heart is at his mouth,[6] and hee doth not know what hee does professe; but a coward in his faith is like a foole in his wisedome; his mouth is in his heart, and hee dares not professe what hee does know. I had rather not know the good I should doe, than not do the good I know. It is better to be beaten with few stripes than with many.

[7. The Christian's Travels][7]

Each true Christian is a right traveller: his life his walke, Christ his way, and Heaven his home. His walke painefull, his way perfect, his home pleasing. I will not loyter, least I come short of home. I will not wander, least I come wide of[8] home, but be content to travell hard, and be sure [to] walke right; so shall my safe way find its end at home, and my painefull walke make my home welcome.

[8. Health of Soul]

As is a wound to the body, so is a sinfull body to the soule: the body indangered till the wound bee cured, the soule not sound till the bodie's sinne bee healed; and the wound of neither can be cured without dressing, nor dressed without smarting. Now as the smart of the wound is recompensed by the cure of the body, so is the punishment of the body sweetned by the health of the soule. Let my wound smart by dressing, rather than my bodie die; let my body smart by correction, rather than my soule perish.

[9. Of Goodness]

It is some hope of goodnesse not to grow worse; it is a part of badnesse not to grow better. I will take heed of quenching the sparke, and strive to kindle a fire. If I have the goodnesse I should, it is not too much; why should I make it lesse? If I keepe the goodnesse I have 'tis not enough; why doe I not make it more? Hee ne're was so good as hee should bee that doth not strive to be better than he is; he never will be better than he is that doth not feare to bee worse than hee was.

[10. Sickness and Health]

Health may be injoyed; sicknesse must be indured: one body is the object of both, one God the author of both. If then hee give mee health, I will thankfully enjoy it and not thinke it too good, since it is his mercy that bestowes it; if hee send sicknesse, I will patiently indure it and not thinke it too great, since it is my sinne that deserves it. If in health, I will strive to preserve it by praising of him; if in sickenesse, I will strive to remove it by praying to him. Hee shall be my God in sicknesse and in health, and my trust shall bee in him in health and in sicknesse. So in my health I shall not need to feare sicknesse, nor in any sicknesse despaire of health.

[26. Of Meditation and Resolution]

Meditation is the wombe of our actions, action the midwife of our meditations. A good and perfect conception, if it want strength for the birth, perisheth in the wombe of the minde, and, if it may be said to bee borne, it must be said to be still-borne; a bad and imperfect conception, if it hath the happinesse of a birth, yet the minde is but delivered of a burthen of imperfections, in the perfection of deformity, which may beg with the criple at the gate[9] of the Temple, or perisheth through its imperfections. If I meditate what's good to be done and doe not the good I have meditated, I loose my labour and make curst my knowledge. If I doe the thing that is good and intend not that good that I doe, it is a good action but not well done. Others may injoy some benefit, I deserve no commendations. Resolution without action is a sloathfull folly; action without resolution is a foolish rashnesse. First know what's good to be done, then do that good being knowne. If forecast be not better than labour, labour is not good without forecast. I would not have my actions done without knowledge, nor against it.

from PART II   [28. Spiritual Gardening][10]

When I plant a choyse flower in a fertile soyle, I see nature presently to thrust up with it the stinging nettle, the stinking hemlocke, the drowzie poppie, and many such noysome weedes, which will either choake my plant with excluding the sunne or divert its nourishment to themselves. But if I weed out these at first, my flower thrives to its goodnesse and glory. This is also my case when I endevour to plant grace in the fertill soyle of a good wit. For luxurious nature thrusts up with it either stinging wrath, or stinking wantonnesse, or drowzie sloath or some other vices, which robb my plant of its desired flourishing. But these being first pluckt up, the good wit produceth in its time the faire flower of vertue. I will not therefore thinke the best wits, as they are wits, fittest to make the best men, but as they are the best purged best wits. The ground of their goodnesse is not the goodnesse of their wits, but the good weeding and clensing it. I must first eschew the evill ere I can doe good, supplant vices ere I can implant virtue.

[29. Improving the Shining Moment]

As it is never to soone to be good, so is it never too late[11] to amend. I will therefore neither neglect the time present nor despaire of the time past. If I had beene sooner good, I might perhaps have beene better. If I am no longer bad, I shall (I am sure) be worse. That I have stayed long time idle in the market-place deserves reprehension; but if I am late sent into the vineyard, I have incouragement to worke: *I will give unto this last as unto thee.*[12]

[30. Benefits of Adversity]

When I see the husbandman well contented with the cold of frost
and snow in the winter, because, though it chilleth the ground, yet
it killeth the charlocke,[13] though it check the wheat somewhat in
growing, yet it choaketh the weeds from growing at all: Why
should I bee moved at the winter of affliction? Why vexed at the
quaking fit of a quartane ague?[14] Why offended at the cold change
of affection in my summer-friends? If as they seeme bitter to my
minde or body, they prove healthfull to my bettered soule. If my
wants kill my wantonnesse, my poverty check my pride, my disrespected sleighting[15] quell my ambition and vaine-glory, and every
weed of vice being thus choaked by affliction's winter, my soule
may grow fruitfull for heaven's harvest, let my winter be bitter,
so that I be gathered with the good corne at reaping time into the
Lord's barne.

[31. A Man for All Seasons]

As oft as I heare the Robin-red-brest chaunt it as cheerefully in
September, the beginning of winter, as in March, the approach of
the summer, why should not we (thinke I) give as cheerefull enter-
tainement to the hoare-frosty hayres of our age's winter, as to the
primroses of our youth's spring? Why not to the declining sunne
in adversity, as (like Persians) to the rising sunne[16] of prosperity?
I am sent to the ant to learne industry;[17] to the dove, to learne in-
nocency; to the serpent, to learne wisedome.[18] And why not to this
bird to learne equanimity and patience; and to keepe the same
tenour of my minde's quietnesse, as well at the approach of calamitie's winter, as of the spring of happinesse? And, since the Roman's
constancy[19] is so commended, who changed not his countenance
with his changed fortunes, why should not I, with a Christian
resolution, hold a steddy course in all weathers; and though I be
forced with crosse-windes to shift my sailes and catch at side-
windes, yet skilfully to steere and keepe on my course, by the cape
of good hope, till I arive at the haven[20] of eternall happinesse?

[32. The Induration of Sin]

The same water which, being liquid, is penetrated with an horse-
haire will beare the horse himselfe when it is hard frozen. I muse

not then that those precepts and threats of God's judgements enter not into the hardned hearts of some old men, frozen by the practice of sinne, which pierce and penetrate deepe into the tender hearts and melting consciences of younger folks thawed with the warmth of God's feare. Hence see I the cause why the sword of the Word,[21] so sharpe that it serveth in some to divide the joyntes and marrow, in others glaunceth or reboundeth without dint or wound from their cristall frozen and adamantine[22] hearts. I cannot promise my selfe to bee free from sinne; I were then no man. But I will purpose in my selfe to bee free from hardnesse of heart by custome and continuance in sinne. I may erre in my way; I will not persist and goe on in my errours till I cannot returne againe into my way. I may stumble, I may fall; but I will not lye still when I am fallen.

[33. Of Revenge]

When I see two game-cocks at first sight, without premeditated malice, fight desperately and furiously, the one to maintaine the injury offered, the other to revenge the injury received by the first blow and to maintaine this quarrell, not onely dye the pit with their bloud but die in the pit with their mutuall bloudy wounds, me thinkes I see the successe of those duëllers of our time which, being ambitious of Achilles his praise,[23] *Pelidis juvenis cedere nescii,* desperatly and furiously adventure their lives heere and indanger their soules heereafter onely for the vaine termes of false honour. I will not say but that being flesh and bloud I may be carelesse of my flesh and bloud to revenge injurious indignities offered me; yet since as a tenant my soule must answer her Landlord for reparations of the house she dwels in, and I have no warrant of God or man for such revenge, I will not kill my owne soule to kill an other man's body. I will not pull the house of my body on my soule's head in a fury, that God may make them both fuell for the fury of hell fire.

[34. A Proper Sense of Glory]

When I view the heavens declaring the glory of God, and the firmament shewing his handy worke, and consider that each little numbred starre even of the sixth magnitude[24] containeth the earth's dimension 18. times in bignesse by astronomers' conclusions, I easily descend to consider the great difference of earthly men's glory and that weight of glory affoorded the Saints in heaven. For what a poore ambition[25] is it to bee the best man in a city? What's a city to a shire? What a shire to the whole island? What this island to the continent of Europe? What Europe to the whole earth? What that earth to a starre? What that starre to heaven? and that to the Heaven of Heavens? And so by retrogradation how little? How nothing is this poore glory. I finde many which say, *hoc nihil est aliquid:* I finde in my selfe cause to say, *hoc aliquid nihil est.*[26] If I needs will bee somebody by my ambition, I will bee ambitious to bee ranged with the Saints in Heaven rather then ranked with the kings on earth; since the least in the Kingdome of Heaven is greater then they.

[35. Of Litigation]

I saw once a jerfalcon[27] let fly at an heron, and observed with what clamour the heron entertain'd the sight and approach of the hawke, and with what winding shifts hee strave to get above her, labouring even by bemuting his enemie's feathers to make her flagg-winged[28] and so escape. But when at last they must needs come to a necessitated encounter, resuming courage out of necessity, hee turned face against her, and striking the hawke thorough the gorge with his bill fell downe dead together with his dead enemie. This sight seemed to mee the event of a great sute in law, where one trusting to his case's potency more then his cause's equity endeavours to disinherit his stubborne neighbour by colourable titles[29] to his land. Heere may you heare the clamorous obloquies of the wronged and see the many turnings and winding meanders[30] in the law sought out to get above his adversary. And lastly when the issue must come to tryall, oftentimes in the grapple they both sinke to beggary by the law whiles lawfully they seeke to get above each other. Hence warned against potent enemies I will alway pray, Lord make mee not a prey unto their teeth; and against an equall or inferiour I will not borrow the lawe's extreme right to doe him extreme wrong;[31] nor fall to law with any body till I fall, by law, to bee no body. I will not doe that to have my will, which will undoe my selfe of what I have by my willfullnesse.

[36. Of Slanderers and Flatterers]

The psalmist doth not slander the slanderers when, in a good description of their bad natures, hee saith, *their throat is an open sepulcher,* etc.; *the poyson of aspes is under their lippes.*[32] For what more loathsome stench and noisome smells can a new opened sepulcher belch out, then these venemous open throated slanderers? And well may their lips containe the poyson of aspes, of which Lucan saith, *in nulla plus est serpente veneni,*[33] when a few words of theirs shall (like a witches spell) charme and strike dead a man's deerest reputation. I will therefore indeavour to make my actions of that vertue, that as an antidote of Mithridates his best confection,[34] they may repell the worst infection those serpents shall spit at mee. And albeit I cannot bee free from their assaults (from which none is freed), yet I will not with Cleopatra[35] set those aspes so neere my heart that they may stop my vitall spirits with their poyson. And since I must passe thorough this Africa of monsters[36] and harmefull beasts, I will carefully feare and shunne the worst of tame beasts, the flatterer; and of wild[37] beasts, the slanderer.

[37. Of Meditation and Resolution]

Meditation is a busie search in the store-house of fantasie for some idea's of matters, to bee cast in the moulds of resolution into some formes of words or actions. In which search, when I have used my greatest diligence, I finde this in the conclusion: that to meditate on the best is the best of meditations; and a resolution to make a good end is a good end of my resolutions.

NOTES

1. *to be best or . . . none:* "Aut Caesar, aut nullus"—a wrong kind of ambition, Warwick's age would have said. 2. *want . . . desires . . . want reason:* lack, fail to achieve; a common meaning still. 3. *the one wanting . . . wants:* This overprecious word-juggling plays a descant on Ovid's "inopem me copia fecit," the discovery of Narcissus (*Metamorphoses,* III, 466). 4. *For hee . . . wants more:* Compare Struther's resolve 23, *lines* 13–17. 5. Resolve 5: This resolve plays with the age-old theme of appear-

ance versus reality, a philosophical problem going back at least to Plato. 6. *the Wiseman's foole . . . mouth:* The Wiseman is Solomon; the reference is to Proverbs 18:6–7 and, by contrast, 16:21–23. 7. Resolve 7: Compare the life-a-pilgrimage theme, Brathwait, note 8. 8. *come wide of:* miss. 9. *criple at the gate:* Apparently referring to Acts 14:8. 10. Resolve 28: Note the elaborate counterpoint of language and figures in this resolve.

11. *never to soone . . . never too late:* Both phrases proverbial; the latter one was, incidentally, used as title for a pamphlet by that late-repentant sinner Robert Greene. 12. *long time idle . . . unto thee:* Jesus' parable of the laborers in the vineyard; compare Matthew 20:1–16. 13. *charlocke:* field mustard (Jim Hill). 14. *quartane ague:* a fever recurring, or peaking, every fourth (third) day. 15. *my disrespected sleighting:* my being neglected. 16. *(like Persians) to the rising sun:* The Persians, before being converted to Islam, were worshipers of the sun (Ormazd, creator and god of light). 17. *to the ant . . . industry:* Proverbs 6:6. 18. *to the dove . . . serpent . . . wisedome:* Matthew 10:16. 19. *the Roman's constancy:* If any particular stoical Roman is referred to, it is probably Marcus Atilius Regulus, consul and general, a hero in the first Punic war. 20. *a steddy course . . . at the haven:* The consistent nautical imagery does not necessarily imply Warwick's experience at sea—but it might be considered.

21. *sword of the Word:* Compare Ephesians 6:17, "the sword of the Spirit, which is the word of God." 22. *adamantine:* diamond-hard. 23. *Achilles his praise:* Reference not found. Translate: "To the young son of Peleus [i.e., Achilles] to give way was unknown." 24. *starre . . . of the sixth magnitude:* Magnitude has to do rather with the intensity of light than with size. A star of the sixth magnitude is about the faintest that can be seen by the naked eye under the most favorable conditions. But distance (and, consequently, size) must also be considered. 25. *what a poore ambition:* For an early and influential statement of this idea, see Boethius, *Consolation of Philosophy,* Book II, prose 7. 26. *hoc nihil . . . nihil est:* Translate, "This nothing is something" and "this something is nothing." 27. *I saw once a jerfalcon:* See Spencer, number 819. The gerfalcon, or gyrfalcon, was used in hunting. 28. *bemuting . . . flagg-winged:* I.e., by befouling the hawk's (falcon's) wings to make them droop with heaviness and encumbrance. 29. *colourable titles:* false, but seemingly reasonable claims. 30. *winding meanders:* In ancient Greece the Meander was a river noted for its wandering, twisting course.

31. *extreme right . . . extreme wrong:* Warwick is playing with the legal maxim "summa jus, summa injuria." 32. *The psalmist . . . their*

lippes: Compare Psalm 5:9 (and Romans 3:13). 33. *Lucan saith . . . veneni:* Pharsalia, IX, 702–3, slightly misquoted. 34. *Mithridates his best confection:* Mithridates, king of Pontus, enemy to Rome, had ingested so many effective antidotes to poison that when captured by his enemies he could not be poisoned but had to be stabbed to death. 35. *with Cleopatra:* Compare Stafford, note 5. 36. *this Africa of monsters:* This was the reputation of Africa among the ancients: "ex Africa semper aliquid novi," "out of Africa, always some new, [strange] thing." 37. *worst of tame . . . and of wild:* It was the saying of Bias, one of the Seven Sages, that flatterers were the worst of tame beasts, slanderers the worst of wild beasts. Compare Guazzo, *Civil Conversation,* tr. Pettie (ed. Sullivan), I, 76. The original seems to have been Plutarch, *Moralia,* I, 327 (Loeb).

John Saltmarsh

d. 1647

TEXT: *Holy Discoveries and Flames* (London, 1640); *STC* 21637. This is a duodecimo of 225 pages. Saltmarsh describes himself on the title page as "Mr. of Arts of *Magdalen* Colledge in *Cambridge*, and Rector *of West Ileslerton* [i.e., Heslerton] in Yorkshire." Beneath the foregoing title on the printed title page are two engraved symbols, a seeing eye (representing the Deity) and a flaming heart (representing man's holy aspirations). In the meditations that form the text, each "discovery" is preceded by a reproduction of the former symbol, each "flame" by a reproduction of the heart symbol. The *Holy Discoveries and Flames,* the author's third publication, had no reissue in the seventeenth century; but it was reprinted in the nineteenth (1811) and was then much admired.

John Saltmarsh (ca. 1612–1647), M.A. at an unknown date of Magdalene College, Cambridge, was one of the most gentle-tongued of religious controversialists, a man of humane and tolerant views and of a mystical turn in religion. As a gesture of conscience, he resigned his living at West Heslerton about 1643 and, after apparently preaching at large, was given the living at Brasted, Kent, "before January 1645" according to the *DNB* account of his life. Later, in 1646, Saltmarsh became an army chaplain under Sir Thomas Fairfax. He presently grew disenchanted with the army (and with Fairfax?), charging that they had "departed from God." Two days later, on his return to London, although apparently in good health, he died.

But during all his brief life Saltmarsh was as busy at writing as at preaching. His first publication, perhaps while he was still at the university, was *Poemata sacra, Latinè & Anglicè scripta* (Cambridge, 1636); and thereafter, in addition to the *Holy Discoveries and Flames,* he published a score or more of religious books, mainly inspirational rather than doctrinal, several of which went into multiple editions.

In the *Holy Discoveries and Flames* the form of the meditations is diffuse and repetitious, the thought entirely pious, the length various. The physical form, or arrangement, is curious and is unlike that of any other book of resolves. In picture and in substance, the reader is often reminded of Francis Quarles's *Emblemes*, a work which preceded Saltmarsh's by only a lustrum. Some, not all, of the meditations in the *Holy Discoveries and Flames* conform fairly closely to the resolve pattern. Of these I have selected a few representative specimens.

HOLY DISCOVERIES AND FLAMES

The strait gate
Matth. 7. 13
Enter yee in at the strait gate: for wide is the gate, and broad is the way, that leadeth to destruction, etc.
[Symbol of flaming heart]

The Flame

Lord, here are two wayes, the one a way of declination, the other of exaltation; the one a broad, a wide, a loose way, a way wherein a soule may be too free, too licentious, too too[1] straying and excursive; the other a narrow way, a strait way, a way to keepe in and hedge in a Christian passenger;[2] such a way as will make him gather up his passions, and gird up his affections, that they bee not excessive nor exorbitant, nor too breaking forth into the broad and open way of wickednesse. Lord, how easie is it to go in this broad way! What freedome, what liberty, what room for disport is here! What associating and heardring[3] is here! what trooping! Every one will have a foot in this way. If I would set forward to any lust, or ambition, or covetousnesse, or any other worldly designe, this way will lead me to it. But, Lord, *I wil think on my wayes and turne* (Psal. 119. 59), and *I will take heede to my wayes,* for here is not onely a wide way to scatter and unloose my selfe in, but a steepe way, and descending way; and if I once slide down this precipice, the returne is painfull, and the recovery desperate. But *I will go stand in the wayes, and see,* etc. (Jerem. 6. 16), and though the way be smooth, and plaine, and easie, and pleasant; the way of the world, though it be strowne with flowers and roses, and spread with carpets of plush, for the pleasure and ease of my feet, yet I will instruct them back unto the strait way. O Lord, though thy way be gravell'd and causied,[4] and uneven, yet I will go in thy paths, for they lead to a new and living way (Hebr. 10. 20). Though they bee strait, that is, strict, and severe, and pinching, and binde my behaviours to thee, yet I will on; though they be toilesome in their ascent, so that I slip back and fall, and decline in my advancements forward, yet I will not go from thy wayes, for *the Lord is my helper* (Hebr. 13. 7),[5] and *he will give grace to helpe in time of need* (Hebr. 4. 16). Therefore into this strait gate will I enter; *bee open yee everlasting gates, that an heire of glory may come in.*[6] I will enter, though I reach but into the portall, for *I had rather be a doore-keeper in the house of my God, then dwell in the tents of ungodlinesse* (Psal. 84. 10). Therefore, O Lord, if any darknesse or clouds of ignorance or impiety would cast me in thy wayes, to muffle or benight me, *direct my pathes* (Prov. 3. 6), for *thou art the God of light, and in thee is no darkenesse* (I. John. 1. 5).

The Mote
Matth. 6. 3[7]
How wilt thou say to thy brother, Let me pull out the mote out of thine eye, and behold, a beame is in thine owne?

[Flaming-heart symbol]

The Flame

O God, how curious[8] are we in the infirmities of others! how officious! how industrious with our eyes to discerne, with our hands to touch, with our tongues to publish. O, that we should be such intelligencers to others, and such strangers at home! so busie abroad, and so sedentarie at home! that wee should light our tapers for others' faults and infirmities, and put them out for our owne! such curious forreigners, and such incurious domesticks! With what partiall eyes do we looke on our selves, so willing to overlook what is amisse! What mercifull courts and consistories do we keepe for our owne offences, and what severe censures and examinations for others! How deceitfull are our glasses! The blemishes and spots which are in our selves shed a shadow upon our neighbours, and makes us beleeve they are in them; how many are the blots and moles in our bodies, and yet how pure and cleare are all our owne representations! And thus we seeme to be religious,

and deceive our owne hearts, and our religion is in vaine (Jam. 1.
26). Oh, my God, how ancient is this errour! how common! Every
religion, and heresie, and schisme, and professor hath a finger for
the eye of his neighbour; *for every way of man is right in his
owne eyes* (Prov. 21. 2), *and there is a generation that are pure
in their owne eyes* (Prov. 30. 12). This generation is our generation,
and of this generation *one passeth and another commeth.*[9] How
direct! how forward are our eye beames! how single! how intent!
how percussive[10] which shoote and beate full upon the eyes of
others! never comming back, nor doubling, nor reflecting upon
our owne weaknesses and offences. How diffusive, and spreading
is this little light in our bodies! how freely disbursed upon other
objects, and how darke at home! how dull to its owne organ! and
if the light that is in me *be darknesse, how great is that darknesse!*
(Math. 6.22).[11] How inquisitive, how finely sighted are wee, even
to a mote or atome in another! Lord, cleare up my sight with some
eye-bright water[12] of contrition, that I may see my owne beames,
my owne motes, and turne back my eyes upon my owne offences.
Turne thou them, O Lord, and they shall be turned[13] (Jer. 31. 18).

Stand without
Matth. 12. 47, 48
*Then one said unto him, Behold, thy mother and thy
brethren stand without, desiring to speake with thee.
But he answered and said, Who is my mother? and
who are my brethren?*
[Seeing-eye emblem]

Discovery

I discover now, that Jesus is upon businesse, and in the heat of
his function, nothing can turn his face or regard out of the way;
a *behold* cannot so arrest his eye-beames, not though the relation
of a mother or a brother put to their hands; *Who is my mother?*
Hee declines his duty and respect, and all relations must bee question'd of their title and interest: *Who is my mother? and who are
my brethren?* Such relations are but now the pauses and interjec-
tions to dispatches and employments, and break off the continuity
which is exacted in businesse of an high and holy nature. *Who is
my mother? and who are my brethren?* hee demands as though

hee would decline his knowledge; indeede, in weighty commissions
wee should put mother and brethren to the distance of strangers,
and open our veines for consanguinity and respects to run out a
while, and leave our bloud and spirits. *Thy mother and thy breth-*
ren stand without, and without must they stand a time; it is not
fit to admit respects into the same roome with employments.[17]

The Sonne of God
Matth. 14. 33, 34

Then they that were in the ship came and worshipped,
saying, Of a truth thou art the Sonne of God.
*   And when they were gone over, they came into the*
land of Genesaret.

[Seeing-eye emblem]

Discovery

I discover, how silent Jesus is now that they worship and applaud
him. Here is not a word of his reply; they call him *the Sonne of*
God, but I reade no answer hee makes; for the verse that followes
is impertinent to this, *And when they were gone over,* etc., I observe, hee refuses not the worship nor sacred applause done him,
nor takes much notice, nor prides himselfe in it. In just and due
applauses, it is a wrong to your merit to denie them, and such
modesty does but whisper to your goodnesse to betray it. I know,
to assume and raise your selfe to the trumpet of another is arro-
gance, and the spirits are too light that are so soone rarified and
advanced. Hee is no wise musician that will make one in the consort[15] of his owne commendation.

They besought him
Luke 7. 4, 5

And when they came to Jesus, they besought him, saying,
hee was worthy for whom he should doe this.
*   For hee hath loved our nation, and built us a syn-*
agogue.

[Seeing-eye emblem]

Discovery

I discover, what an interest and obligation publick favours lay
upon those they concerne! How many here come to Jesus in the

Centurion's behalfe![16] *They came to Jesus;* they, even they who had a common interest in the courtesie he did, *He loved our nation, and built us a synagogue,* and for this love of their nation, they returne him love againe, for *they came to Jesus* for him; and for his *building a synagogue,* they build him a good reputation, *saying, that hee was worthy;* and why? because *hee loved our nation.* If you would gaine a people, you must doe something that is popular. Nothing wins a nation so as a nationall favour, and to doe this, you must raise your courtesie a story or two higher then the ordinary heighth: *hee built us a synagogue.* You must build something, that is, doe something of eminency, of notice, of duration, that may towre, and may continue above a private favour: you must build, that is, lay things together, reconcile, and cement, and unite; and such structures of friendship and charity are such synagogues as would be built both in civill and holy societies.[17]

Hee set his face

Luke 9. 51

He stedfastly set his face to goe to Jerusalem.

[Seeing-eye emblem]

Discovery

I discover here a firme resolution in Jesus. If hee look towards a place or purpose in earnest, hee goes on for it, and turnes not back on his way: *Hee set his face to goe.* His very looks and face shall steere him, and his countenance shall bee set, that his feet may goe the more firmely: *hee set his face.* Those that are unstable in their wayes, have their faces running and stirring, not well set, not stedfastly; and they that goe back and apostate[18] in their resolutions and purposes, never had their faces stedfastly set. *He stedfastly set his face,* and whither, but for Jerusalem, a place hee was to suffer and die at? In necessities and occasions which we cannot avoide, it is good to set our face, and stedfastly to conforme and confirme our resolutions. Never a martyr nor holy saint in their suffering, or way to the heavenly Jerusalem, but they had this holy feat of setting their face, and stedfastly to go; for no man looking back[19] is fit for the kingdome.

A Kingdome divided
Matth. 12. 25
Every kingdome divided against it selfe is brought to desolation.

[Seeing-eye emblem]

Discovery

I discover, that division is the way to desolation. Divide and rule[20] then is no aphorisme here; discord does well in any musick of soveraignty. Whatsoever the kingdome then or empire bee that wee have, let us keepe it from being divided: nothing spoiles our kingdom of nature so much as factious humours, and distempers, and bruisings, and breakings; for these set up unwholsome states, and infect, and corrupt the good provinces and shires of our flesh and bloud; and by this wee are soone brought to desolation. Or, if our kingdome be a kingdome of grace that wee have, let us keepe it from being divided; nothing brings this kingdome to desolation sooner then *a law in the members warring against the law of the minde.*[21] For in every kingdome there should bee a continuity, and concatenation, and consolidation, and where the kingdome is divided, there must needs be a dissolution and parting of the parts continued, and a breaking and rupture of the links, and lawes, and firme combination. And now all is divided, and there are so many flawes and chinkes, that any thing may flow in: division is the leekes of the kingdom, and where these are open, there may soon spring in a tide which may drowne all.

NOTES

1. *too too:* A frequently encountered intensive in our earlier writers; compare Hamlet's "O! that this too too solid [sullied] flesh would melt" (*Hamlet,* I, ii, 129). 2. *passenger:* Here, as elsewhere in these resolves, "a wayfarer," "one who passes by." 3. *heardring:* gathering in herds. 4. *causied:* paved with small stones, or cobbles; bumpy. 5. *(Hebr. 13.7):* The reference should be Hebrews 13:6. 6. *Bee open . . . come in:* Psalm 24:7. 7. *Math. 6.3:* Should be Matthew 7:4. 8. *curious:* inquisitive (in an unfavorable sense). 9. *one passeth and another commeth:* Ecclesiastes 1:4. 10. *percussive:* striking, beating upon; much earlier than any instance of the usage cited in *OED.*

11. *Math. 6.22:* Should be Matthew 6:23. 12. *eye-bright water:* a medication used as a remedy for weak sight (*OED*). 13. *Turne thou . . . turned:* Much modified from Jeremiah 31:18. 14. *to admit respects . . . employments:* Another way of saying that God is no respecter of persons; compare Acts 10:34. 15. *consort:* concert. 16. *in the Centurion's behalfe:* Compare Tuvill, note 47; Henshaw, note 16. 17. *civill and holy societies:* state and church. 18. *apostate:* to renege, desert a cause; now obsolete as a verb, but current in Saltmarsh's time. 19. *no man looking back:* Luke 9:62. 20. *Divide and rule:* See Hall, note 12. 21. *law in the members . . . minde:* Romans 7:23.

Thomas Manley

1628-1690

TEXT: *Temporis Angustiae: Stollen Houres Recreations. Being Meditations fitted according to the variety of Objects* . . . [two Latin quotations omitted] *By Tho. Manley, Jun. Gent. and Student, Anno Aetatis 21* (London, 1649); Wing M449. This is a thin duodecimo (Pref. + 127 pp.) containing an even one hundred numbered "Meditations." An engraved portrait of the young author figures as frontispiece. So far as can be determined, posterity has never demanded a reprint of these resolves.

Thomas Manley (1628–1690) was a miscellaneous writer upon religious and legal topics. The *Temporis Angustiae* seems to have been his first publication, deprecatingly described in the *DNB* as "a collection of boyishly sententious essays on religious subjects." The same source says that he "was called to the bar at the Middle Temple about 1650, and became king's counsel 18 Sept. 1672." His legal interests continued, for as late as 1676 he was still writing on the duties of executors (Wing M442). Yet in between 1649 and 1676, and after, he found time to concern himself with non-professional matters such as biography, history, and the current state of European affairs. As he said—in a different sense—in his "Meditation 100": "I like the law well, but yet I will not follow it wholly." Possibly his most significant achievement was his strong and influential advocacy of the use of English instead of Latin in legal literature.

If the overall temper of Manley's resolves is religious, the illustrative anecdotes, commonplaces, and proverbial sayings upon which the thought turns, or around which it weaves its patterned way, are commonly secular rather than biblical. And if his resolves are as jejune as the vapidities of the young Alexander Pope, writing on criticism before he was dry behind the ears, the cause is that they emanate from his reading, not from his experience of life. The verses with which some of Manley's resolves end seldom rise above mediocrity—or, sometimes, to it.

TEMPORIS ANGUSTIAE:
STOLLEN HOURES RECREATIONS

Med. 3

Who would ever trust him that loves to break the trust reposed on him, and will never do any good, unless it be to satisfie some private ends, some selfe-interest? As[1] such men deserve not to be trusted, so neither ought they to live, for in stretching my conscience to harme others, I deceive my self, and while I strive by wicked and sinister ends to rob others of their hoped and sought earthly good, I barre my self from an everlasting, by shutting heaven against my self. As I would not promise more then I mean to perform, break my faith, so I would not do more then I could with conveniency, least regard of my faith breake me.

Med. 12

Love is a voluntary affection and desire to enjoy that which is good; love wishes, desire enjoyes. Now if there be so much sweetnesse in the theoretick part, how much more is there in the practick; if there be so much pleasure in the journey, how much greater joy at the end? If it somewhat tends to vertue, to wish good, then it is vertue it selfe to do, to enjoy good; if desire of good make a man vertuous, then the full enjoyment of it, makes a man perfectly happy. O divine and heavenly passion, that canst at the same time make a man both vertuous and happy! Let me now begin to love, that I may begin to be vertuous, and proceed in affection, that I may be truly happy. What happinesse greater then true love? What Paradise more glorious, then that of affection? Let me then love truly, that I may enjoy happinesse, and let me devote my selfe to a vertuous affection, that I may have a share in the terrestriall Paradise.[2]

> *Thou conquer'st all, Love,[3] let not me be free,*
> *I will devote my self wholy to thee;*
> *Thou canst make happy, yea, and vertuous too,*
> *Accept me then, Ile be a servant true.*

Med. 34

When I come among a company of musitians, and see every one playing on a severall instrument, and singing thereto, with various voyces, and yet heare what a melodious harmony ariseth out of that discord, which pleases mine eare, delights my fancy, and luls my senses, as it were into a sleep with content; I cannot but thinke of that heavenly joy among the Saints, where all sing allelujahs with one consent.[5] What a supernaturall content they enjoy! If then our inferiour musick can so ravish my senses, what shall I say of those superiour? whose least harmony as farre surpasses ours, as the golden ore excels the contemned[6] sand; the least sounding of whose angelical voyces as farre exceeds the sweetest melodie and most delightfull symphonie of our best tuned notes and instruments as the purest diamond, and most hard adamant[7] doe the britlest glasse. Lord make mee one of that heavenly quire, that sing perpetuall prayses in thy presence, that my voice may chant forth allelujahs to thy name. Oh heavenly joyes, filled both with content and happinesse!

> *Lord raise my spirit that I may attaine*
> *To chant forth prayses with thy heavenly train,*
> *Ravish my senses, my dull notes inspire*
> *With holier fancies, make me of thy quire.*
> *The greatest discords shall, that now appeare*
> *Be then melodious harmonie; Lord heare.*

Med. 44

How much that candle steeds me at night, which at noon day was of no use? Yet not that now it hath more light, but that there is more need of it. Every man will be my friend in the noone, the time of my prosperitie, but he is a true friend, that stickes to me, and helps me with his counsel in the night of my adversitie, when ill fortune hath cast me downe: *amicus certus in re incerta cernitur*.[8] I will always love, and desire friends; but a friend at a dead lift[9] is really *alter idem*.[10]

Med. 47

What a various disposition of minde and speech doth every climate affords [sic] its inhabitants; and not only so, but the very same clime stamps a several character of body on every particular native thereof, insomuch, that in almost the whole world one shall never see two men alike in feature and condition; nay, some are by nature so contrary to us, that they are made black, drawing our wonder after them wheresoever we see them, as having in them somewhat monstrous; *rara avis in terris nigroque simillima cygno*.[11] And though every man be thus bodied, and vizaged severally, yet hath God made the heart of like forme in all, thereby shewing, that though we differ in all outward parts, yet our hearts should all agree, tend to one center, *viz.* the prayse of our creator. I will, since God hath given our hearts one forme, endeavour to reduce them to one affection, to doe the worke for which they were created. I will never raise severall opinions in that which God created but for one.

Med. 51

It is the foolish ambition of too many, in this last and worst age of the world, either to be best, or not at all;[12] and if they cannot attain the perfection of their desires, they wil not desire to be perfect. I am not of their mindes, but since I cannot doe as well as I would, I will doe as well as I may, and what I want in my actions, I will performe in my desires. It was pride that transformed *Lucifer*,[13] once a glorious angel, into a devilish fiend.

Med. 62

The poor Publican was sooner heard, that said little and stood afar off, then the proud-loud-boasting Pharisee:[14] 'tis not the multitude of our words, but the zeal of our hearts that God affects. The righteous man in the midst of trouble can fly to God by his prayer, when the abundant prosperity of the wicked makes him guilty both of neglect and infidelity. The prayer of the heart is the heart of prayer, and where my faith fails, my prayer falls; our infidelity stops God's eare, and makes us that we cannot heare when he calls. I will be humble in prayer, but not fearefull: *Qui timide rogat*,[15] *docet negare.*

Med. 66

When a sudden storme arises, how fast will the harmelesse sheep runne to the next brambles, where thinking to save her selfe by its shelter from the fury of the storme, it is deceived into a greater ill, and returnes with some losse of its fleece.[16] Just such thinke I, many times proves the friendship of some ingrateful, and self-seeking friends, to whom, when driven by the adverse blasts of a contrary fortune, I retire my selfe for help and comfort. They either altogether cast me off, or prey upon my necessitie, so that such help proves more fatall to me then my worst calamitie. I may patiently beare all outward miseries, and though I am wet to the skin, I can drie my selfe againe; but when my professed friend, instead of love, works my woe, this, this cuts me to the heart.[17] *Brutus'* one stroke[18] went neerer Caesar's heart then the stabs of all his other enemies.

Med. 75

See you that dust with which the sportive winde does play the wanton? now framing it in curles, anon disperseth it abroad, throwing it now here, now there. It is perhaps the remaining reliques of some fallen beauty: see, even in death it has not lost its nature, but as before so still, does fly about to trouble our weaker sight. O insolent,[19] yet empty boast of flesh! Though we be ennobled with the greater honor, and set on the top of Fortune's wheel[20] in our life, though we leave heires behinde to maintain our name, which will with everlasting monuments (as much as in them lies) eternize our dying, nay, dead memory, yet will death betray for all these things our dust to every blast! Alas, poor relique of our glory, wilt thou still swell with glorious ambition; or rather not to mock weake, yet proud man, who rises straight above his center by the meanest blast of common praise, ready to think himself now weak and falling, stable, yea even immortall.

> *Leave off this pride fraile man, for all thy lust*
> *To beauti's madness, for it courts but dust.*

Med. 76

Expectation in a weak and wearied minde makes an evill greater, and a good less, but the constantly resolved minde diverts an evil, being come, and makes a future good present before it come. I expect then the best, I know the worst; worst and best will arrive both at their end.

Med. 81

I can never reade that portion of Scripture,[21] where Jacob cunningly gaines the blessing from his brother Esau, and his vaine seeking, and fruitless begging it even with teares, but it drives me to think, how just might God be to cast us off, who sin with so high a hand against him. If with Esau we sell our birthright for a messe of pottage, if we forfeit, and that willingly, our everlasting heavenly inheritance for the deceitfull momentany[22] pleasures of sin, it is but just with God to cast us off as illegitimate. I will not therefore hunt after worldly pleasures so long with Esau as to forfeit my blessing for my long stay; ere vengeance begin, repennance [*sic*] is seasonable, but if judgement be once gone out, we cry too late. While the Gospel solicites us, the doores of mercy are open, but if we neglect the time of grace, in vaine shall we seek it with teares. God holds it no mercy to pity the obstinate.

Med. 84

When I see two game-cocks[23] fighting in the pit, and each striving by the death of the other to remaine sole conquerer, I cannot but take notice of the vaine strifes of great men, who without any cause at all seek the destruction of each other, endeavouring to make great the plumes of his owne ambition, with the feathers of his adversarie's downfall, as if it were glory enough to enrich himselfe by [the] other's ruines. I am not of that minde: but if I strive to be great, I will desire to be good, for great goodnesse is the best greatnesse, and I will not with Aesop's daw trick up my pride with stollen feathers,[24] least I be served like her, that when every man takes his owne, I appeare not only naked, but ridiculous.

Med. 87

I can never see a flatterer framing all his actions and gestures according to the humours of whom he flatters, but I thinke the polypus[25] a fit resembler of such a person, who changes his colours as often as the various objects he touches doe. Art thou sick, so will he counterfeit himself? Art thou prodigall, he will tell thee it beseemes thy birth? Whatever thou dost or sayest, thereafter will he frame both his words and actions, till he hath so far compassed his

own ends, as thou must either trust him, or he will undoe thee.[26]
I will not then looke altogether at the outside of a faire word,
nor trust too much to the subtle daubings of a cunning flatterer,
for outward appearances are but deceitfull guides to our judgement, and they are worthy to be deceived that value a flatterer
above a true friend.[27] A smiling malice is most deadly,[28] and hatred
doth most rankle the heart when it is kept in and dissembled.

Med. 97

Hodie Croesus, cras Irus.[29] Though thou sittest today on a throne,
thy will standeth for law, and dominering with a proud tyranny
over thy inferiors, thou mayst to morrow lye with Job on a dunghill.[30] See the inconstancy of fickle fortune, making, as it were, a
tennisball of the world. Who would be a servant to so wavering a
mistress? Who would rely on that which is constant to nothing but
inconstancy? I will therefore bare my affliction[31] like my self, as
one subject to chance, but resolved in the change of my fortune.
Though I may bewaile my fortune, and lament my fall, yet will
I not dismay my self, since I know that all corporall damages
that betide mortall men are either by means remedied, by patience suffered, by reason rectified, by time cured, or by death
ended. There is a power above the capacity of men, and comfort
may descend beyond the expectation of men.

Med. 100

Dimidium facti, qui bene coepit habet. Though it were said of
old, He has done the better half of his work that hath begun well,
yet we know that *non progredi est regredi,* he that goes not forward goes backward. It were as good he had never set out, who
sits down in the midst of his journey; Jacob's ladder[32] hath many
steps; it is[33] not enough to begin to be good, but to proceed in
goodness. It is as true as common that *exitus acta probat,* the glory
of a thing lies in its ending. It was a law in Rome, that when a
souldier was fifty years old, he should no more beare arms; a
Senator having attained to threescore years was no more bound to
attend the Senate. What should be the reason, but that after the tur-
moyles of their tedious life, being freed from the cares of the world,
they might think of their end? I like the law well, but yet I will not

follow it wholly, for I will not put off the thought of my death till old age, but will always prepare for it: since ever to meditate on my end is the best end of my meditations.

NOTES

1. *selfe-interest?* *As:* original reading; selfe interest; as. 2. *terrestrial Paradise:* It may be questioned here whether Manley means "terrestrial" or "celestial." 3. *Thou conquer'st all, Love:* Probably a conscious translation of Virgil's "omnia vincit amor." 4. *a severall:* a different. 5. *consent:* musically, *concent* is "harmony of sounds." 6. *contemned:* despised, not valued. 7. *diamond, and . . . adamant:* The two words were often used interchangeably, although *adamant* could mean any exceedingly hard metal or stone. 8. *amicus . . . cernitur:* Translate, "A sure friend is revealed in a shaky circumstance"; attributed to the ancient Latin poet Ennius. 9. *at a dead lift:* I.e., "when the chips are down." (For a more precise definition, see *OED, s.v.,* 2.) 10. *alter idem:* Stafford, note 12.

11. *rara avis . . . cygno:* Juvenal, *Satires,* VI, 165. Translate, "A rare bird on earth and most resembling a black swan." Juvenal's swan is *cycno.* 12. *It is . . . at all:* For the "foolish ambition," see Warwick's *Resolve* 1. The notion that the present age is the "last and worst age of the world" goes back to the classical myth of the four ages: the golden, the silver, the brass, the iron—each successively a falling-away from the desirable qualities of its predecessor. Thomas Heywood, a playwright nearly contemporary with Manley, wrote a series of four plays, each dealing with one of these "ages." 13. *pride that transformed Lucifer:* Milton tells the whole story, *Paradise Lost,* Books V–VI. 14. *The poor Publican . . . Pharisee:* Compare Luke 18:10–14. 15. *Qui timide rogat:* Translate, "He who asks faintly invites denial." 16. *the harmelesse sheep . . . fleece:* An illustration often used by moralists, and in nearly these words. See Henry Smith, *Works,* ed. Thomas Smith, 2 vols. (Edinburgh, 1866–1867), II, 75; Barnaby Rich, *The Honestie of This Age* (1614), sig. G1 verso. 17. *my professed friend . . . heart:* Compare Tuvill, *Essays,* pp. 47–48. 18. *Brutus' one stroke:* Compare Plutarch, *Parallel Lives,* tr. Dryden (Modern Library ed.), p. 893, and Antony's elaboration of it in Shakespeare's *Julius Caesar,* III, ii, 177–87. 19. *insolent:* swollen, puffed up. 20. *top of Fortune's wheel:* A favorite image with emblematists and writers on the *de casibus* theme. The original is Boethius, *Consolation of Philosophy,* Book II, prose 1.

21. *that portion of Scripture:* Genesis 25:29–34. 22. *momentany:* fleeting, of a moment's duration; now obsolete. 23. *When I see two*

game-cocks: See Warwick, resolve 33, "Of Revenge." 24. *Aesop's daw
. . . feathers:* The daw (or crow) in borrowed feathers was one of the
most widely known of the Aesopic fables; for an English version nearly
contemporary with Manley, compare *The Fabulist Metamorphosed*
(1634), Fable 52. To *trick up* means to "decorate, adorn." 25. *the polypus:* Our early writers were much confused about the identity of the
polypus and about the undesirable characteristics that could be attributed to it; compare *OED, s.v.* Manley would have done better here
if he had used the chameleon for his comparison; but see also Lucian,
Dialogues of the Sea-Gods, tr. H. W. and F. G. Fowler (Oxford, 1905),
IV. 26. *thou must . . . undoe thee:* Tuvill offers an illustration of this
principle in the case of Augustus and Agrippa; see *Essays,* p. 124 (and
note). 27. *value a flatterer . . . friend:* The classic statement on dis-
tinguishing the one from the other is found in Plutarch, "How to Tell
a Flatterer from a Friend"; compare *Moralia,* tr. Holland, pp. 83–116.
28. *A smiling malice . . . deadly:* Compare Shakespeare's "one may smile,
and smile, and be a villain," *Hamlet,* I, v, 108. 29. *Hodie Croesus, cras
Irus:* Translate, "Today [you may be like] Croesus, tomorrow [like]
Irus," i.e., rich today, poor tomorrow. A parallel saying, often associated
with the summons of "that fell sargent Death," is "Hodie tibi, cras mihi,"
"for you today, for me tomorrow." 30. *lye with Job on a dunghill:*
Compare Job 2:9. Job's seat of suffering was the ash-heap, or city dump,
outside the walls of his city.

31. *bare my affliction:* for *bare* read *bear.* 32. *Jacob's ladder:* In
Jacob's dream, the ladder ascended into heaven; see Genesis 28:12. 33.
it is: original reads *its.*

Edward Waterhouse

༺ᖶᗦᑗᑉ༻

1619-1670

TEXT: *An humble Apologie for Learning and Learned Men* (London, 1653); Wing W1048. Octavo, in three parts, since the two *Meditations* following the *Apologie* are both separately paged and carry separate signatures. A glance at the title of Waterhouse's book, without opening the work itself, might easily mislead the reader. The book is learned enough—the margins are loaded. But the "apology" is not so much for *learning* as for a learned clergy; and the tone is prevailingly pious, notwithstanding occasional secular allusions. Bacon, who might have been expected to figure here is cited, as nearly as I detect, but twice.

Waterhouse was a man of curious and irregular erudition. He was an LL.D. (1668) of Cambridge, *per literas regias,* but is said to have studied also at Oxford. He was elected to membership in the Royal Society; and late in life he took holy orders and began preaching. His piety and obvious orthodoxy, however, were no late arrivals: they are abundantly present in the *Apologie* and in the two *Meditations* that were published with it.

I excerpt from the *Apologie* three passages in which the author seems to make use of his own inverted form of the resolve. In Waterhouse the resolve has ceased to exist as an independent form and has become an incidental instrument of polemics.

AN HUMBLE APOLOGIE FOR LEARNING AND LEARNED MEN

[A Word to the Envious and Carping Unco' Guid]

Me thinks I hear one bethinking[1] me this motion, and taxing me as too bold to crave this boon for the clergy, while the gifted men (as the term is) who are all honey and no gall, all gold and no drosse, all beauty and no deformity in their eyes, stand competitors: as if I were injurious to beg away the children's bread for aliens from the Common-wealth of Israel, and men without God in the world, who are formalists, worldly wise, enemies to free grace, and branded by such like insinuations.

Truly, were the ministers such, I would confesse their charge, and plead guilty: But when I know the contrary, I cannot but wonder at the agreement they would make 'twixt Christ and Belial in one tongue; while with the same mouth they blesse themselves and all of their own way, and curse others, perhaps (I am unperemptory) not lesse holy then themselves.

To this objector I shall answer in the words of God himself, Gen. 4. 6.[2] Why (man) art thou so wroth? why is thy countenance changed? why lookest thou upon thy brother as one born out of due time, as one to eat of the husks, when thou thinkest the fatted calf[3] little enough for thee? *What hast thou which thou hast not received,* not onely from God *(from whom every good and perfect gift cometh),* but from men, perhaps those whom thou despisest, to whose ministry, writings, discourses thou owest what thou hast? Dost thou do well to be angry?[4] to rage against, and revile those who have with the phoenix,[5] spent their lives to beget the life of grace (if any thou hast) in thee? How canst thou without shame (in St. Jerom's words)[6] accuse that cook as unsavory-handed, from whom thou tookest thy wholsome diet? or how can that Church be dark, at whose lamp thou lightest thy farthing candle? or that eye be blinde which gave thee light? If Christ be formed in thee, if the life of grace has its perfection in thy soul, if thou art one with Christ, as thou saist thou art, and those are that thou preferrest; who were instrumentall in this work? Was it not the minister of God who applyed the corrosives of the Law, and cordials[7] of the Gospel to thee? Did not his hand conduct thine eye to such a menace, and such a promise? And didst thou not heretofore, when thou was as much thy self as now, blesse God for him, and rejoyce under the wings of his ministry? Whence then comes the change? while he continues the same, why alterest thou? While hee opens his treasure to thee, and bids thee welcome to his fat things, why dost thou nod the head, and bend the fist? Why lookest thou upon him as reprobate silver which the Lord hath rejected? Doth this manifest Christ in thee, and not rather sin raigning and precipitating thee into ruine? Do not boast thyself, that in Christ's name thou hast prophecied:[8] if the Divel and evill spirit of pride be not cast out, there is nothing of Christ in thy soul; *His soul which is lifted up is not upright in him.*[9] 'Tis not great words, devout looks, that makes a Christian: to live what we beleeve, is to walk to well pleasing; for as Justin Martyr excellently,[10] If shewes and semblances were true proofes of vertue and holinesse, Christ would never have reproved those as unworthy his familiarity and acceptation who said, Have we not in thy name prophesied, and in thy name cast out divels, etc.

I will not follow the method of many men, to right some with the wrongs of others. I will exhort, rather then recriminate. Those which have most of Christ in their lips and lives, shall be the Saints in my kalender. If the "gifted men"[11] (as they are called) are more holy, more learned, lesse leavened with pride and uncharitablenesse, lesse versed in craft; if they are more in fastings, prayings, watchings, weepings, charitie; if they discourse with more evidence and demonstration of the Spirit; if they forgive more throughly, converse with God more closely then the holy ministers of the Church do, or can, then let them bee owned as the living temples of the holy Ghost.

But if they which are good amongst them, are as errable[12] and imperfect (not to say ought else) as others; yea, if they do not abhor, and declare against persons, who in Justin Martyr's phrase,[13] teach blasphemies and untrue things, under the name of divine truths, when as indeed, they are but the obtrusions of Satan upon their impure heart; if[14] they persist in disesteeming and undermining the ministry, which they ought to honour as Christ's ordinance, and the Churche's glory and comfort; if they shew not a better warrant for their singularity, then yet they have—let[15] them pardon us, if we follow them not, though a multitude; and I promise them, they shall have my prayers, that God would (if they be not in it, which they better know, who say they have the Spirit, then I) shew them what is his good and acceptable way. That's all the harm I wish them, that shall be all the vinegar and gall[16] I'll give them. (Pages 166–69)

[Cautions in the Reformation of Religion]

I will declare myself to all the world for one who approves[17] reformation in religion and learning, as an act of piety and uni-

versal good; but truly, O Powers, there is much heed to be taken
in a matter wherein miscarriage is so easy and fatall. *Cassiodore*
sayes[18] *omnia deliberata sunt robusta;* and I have ever judged
things done in haste, fit to be repented of at leisure.[19] In the
Counsell of Basil consultation was had about reforming religion,
and the Counsell concluded to begin with the Minorites, one of
the meanest Orders; but the Emperour Sigismund cryed out, *Non
à Minoritis sed à majoritis.*[20] Take down those top-sayles of defy-
ance, that are hoysted up against principles of art and sober
science; polish off that rust and canker which time and impudence
hath forced upon religion and art; imploy[21] learned and unpreju-
dic'd men to prepare things for your deliberation and authoriza-
tion, and then there is hope to come to anchor, and to make a
successfull port the haven[22] of truth and honour. (Pages 198–99)

[That the Vulgar Many Should not Govern]

Let those who will cry up multitudes, I shall not; for I find them
disorderly, vain, injudicious, cruel, like rivers, sinking everything
that is solid, and bearing up whatever is light;[23] their traffick is
in the nothings of bubbles, swellings of waves, and bladders of
words; and those governours neglect themselves and their people
who do not answer their mutinies with punishments, and en-
courage their obedience with justice, protection, and honest ease
and liberty. But[24] if they desire more then is their due, or they
know how to be happy with, let them have that reproof which
St. Basil gave[25] Valens, the Emperor's prattling cook: *Look you to
your pot and dresse, that they be savoury;* or which Alexander
gave[26] his mutinous rabble; otherwise there wil be no hoe with
them, as the phrase is. Not that I think it safe or honourable to
rule with rigour, but for that it is more to good men's peace to have
government tite and stiffe girt, and more to their content to live
where nothing, then where every thing is lawful. That noble grave
Roman Appius Claudius gave gallant counsel to the Senate,
against submission to the vulgarity, telling them of many Graecian
cities, who by yeilding had ruin'd themselves, and been a president
of ill to the world, while they suffered evils to grow through im-
punity: and assure them, that if they resign the government
to the rude people, 'twill be all one as if the body should rule

the soul. And therefore he wishes them *not to perplex well ordered government, not to change laudable customs, not to take away fidelity, the firmest bond of humane societies* (and that which makes us differ from beasts, who prey one upon another), *but to stand for order, and maintain that peace which just and wise governours ought to labour for, and to overthrow which, rude multitudes do ever aim.*[27] Thus he, and wisely to: for to give people way, contrary to law, and judgement, is to make power become their minister to spoils, furies, and inhumanities; and therefore every good magistrate should resolve if he perish, he'l perish in doing his duty; for in so doing, he may expect God's custody. While the mid-wives of Egypt feared God, they had houses built for them. Power and honour is never better founded, then when on true religion and zeal for God, on justice and moderate liberty to men-wards: the Covenant of peace followed Phineas his zeal, *and continued the everlasting Priest-hood to his seed after him.* Numb. 13. 25.[28] (Pages 242–43)

NOTES

1. *bethinking:* begrudging, conceding unwillingly. 2. *Gen. 4. 6.:* See the account of Cain and Abel at this passage in Genesis. 3. *the husks . . . the fatted calf:* The reference here is to the grumbling elder brother in the parable of the prodigal son; compare Luke 15:11–32. 4. *What hast thou . . . to be angry:* The main reference here is to the angry and rebellious spirit of Jonah (Jonah 3–4), with an intruded passage ("every good and perfect gift") from James 1:17 and the *Book of Common Prayer.* 5. *the phoenix:* fabled bird whose self-immolation provided the ashes from which arose the next phoenix, only one of these long-lived birds living at a time; symbolic of the sacrifice and resurrection of Christ. 6. *St. Jerom's words:* Not found. 7. *corrosives . . . and cordials:* Contrasting the harsh remedies of the Old Testament (Law) and the soothing ones of the New (Gospel). 8. *Do not boast . . . prophecied:* Compare Matthew 7:22–23. 9. *His soul . . . upright in him:* Habakkuk 2:4. 10. *as Justin Martyr excellently:* See "The First Apology of Justin," tr. Marcus Dods, *The Writings of Justin Martyr and Athenagoras,* Ante-Nicene Christian Library (Edinburgh, 1867), II, 20–21.

11. *the "gifted men":* I.e., evangelical dissenters, enthusiasts; extempore preachers. 12. *errable:* subject to erring, fallible; an earlier use of the word than any cited in the *OED.* 13. *in Justin Martyr's phrase:*

Justin Martyr, *Writings,* pp. 29–30.   14. *impure heart; if:* Original reads
"impure heart: If."   15. *they have—let:* Original reads "they have; Let."
16. *vinegar and gall:* The bitter drink tauntingly offered to Jesus on the
Cross; compare Matthew 27:34.   17. *approves:* Original reads *approve.*
18. *Cassiodore sayes:* I have not found this needle in the copious hay-
stack of Cassiodorus's *Opera omnia.* Translate "All propositions well
considered are firm."   19. *things done in haste . . . leisure:* Marriage, for
instance; see Tilley, *Proverbs,* M694; and Congreve, *The Old Bachelor,*
V, viii.   20. *Counsell of Basil . . . majoritis:* The antipapal Council of
Basle was held, with some interruption and a transfer of locale, from
1431 to 1439. The emperor's pun may with some clumsiness be translated as "Not with Minorities, but with majorities," i.e., not with the
defects of the Minorite Order, but with major evils.

21. *and art; imploy:* Original reads "and art: Imploy."   22. *top-
sayles . . . anchor . . . haven:* Note the consistency with which this nautical
figure is developed.   23. *like rivers . . . light:* Compare Bacon, *Advancement of Learning,* in *Selected Writings of Francis Bacon,* ed. Hugh G.
Dick (New York, 1955), p. 190.   24. *ease and liberty. But:* Original
reads "ease and liberty; but."   25. *reproof which St. Basil gave:* Basil
does write to (and about) one Demosthenes, superintendent of Valens's
kitchen and incidentally Vicar of Pontus; but if the present quip appears
in Basil's *Letters,* 4 vols. (Loeb), I have not found it.   26. *or which
Alexander gave:* See Plutarch, *Parallel Lives,* tr. Dryden (Modern Library
ed.), "Alexander," p. 851.   27. *That noble . . . ever aim:* For Appius
Claudius, see Livy, *A.u.c.,* III, lvi–lviii. The verbs in this passage are
highly inconsistent in tense and number; but since Waterhouse's meaning is clear enough, it has seemed better to let them stand unchanged.
28. *Numb. 13. 25.:* More intelligibly, Numbers 25: 12–13.

John Spencer

d. 1680

Text: *KAINA KAI ΠΑΛΑΙΑ. Things New and Old. A Storehouse of Similies, Sentences, Allegories, Apophthegma, Adagies, Divine, Morall, Politicall, &c. With their severall Applications. Collected and observed from the Writings and Sayings of the Learned in all Ages to this present. By John Spencer, a lover of Learning and Learned Men* (London, 1658); Wing S4960.

Nothing about this curious folio facilitates reference. Each of the lucubrations is numbered—but very carelessly and inaccurately. The final one carries the number 2004 and is entitled "Honesty, the best Policy," though the vexed reader may feel that a little more "honesty" might have been exercised in the count. Actually, because of the large blocks of repeated numbers, the count should be considerably higher—possibly as much as five hundred more; I have not bothered to make a private count. Nor does the pagination help, for there the numbering is hopelessly jumbled. Even the signatures are irregular. For purposes of identification, therefore, I have given the heading, the numbering, the page, and the signature of each entry.

Spencer's vast compilation is a sort of commonplace book, intended (as most such personal gatherings were not) for publication. The resolve, if successful, obviously lent itself to such excerption and reproduction. A long list (7 pp., double column) of "the severall Authors cited" is prefixed to the volume. Several resolve writers appear in this list: Feltham, Hall, and Warwick (whose first name is given as Anthony). Tuvill (or Tutevile), though not in the list, is cited several times from the *Essays* but apparently not from the *Christian Purposes*. Numbers 1976, 1977 (p. 668) cite Hall's *Meditations and Vowes*, the third century. The pieces numbered by Spencer 819, 822, 823, and 824 all take their impulse from Warwick. I reproduce No. 819 so that the reader may compare it with the original (p. 140 of my text) and thus see how subtly the form is altered.

Not many particulars are known of the life of this quiet "lover of Learning and Learned Men," who was for many years librarian

of Sion College, London. His only other known work is a catalog
of the books in that library (Wing S4959), published in 1650. The
preface "To the Reader" in the present work was written by
Thomas Fuller, who says of the author that he was "no Scholar
by profession." Since Fuller was at that time resident in Sion
College and presumably well acquainted with Spencer, we may
let the matter rest in that pronouncement.

Few, if any, of Spencer's selections can be said to represent the
ideal form of the resolve. But that he knew the form is clear from
his dependence upon the aforementioned writers of resolves.
Where he comes closest is in the double nature of each composition: a meditation or observation which is then given an application to Christian life. Some degree of preacherly exhortation is
normally involved here; and if not implied in the conclusion of
the entry, the desired "resolution" is commonly explicit in the
title.

ΚΑΙΝΑ ΚΑΙ ΠΑΛΑΙΑ. THINGS NEW AND OLD

819. *The great danger of Law-suits*

It is the relation of a gentleman, that seeing a jer-falcon let fly
at a heron, he observed with what clamour the heron entertained
the sight and approach of the hawke and with what winding shift
he strove to get above her, labouring even by bemuting his enemie's feathers to make her flag-wing'd, and so escape; but at last
when they must needs come to a necessitated encounter, resuming
courage out of necessity, he turn'd face against her, and striking
the hawke through the gorge, both fell down dead together.[1] This
fight doth much resemble some great suit in law, where one trusting more to his cause's potency, than his cause's equity, endeavours to disinherit his stubborn neighbour by colourable
title to his land. Here[2] you may hear the clamourous obliquies[3]
of the wronged, and see the many turnings, and winding meanders of the law, sought out to get above his adversary; and then
when the issue must come to tryal, oftentimes in the grapple they
both sink back to beggery, whilst lawfully they seek to get one
above the other. (Page 207, sig. Dd4ʳ)

916. *A Man full of talk, full of Vanity*

A prating barber[4] asked King Archelaus how he would be trimmed, the King replyed, *Silently.* Surely in much talk there cannot chuse but be much vanity. Loquacity[5] is the fistula of the mind, ever running and almost incurable; let every man therefore be a Phocion or Pythagorean, to speak briefly to the point or not at all. Let[6] him labour, like them of Crete, to shew more wit in his discourse then words, and not to powre out of his mouth a floud of the one, when he can hardly wring out of his brains a drop of the other. (Page 235, sig. Hh2)

1215. *The good of Quietnesse, and evill of Contention*

Look but upon a pleasant pond, full of sweet fish, how do they sport themselves up and down in it, and multiply continually unto a great encrease? But let the sluce be once taken up, the fishes are quickly gone, the waters stay not till they be gone also, and nothing but mud and mire is left behind. So it is that in a quiet life, the affairs and endeavours of men do prosper, and their estate is encreased to plenty and abundance, so that they even bathe themselves in the comfort and contentments that they find therein; but let the waters of strife break in, the gap of contention be opened, all comforts fleet away, and usually the estate sinks lower and lower, untill it be dried up to beggery and misery. Such is the good of quietnesse, and the evill that attendeth upon contention. It[7] is therefore good counsell to make up all breaches assoon as they doe appear, or rather by watchfulnesse keep all so firm, that no breach may appear, for the evill of contention is a great deal better prevented then remedied. (Page 331, sig. Vv2)

1293. *Consideration of our secret Sins, a motive to Compassionate others*

We may read[8] of a judge in the primitive times, who when he was seriously invited to the place of judgment to passe sentence upon another, withdrew himself; and at last, being earnestly pressed, came with a bag of sand upon his shoulders to the judgment seat, saying; *You call me to passe judgment upon this poor offender; How can I do it, when I my self am guilty of more sins then this bag hath sands in it, if the world saw them all?* This[9] was not so well done as a publique magistrate, being invited to do justice; yet as becoming a conscionable Christian. And thus ought all good men to do. The[10] consideration of their bosome sins should work in them compassion towards others, saying within themselves, Can I be as Judah to cry out upon Tamar, *Let her be burnt,* when I remember the ring and the staffe, laid in pawn to her in secret?[11] How can I be extream against my weak brother, when if my faults were written on my forehead, I might deserve as severe a censure my self. (Page 457, sig. Mmm^r)

NOTES

1. *It is the relation . . . together:* Adapted from Warwick, resolve 35. 2. *his land. Here:* Original reads "his land; Here." 3. *obliquies:* detractions, calumnies. 4. *A prating barber:* Spencer's marginal note refers to Feltham's *Resolves;* the original is probably Plutarch, *Moralia,* tr. Holland, p. 408; see also Tuvill, *Essays,* p. 147. 5. *much vanity. Loquacity:* Original reads "much vanity, Loquacity." 6. *at all. Let:* Original reads "at all; let." 7. *contention. It:* Original reads "contention, It." 8. *We may read:* Source not found; but compare Babrius's Aesopic fable of the two wallets, Fable 66 (Loeb). 9. *them all? This:* Original reads "them all: This." 10. *to do. The:* Original reads "to do, the." 11. *be as Judah . . . secret:* The curious familial tale of Judah and Tamar may be read in Genesis 38:12–26.

Henry Tubbe

1618-1655

Title: *Meditations Divine and Morall. By H. T. M. A. and some-times of St. Johns Colledge, Cambridge* (London, 1659); Wing T3208. This posthumously published thin duodecimo ("Preface to the Reader," 31 pp.; meditations, 189 pp.) contains one hundred numbered meditations, many of which are cast in recognizable resolve form. I reprint fourteen of these. A reissue of this 1659 set of meditations appeared in 1682 from the same press, with the type not reset, and with the preface omitted.

Henry Tubbe (or Tubb), 1618–1655, has no entry in the *DNB;* I am indebted for such information as here appears to a study by G. C. Moore Smith, *Henry Tubbe* (Oxford, 1915). Moore Smith informs us that Tubbe, son of Captain John Tubbe and his wife Anne, was born at Southampton, where the family had substantial connections with the Spencers, the Wriothesleys, and the Dever-eux. Henry Tubbe was admitted to St. John's, Cambridge, June 3, 1635, proceeding B.A. in 1638–1639, M.A. in 1642. While Tubbe was still a child his father was killed (May 1625) in the attack upon Terheyden, in the Netherlands; and his widowed mother then moved to Croydon, where she died in 1629. Efforts were made in 1642 and 1643 by noble patrons to secure a Fellowship for Tubbe at St. John's, but without success. It is not known for how long, or even whether, he remained at Cambridge after taking the M.A. degree. A few of his letters dating from 1644–1655, selectively re-produced by Moore Smith, give some particulars of his where-abouts and state of mind—the latter firmly Royalist. But the best record of his activities is probably that provided in the contents of his holograph manuscript preserved in the British Museum (Moore Smith, pp. 56–59) which contains epistles (prose and verse), elegies, hymns, miscellaneous prose, satires, epigrams, char-acters, and the Devotions (i.e., Meditations)—there present in *three* centuries rather than the one of the printed version. There is va-riety enough to show that Tubbe was alert to the literary forms popular in his day.

Tubbe's literary performances in prose and in verse were frequently derivative and of no exceeding brilliance; but, says Moore Smith (p. 51), speaking of the original manuscript, "The Meditations are by no means without merits of thought and pointed expression, and show Tubbe perhaps at his best." Moore Smith prints (pp. 104–6) five—Nos. XI, XXV, L, LXI, LXXXVI—of these meditations from the printed edition of 1659. But neither in his introduction nor in his notes does he give the faintest indication that they belong in the resolve tradition. In the notes (p. 116) he asks only, "Is it possible that the form of T. Traherne's *Centuries of Meditations* was in any way suggested by Tubbe's work?" To which one might answer: Possible, of course; but not likely. That Tubbe possibly knew Feltham's *Resolves* may be inferred from the fact (Moore Smith, p. 57) that one of Tubbe's verse-epistles in the B. M. Harleian MS 4126 is "an adaptation of Randolph's poem, 'To Feltham on his book of Resolves.' " The point is of no great moment.

MEDITATIONS DIVINE AND MORALL

VIII

Boldness is an ornament to a vertuous man; but when 'tis put on to boulster up a vicious act, nothing more odious. Bashful vertue 'tis a foolish sin, and bold vice is a sinful bravery. Too much modesty intangles the soule with many impediments; and over-daring drives headlong into infinite dangers. Remorse for sinning is a divine grace, but to be ashamed of goodnesse is the next way that leads to impiety. How many good natures have betray'd themselves for want of courage to deny an unreasonable importunity? As I would not stubbornly reject the worst request, so I shall never grant the best without some intimation of power in the libertie of a denial. I will neither accept nor afford any thing in such a manner, but that the world shall see, I could easily forbear to confer, and as easily refuse a benefit.

XII

In experience I shall observe this rule: Rather[1] spend too little then too much. For covetousness there may be some satisfaction, but the prodigal is lost beyond all redemption. He that spends above his abilities will never be able to make himselfe amends. I had rather deceive the expectations of others, then cosen my self. He that straines his estate to be accounted liberal, may be thought covetous when all's spent: for the world is most apt to censure those that decline their former course. Give God his due in tythes, the poor in almes, and thy self in necessaries, and there will remaine no great superfluitie of wealth to cast away in vanity.

XVI[2]

Beauty is a grace that proceeds from the proportion, agreement, and harmony of things; it is then most seemly in the body of man when it follows nature alone without any blemish or defect. How far we may use the help of art, and disguise a deformity to appeare more comely, then we are by our creation, a sober Christian may easily resolve. As God is not pleased if we mangle and macerate our bodies with cruel tortures, so he cannot but be offended when we over-garnish them with gaudy colours, and lay on the varnish of a deep complexion. It is to be feared that they can hardly speak from their heart, that cannot blush from their own blood. When the face can dissemble so well, the tongue may be suspected too. A painted feature is the emblem of vice, which would seem to be adorned with the blushing colours of vertue, when she intends nothing but temptation. We are not to disfigure our faces when we fast in our greatest sorrow; nor reform them too much when we feast in our highest mirth; we must not mar God's work; we must not mend it so as if it should need no additions of glory hereafter.

XXXI

The want of things makes them precious. We are scarce sensible of a benefit which we enjoy. Before possession we think our selves miserable; and when our desires are satisfied, we growe weary of our happinesse. The fond lover can court his mistris with oaths and protestations, whom afterwards he esteemes no better then his necessary drudge. A poor man knows the value of a penny, when the rich prodigal throwes away his pounds. How sweet is liberty and redemption to the captive? Health and strength to the diseased? We are eager for those blessings which are denied us, and unthankful for those which we obtain. The apprehension is still fixt upon the object which is absent, as not thinking that which is present worth a serious and stedfast view. But certainly that man is most true to his owne content that can rightly value a blessing enjoyed, and comfortably use those favours which God and nature have bestowed upon him. As I would not overvalue any thing, least I bee too much affected with grief in the loss, so, I will learn to know the just price of what I have, least my desire of more increase beyond all measure of satisfaction.

XXXIV

I will be kinde and courteous to all, but familiar with none but my intimate and equal friends: for the love of inferiours often-times degenerates into contempt. Yet I had rather my carriage should savour of too much humility then over-much state: for the affections which proceed from popularity are not so dangerous as those passions of feare and envy which alwayes attend the proud. I will not think my self too good to looke upon any man; but I will be sure that he whom I receive into my bosome acquaintance shall be at least as good a man as my selfe.[3]

LII

When God resolves to make his wisdom knowne by suppressing the counsels of wise men, it is commonly done by small means, and weak instruments;[4] thus the poor man shall save the City: thus Jaell shall prevaile[5] against Sisera above an army of men: thus the folly of preaching hath confounded all the learning of the world—to teach us that nothing can be done without him. The streames of our strength runne dry unless the spring of his bounty be full. The best knowledge, if not attendant to his grace will faint and tire at last, but the least spark of wit animated by his goodnesse shall mount up with eagles' wings. Nothing can act rightly except he inspire the motion; yet he that looks for revelations, and expects a divine assistance to his undertakings, without all endeavour on his own part, intends but to deceive himself and others. As too much confidence in the external helps of devotion brings in superstition, so too much neglect doth but advance profanenesse. The very name of a university is hateful to ignorant atheists; and heresies thrives [*sic*] best in the suppression of all learned diligence. Industry and grace will stand well together; strength and glory have a mutual complyance. Let us not trust overmuch to the one, nor caution our selves with a conceit of the other.

LVI[6]

I will ever suspect that man that makes too much haste to gaine my acquaintance. A violent affection goes away as fast as it comes; a fire of straw is easily kindled and quickly out. Love that is ripe too soon, like summer fruit, will not hold out in the winter of affliction. A durable friendship is built upon consideration. He that thrusts himself upon me may be presumed to want honesty or judgement: either he hath some designe upon my person, or else is not worthy of my knowledge. Religion is the best ground of a familiar society: and I shall think that he hath but little in himself, that will venture upon me, not yet informed of mine.

LXI[7]

We may observe that in times of danger and destruction, good men are little regarded and for the most part live obscurely. In this injustice of the world the goodnesse of God is most conspicuous. When the birds of prey are fluttering abroad, the careful hen calls in her chickens to the safe protection of her wings; when the street is filled with violence and tumults, the tender parent locks up the children within doores, not denying them their liberty, but thus providing for their safety and security. What greater happinesse then a quiet close retiring roome, when blood and ruine are making merry without? Can we complaine of obscurity, when scarce any open place is secure enough? How happy was the Church under ground,[8] when in that darknesse there was light enough to see heaven? In that narrow imprisonment they were yet free from persecution. Those seven thousand which Elijah [Margin: I King. 19 18] knew not of were well known to him that preserved them. And when Elijah himself was sought for by Jezabel,[9] where had he been if he had been every where? They that have strength enough to burn in glorious flames, may scorne to save themselves by flight; but if God afford this help to our weaknesse, we have reason to be thankful for an easie judgement, which appointed as the means of our deliverance turns into a blessing. Let me be separated from the comfortable society of my dear friends, deprived of the benefit of my owne countrey aire, exposed to misery and the contempt of strangers, always forgotten, never observed; let[10] me be an obscure dark inmate, a son of earth, an ignominious bastard in the world's opinion, a neglected slave; I shall think this disgrace a great honour, if I may rest safely under the shadow of the Almighty.[11]

LXVIII[12]

There are secrets that cannot well be communicated to our dearest friends, nor will any reasonable man desire to know all that another man knows; yet some men are of such a searching nature that they will sift every corner of the heart, and never rest satisfied till informed of that which perhaps will but trouble them when revealed. This is a mistake of those that think there is no greater obligation of friendship then a mutual participation of each other's thoughts; and indeed the relation must needs be very great that depends upon such a trust. Yet there may be that in the minde which cannot be imparted without a wound to the receiver, nor extracted without violence; and such importunity doth mar the peace and content of affection. I will ever reserve in my self a power of concealment whether the matter concerne me alone or another. There are some griefes that finde ease, others that grow worse by discovery. I will give my sorrows vent if the vessel be two [sic] full; but if there be no danger of dissolution, 'tis best without meere harm to let them lie still smothered up within a silent breast, lest breaking loose they get fresh aire, and maintain a new life to encrease my affliction.

LXIX

Good order is the life and soule of government. In the external frame of nature we may observe a regular disposition and uniformity of creatures. The heavens walk in a constant course of circular motion. The sea ebbes and flows at certain seasons. All things have their just beginning, progress and dissolution; confusion and disorder dwell no where but in Hell; and the wicked man is but an irregular limb of that region. Disorderly tumults proceed from the Prince of darknesse, whose kingdome is but a medly[13] of violence and rebellion. Factious men are of the Devil's kindred; still perplexed[14] in disturbing others. One jarring string puts all the rest out of tune; one unruly companion will spoile the peace of a faire society. I shall endeavour to keep my mind within a reasonable compass; for if the least passion once usurp upon the intellectual faculties, I shall be no more able to governe my selfe then a little infant or a mad-man to hold the reynes of a common-wealth.

LXX

There is a moderate use of the creatures which exceed [*sic*] not the bounds of temperance; and he is most miserable that denies himself this freedom. Mirth is a jewel if beset with modesty, other-wise but a light toy to please trivial apes and wanton girles.[15] Nothing doth lesse become humanity then a scurrilous and abusive wit. To laugh at the imperfections of others implies a kind of malice that must be fed and maintained with continual mischief. Charity commands a strict inquiry into our neighbour's good-nesse; which by a liberall commendation must be discovered unto the world, while defects and errors are laid up in a silent grave and[16] may sooner be reformed by example, then confined by dis-grace. If the heart be clear, the brain will not run in a muddy channel. If my thoughts be disposed to entertain some sport and mirthful solace, I will be sure not to transgresse the limits of a charitable indulgence, a chast behaviour, and a religious integrity. I will play within the lists,[17] and not rang[e] abroad; then I shall not need to say, I am sorry for what I have said; or follow my invention with this unprofitable complaint, Wit, whither wilt thou?

LXXI

Of all afflictions, poverty is none of the least, which to some is more terrible then death it self. And truely, what can more afflict a generous mind then a penurious want?[18] Yet against this and other miserable events of our various life I have a sufficient cor-

dial[19] from the powerful vertue of my religion. I have learnt
therefore to be thankful in the lowest condition.[20] The course of
this world is full of change, so that I am never dejected with the
terror of my own wants, knowing that the next day or houre may
make a prize. Our happinesse is no exhalation drawn from any
earthly matter, but like the sunne in the circle (sometimes clouded,
never put out),[21] continues an everlasting race of glory. Poverty
is not the object of my feare, which though unexpected may finde
chearfull entertainment: nor shall the tyranny of a cruel want
make me sacrifice my soule in sighs and tears. Brown-bread and
the Gospel is the best fare said Master Bradford.[22] However if I
cannot fancy so great a happiness, I will yet keep fast my integrity. The greatest crosse shall not force me to be dishonest. I
think I should rather starve then play the parasite for a morsel of
bread.

LXXIII

I know the separation of the body and soul in regard that nature
abhors all evacuation, dis-union, and dissolution, may be said to
be unnatural: yet I can apprehend this disjunction as a necessary
means to a more glorious redintegration and incorruptible union.
I know that there is a mutual relation and commerce, a friendly
society and interchangeable conversation betwixt these two: yet
I can see an image of divinity, a picture of heaven, an impresse of
eternity,[23] in the inward part, which cannot appear and shine
forth in its true lustre, in that genuine purity and brightnesse till
this dirty clay, this red earth, this body of dust be scoured off and
refined for a resurrection. I know that both shall meet againe so
purified, so rarified, so together glorified, as now I cannot conceive
an expression to certifie my understanding, but can understand
enough to strengthen and confirme my faith. I believe and know
that both shall be renued with such perfection and absolute grace
that there shall be no roome left fit for a temptation, for a disease:
the soul without hope, or fear, or anger, or grief; free from all
tumultuary passion, and rebellious lusts; the[24] body free from
all paine, and anguish, and sicknesse; the whole man void of all
necessity of sin and misery. I will not fear death that is the occasion of all this blessednesse. Life is nothing else but a progresse
unto death; and death is nothing else but an entrance into life.[25]

I know it is the end of all misery, and the beginning of all happiness. Against the *fear* of death, and the *desire* of death, I do thus conclude. I wil so live that I may die happily; I will so die that I may live eternally. Lord, give me thy grace here, and I will not doubt of thy glory hereafter.

LXXXIX[26]

A true jeere is a jest in earnest: which is worse then down-right railing. A smiling cut-throat[27] is the most injurious villain. To turn truth into a matter of mirth is to banish all favourable compassion, which is the bond of society and friendship. An abusive wit is but a sweet poyson, which though for the present it affect the taste, yet afterwards it infects the heart. A generous spirit scorns to solace himself with the disgrace of another. I will not triumph in the wounds of an enemy, nor insult upon the weaknesse of a friend. For the common frailty of our nature is such that we may condemne our selves when we laugh at others.

NOTES

1. *this rule: Rather:* Original reads "this rule; rather." 2. Resolve XVI: Compare Tuke, "Of painting the face." 3. *I will be sure . . . my selfe:* Compare the ending sentence of Hall's resolve VIII. 4. *When God resolves . . . instruments:* Compare 1 Corinthians 1:27–29. 5. *Jaell shall prevaile:* How Jael, wife of Heber the Kenite, treacherously slew Sisera is related in Judges 4:11–22. 6. Resolve LVI: Note that this highly sententious resolve, though patently built upon commonplaces, actually does not contain a single identifiable proverb. 7. Resolve LXI: Reprinted in Moore Smith without notes. 8. *the Church under ground:* I.e., in the catacombs, or sacrosanct subterranean crypts, during persecutions in pagan Rome (and elsewhere). 9. *when Elijah . . . by Jezabel:* Compare 1 Kings 19. 10. *never observed; let:* Original reads "never observed, let."

11. *rest safely under . . . Almighty:* This imagery is characteristic of the Psalms; compare 17:8, 36:7, 57:1, 63:7. 12. Resolve LXVIII: With this secrecy in friendship, compare Hall, resolve XXXIX; Henshaw, p. 125. 13. *medly:* medley, mixture. 14. *still perplexed:* always involved. 15. *Mirth . . . wanton girles:* Compare Spenser's picture of immodest mirth in his Phaedria, *Faerie Queene,* II, vi, 3 ff.; "girles" here probably means young people of both sexes. 16. *silent grave and:* Original reads

"silent grave; and." 17. *play within the lists:* I.e., observe the rules, stay within bounds. 18. *Of all afflictions . . . penurious want:* Compare Juvenal, *Satires,* III, 152–53: "Nil habet infelix paupertas durius in se/ quam quod ridiculos homines facit." And Dr. Johnson (Boswell, *Life,* under date 7 December 1782): "Poverty is a great enemy to human happiness; it certainly destroys liberty, and it makes some virtues impracticable and others extremely difficult." 19. *a sufficient cordial:* an effective remedy. 20. *I have learnt . . . condition:* Compare Paul's statement, Philippians 4:11.

21. *(sometimes . . . out):* Punctuation supplied, replacing comma before "continues." 22. *Brown bread . . . said Master Bradford:* The "Master Bradford" referred to is doubtless John Bradford (1500?–1555), Protestant martyr. Bartlett, *Familiar Quotations,* 13th ed. (Boston, 1955), p. 292b, cites Matthew Henry's commentary on Isaiah: "It was a common saying among the Puritans, 'Brown Bread and the Gospel is good fare.' " 23. *an impresse of eternity: Impresse,* here, probably means "imprint"; but it might also be considered as an *impresa* (Ital.), a verbal (and sometimes pictorial) symbol akin to an emblem. 24. *rebellious lusts; the:* Original reads "rebellious lusts: the." 25. *Life is nothing . . . into life:* Compare Stafford, resolve iv. 26. Resolve LXXXIX: Like resolve LVI, this wittily sententious resolve suggests the proverbial without really incorporating actual proverbs. 27. *A smiling cut-throat:* Compare *Hamlet,* I, v, 108: "One may smile, and smile, and be a villain." See also Manley, above, p. 158.

Caleb Trenchfield

1625?-1671

TEXT: *Historical Contemplations as also Scriptural and Occasional Observations: together with their Divine Improvements and Applications* (London, 1664); Wing T2123. The first part of this small octavo, the *Historical Contemplations* (or, running head, "History Improved") occupies pp. 1–111, and the contemplations are ostensibly 200 in number, though the count is faulty. This rounded number may reflect Feltham's "duple century," for many of the contemplations follow the resolve pattern. The *Historical Contemplations* part of the volume is headed "Christian Chymistrie." The chemistry by which these snippets are applied to the Christian life and moralized is much like that in the *Things New and Old* of John Spencer. Another edition of the book is said to have appeared in 1679.

Information about Caleb Trenchfield (1625?–1671) is hard to come by; there is no *DNB* article. On the title page of the present work he is identified only as "C.T. late Minister of Chepsted in Surrey." Calamy, *Nonconformist's Memorial* (London, 1803), III, 330, records that Trenchfield, former incumbent of Chipsted, Surrey, "returned to this living in 1660. Mr. *Trenchfield* having an estate at *Eltham* in Kent, went and lived there, and kept a school, and there he died." Perhaps that is as much as we need to know.

Trenchfield's only other major work seems to have been a *Cap of Gray Hairs for a Green Head* (Wing T2118), 1671, which went into a fifth (sixth?) edition in 1692. Wing's T2121 (which I have not seen), entitled *Christian Chymistrie* is probably identical with or little different from the first part of the *Historical Contemplations;* and his T2122, *The Father's Counsel* (1676) sounds like a variant title for *A Cap of Gray Hairs*. In any case, on the title page of the fourth edition (1688) of the *Cap*, Trenchfield styles himself (or is styled) "Gent."; and if he is indeed the father of the apprentice to whom the work is directed, then that son was one of at least ten children (p. 47).

In his resolves Trenchfield, whatever the secular historical situation alleged, or whatever the "occasion" viewed at firsthand, always manages as relentlessly as Spencer to bring them to a "divine improvement and application."

HISTORICAL CONTEMPLATIONS
AND OCCASIONAL OBSERVATIONS

2

Agesilaus playing[1] with his young son, and riding upon a reed to make him sport, was dirided by one of his familiars as being too vaine; to whom he answered, *hold thy peace till thou thy self art a father, and then we will heare thy advice.* When we meet with infirmities which have befallen some of the servants of God in their exigencies, we are ready to deride their weaknesse, or suspect their sincerity; but let us suspend our judgements till our soules be in their soules' stead.

3

The Minturnians[2] changing their purpose of slaying Caius Marius into purposes of conveighing him to the sea side were in their passage thither either to go a great way about, which his danger would not allow, or to go through a wood which they accounted sacred, and the highest sacriledge to carry any thing out of it that had been once brought into it. In this exigency, an old man among them steps out and resolves the doubt, saying, no way was to be scrupled whereby Marius might be saved. Our dayes have shewn us many of that opinion, that nothing should be accounted holy which stood in the way of their ambition; but Lord, make me alwayes willing rather to go about for the obtaining of my purposes, then to tread over where thou has[t] set bounds.

30

Sir Edwin Sandys reporteth[3] upon his own knowledge of devout Papists who have dared to perjure themselves in judgement, presuming upon the present and easie remedy of confession. Lord, thou hast in thy Word discovered repentance and faith in the bloud of thy Son as the meanes of blotting out the sins of my soule; and how apt is my heart to take liberty to sin, with purpose of applying this remedy against the evill consequences of it? But let me not so trample under my feet the bloud of thy covenant as an unholy thing, but keepe me that such presumption may not prevaile over me.

49

The Germans, knowing themselves no matches for the Italian, in respect of their craft and subtilty, make amends for that want by a peremptory sticking to those resolutions which they had before considerately taken up. I find my selfe no wayes able to deal with that old Serpent, who hath so many methods of deceit; but let him say what he will, or can, Lord, do thou fix me irremovably on this resolution, *I have said I will keep thy commandements alwayes, even to the end.*[4]

73

The Commons of England[5] being very importunate with Edward the Fourth to make war on France, he consented to satisfie their importunity; though willing, rather, to enjoy the fruit of his wars and toiles and spend the rest of his dayes in peace. Therefore he takes with him a dozen of fat capon-eating burgesses who had been the most zealous for that expedition. These he imploies in all military services, to lye in the open fields, stand whole nights upon the guards, and causes their quarters to be beaten up[6] with frequent alarmes. Which was so intollerable to those fat paunches, accustomed to lye on their soft downes, and that could hardly sit on a Sessions bench[7] without their nods, that a treaty being motioned by King Lewis,[8] none were so forward to presse the acceptance of his offers, and hasten their returne into England, as they; and when there, to excuse so little done by the King with so great preparations. Lord, how shall I be able to keep way with the horsemen, if I cannot hold out with the foot? How shall I be able to stand in the day of battell, when in the cause of thy truth there must be a resisting to bloud, if I am nothing active in resisting of sin now? Am I like to abide in the watch tower whole nights, that like the Disciples[9] cannot watch one houre to prevent temptation? Oh, let me be therefore much in spirituall exercises now, and in cutting off the right hands and plucking out of the right eyes[10] of corrupt desires, that I may be ready to deny the conveniences and preciousnesses of life when the emergences of thy interest shall call me to it.

117

In the conspiracy of Otho[11] against Galba, when Otho had invaded the army and was acknowledged by it, there was a strong report that Otho was slaine; which very many of the Senators and Knights of Rome hearing presented themselves to Galba, professing their sorrow that the occasion to shew how much they would have done for his security was taken away, of which yet (when the truth proved otherwise) not a man did once appeare in his defence. Lord, when thy justice seemes to be suspended, and because thou punishest not speedily [it seems that] therefore thou wilt not at all, how daring and presumptious is this heart? What promises of pleasure and security in sin doth it make? But when conscience is awakened, and the expectations of thy vengeance received, it is not lesse ready to despond then it was before presumptious and daring. Therefore, Lord, though I desire to serve thee out of a principle of onenesse with thee, and affection to thee, yet no bonds are too many to restraine rebellious corruptions; and I had rather the rod should be ever held over me then I should grow wanton through want of it.

127

'Tis said of Galba[12] that *he could not so well be accounted vertuous as without vices.* 'Tis not seldome that civility is mistaken for grace, and we please our selves that we are not as others are then that we are what we should be. Peter, speaking of those that may apostatize, expresseth them not by their actings of grace but *their escaping of the pollutions of the world.*[13] The sinfulnesse of some sins may be discovered, and through the light of conscience there may be an abhorring against them, where yet there is no hearty closing with good nor affectionate application to the wayes of righteousnesse. Lord, let therefore the new creature be formed in me, whereby I may not onely *be purged from dead workes, but purified to serve the living God.*[14]

200[15]

Neer the Lake Agnano[16] there is a cave into which (for the experience of travellers) the neighbouring inhabitants are wont to put their dogs, which are no sooner in but they are as dead immediately, with eyes set and tongues hanging out; but taken thence presently and thrown into the lake they recover; for which cause those dogs no sooner see a stranger coming but, if not prevented, away they get them packing to the adjoyning mountains, not to be got again to make a new experiment. Lord, thou saidst, *In the day that thou eatest thereof thou shalt dye the death;* and we never descend into acts of iniquity but we are afresh dead in trespasses and sins, and that irrecoverably, if not washed by faith and repentance *in the fountain*[17] *opened for sin and for uncleannesse.* But if we have so escaped, when temptation again presents it self shall we not get us packing, by no means to be brought to another tryall?

from the OCCASIONAL OBSERVATIONS

31

I saw an orchard planted with choice of, and the choicest of fruits, but no good husbandry bestowed upon it afterwards, but suffered to lye undigged and over-grown with nettles and cropt by cattel, so that the trees were hinderly and shrubbed,[18] having nothing neer attained that growth which otherwise they would. I heard a sermon the other day wherein I heard such smart and seasonable exhortations as possest my soul with many pious purposes, which yet, alas, wanted that good husbandry which should have caused those thoughts to flourish into good works. I am sensible I have lost a precious advantage; I will therefore bestir me to recollect them out of the rubbish of impertinencies which lye in my heart and will take care of them that they be fenced with circumspection, stak't with resolution, digged about with religious exercise, wed[19] with caution, and watered with prayer.

NOTES

1. *Agesilaus playing:* Plutarch, *Parallel Lives,* tr. Dryden, p. 729. 2. *The Minturnians:* Original reads "Miuturnians." For Marius, see Plu-

tarch, *Parallel Lives,* "Caius Marius"; his capture and treatment by the Minturnians, pp. 518–79. See also Sallust, *War of Jugurtha,* chapts. 20–36; and, for the Minturnian episode, Livy, *A.u.c.,* XIV, 97 (Loeb).   3. *Sir Edwin Sandys reporteth:* In his *Relation of the State of Religion* (1605), sig. Bl verso.   4. *I have said . . . end:* Restating Psalm 119:33. 5. *The Commons of England:* The French war and treaty of Edward and Louis form part of the later acts in Thomas Heywood's First Part of *King Edward the Fourth* (1600), but the discomfiture of the "commons" is not there. Trenchfield is perhaps recalling (and elaborating) Holinshed, *Chronicles* (London, 1808), III, 329–35, who remarks concerning the treaty: "The king . . . was the more easilie induced to agree by those of his councell, that loved peace better than war and their wives soft beds better than hard armor and stonie lodging."   6. *beaten up:* disturbed, aroused.   7. *sit on a Sessions bench:* I.e., perform their duties either in a court of quarterly sessions or, more probably, in a session of Parliament.   8. *King Lewis:* Louis XI, Edward's opponent.   9. *like the Disciples:* Asleep in Gethsemane; compare Matthew 26:40.   10. *right hands . . . right eyes:* Compare Matthew 5:29–30, reversed order.

11. *the conspiracy of Otho:* See Plutarch, *Parallel Lives,* "Otho"; Dio, *Roman History,* Book XLIII.   12. *'Tis said of Galba:* See Plutarch, *Parallel Lives,* "Galba"; and compare Tuvill's statement, *Essays,* p. 69: "He is thought to do good enough who, when he is in place of authority, doth but little ill."   13. *Peter, speaking . . . the world:* 2 Peter 1:4.   14. *new creature . . . living God:* A combination of 2 Corinthians 5:17 and Hebrews 9:14.   15. *(200):* Two of the resolves are given the number 200. This is the second of those so numbered.   16. *Neer the Lake Agnano:* I have not discovered the "traveliar" responsible for this charming *conte drolatique.* 17. *in the fountain:* The sacrifice of Christ, of course. The idea finds expression in two familiar hymns, in Toplady's "Rock of Ages": "Foul, I to the Fountain fly; / Wash me, Saviour, or I die;" and in Cowper's *Olney Hymns,* 15: "There is a fountain fill'd with blood / Drawn from Immanuel's veins; / And sinners plung'd beneath that flood, / Lose all their guilty stains."   18. *hinderly and shrubbed:* retarded and stunted. 19. *wed:* past participial form of the verb "to weed."

Dudley North, fourth Baron North

1602-1677

TEXT: *Light in the Way to Paradise: with other Occasionals* (London, 1682); Wing N1281. There is in the Perkins Library of Duke University a manuscript of miscellaneous *Works* by this Sir Dudley North which contains, among his poems and other items, a copy of the "Occasionals." Since a close comparison of that manuscript and the printed version reveals no substantively different readings, I have elected to reprint the more regularized printed form. The copy used is that formerly belonging to Edmund Malone, now in the Folger Library.

Sir Dudley North, fourth Baron North (1602–1677) was the son of Dudley North, third Baron, whose work (*A Forest of Varieties,* 1645) shows him also to have known the resolve writers. The fourth Baron, like other members of his distinguished family —and notably like his father—moderately eminent in politics, was a lover of music and of studies and was gifted with his pen. His son Roger is well remembered for his family history, *Lives of the Norths.* The long life of his father (d. 1666, at age eighty-five) kept Sir Dudley overlong from his inheritance and title but did not greatly perturb his equanimity.

A life-and-works study, together with an edition of Sir Dudley's poems in the Duke manuscript, is in final stages of preparation by my friend and former colleague Dale B. J. Randall.

From internal evidence the "Occasionals" seem to have been composed during the 1650s and 1660s. North does not call his "Occasionals" resolves; but the reader who has followed the present set of writers thus far will have no difficulty in recognizing the underlying resolve pattern. In the general preface to the printed volume, "To the Reader," North describes his efforts thus:

To these following Discourses of mine (or *Occasionalls* as I style them) I have no more to say but this. That if any shall think them worthy of a Perusal, there must not be expected, either Method or curiosity of expression, for they are no other than a mere after-birth to some of my serious thoughts, which I have thought fit to preserve in being, rather for the satis-

faction of my self than of others. For their matter, I have no reason to
think that it will receive good entertainment, for in many things I have
been far from confining my self to the common received opinions; nay, I
have gone cross to very considerable Interests: yet I hope there will be
found in them, neither great deviations as to Truth, nor the least offence
in relation to any of the fundamental points of Religion.

Occasional numbers X and XI are included here. It should perhaps be recalled that part of Trenchfield's title had been "Occasional Observations."

LIGHT IN THE WAY TO PARADISE

[Occasional X]

I have read in an Italian writer[1] of some estimation to this effect,
that a desire and endeavour of attaining fulness of power over
others, is very commendable, because it giveth men some measure
of likeness unto God, the fountain of all perfection, one of whose
chief attributes is his omnipotence. The assertion admits of some
justification, as I conceive, but not the reason, for though we may
take God for our pattern, in respect of his ethical and intellectual
excellences (if I may so call them,) yet it savours too much of
the Luciferian presumption,[2] to bear an emulating eye in the least
measure, either towards his glory or his power. And as to the desire of power, the edge of it may be somewhat abated in the lovers
of vertue and goodness, when they take into consideration, that a
state of mortality shall always want that infinite wisedom, and
purity of intention, which resideth in the Deity, and which makes
power to consist inabusively only there, as in its proper sphere.
For that power which men enjoy, is none of their own,[3] and they
must yield an account to the true proprietary,[4] not only of the
use, but of the very having of it. And as among men, he who in a
way of violence and illegality, possesseth himself of that which
is the property of another, (though his equal or inferiour) becomes an offender against the civil magistrate; so it is, but much
more unpardonable in relation to the Deity so infinitely tran-
scending our capacity, with those who assume power to themselves
in an unwarrantable manner. I doubt not but divines will step

in further, and assert, that a mere desire of power, with a sinister intention, is no small sin; and what may it then be to desire, assume, and use power corruptly? The true end of all external power can be no more than this, to propagate the peace and happiness of mankind, and every individual person, as far as may be done without a more publique prejudice: and from hence it comes, that a desire of rewarding becomes more natural to a noble nature, than of punishing (though an approach may be made even to the latter with chearfulness of spirit), for remunerations answer to both parts of the above-mentioned end; whereas punitive justice for the present satisfieth only the former, bringing with it always harm to the offending person, and sometimes ruine total and final; yet as I said, this may be proceeded in with comfort, because the extirpation of one may be a means of reforming many; and sometime there is no other way to save them from destruction, and that not only by terrour in the example, but by prevention of ruinous and destructive designs inherent in (or affixed to) the person of him who is cut off.[5] But that magistrate, who useth severity to torment or destroy the offender with any intention whatsoever, other than those above-specified, either with Pilate sells[6] the indolence and safety of others for favour and particular advantage, or out of a mere Satanical spirit, takes delight in the sufferings of others, and at the best, makes the hands of justice to become (upon personal provocation) an instrument of revenge, which is the peculiar of him, who hath said[7] Ἐμοι ἐκδικησις, or *Vengeance is mine,* so as men can have no other part in it than to become instruments, and are no otherwise justified in being so, than either by the rule of God's revealed will exprest in the written Word, or by some immediate and miraculous precept from him. For my part, though I conceive it to be the strongest of temptations to an active and knowing spirit, to be courted by an opportunity of having great power over others; yet I shall rather choose to become the mark (or anvile, if you will) of injurious power, than to exasperate my Creator either by an usurpation, or by the revengefull use of so dangerous a weapon.

[Occasional XI]

Ever since our first father Adam sought to palliate his first transgression, by laying upon another the iniquity which proceeded

chiefly from the determination of his own will, we of his posterity
have applied our selves to doe the like; and for the most part
when better evidence fails us, we lay the crime to the charge of
fortune, who very fitly by the fabulist[8] is represented with a great
complaint in her mouth upon that occasion. Among the heathens,
Fortune was esteemed a goddess,[9] and with us Christians she is
little less, if rightly understood; for what squareth better with the
notion meant by fortune, than the providence of God, which
being one of his chief attributes, is hardly severed from his person?
We should therefore be very carefull not to make complaint in
that kind, considering the person against whom our complaint is
levelled; nor to doe like some men, who to excuse their own folly,
for yielding to temptations in the way of excess by which their
body or estate is impaired or ruined, lay all the blame on Fortune.
Certainly complaints of this nature can be no other than a high
provocation of the Almighty, who hath the absolute dominion over
his creatures; for no temporal thing is necessary, if the want of it
be not an absolute hindrance to the end whereunto the vessel (to
use St. Paul's expression)[10] is designed, which design is only known
to the Creator. Neither are worldly wisedom, riches, power, and
such like, any ways necessary to the attaining of the chief end of
our life, for there is as ready a way to it from the lowest condition
as from the highest: and if so, then why do we complain? It was
the opinion of some philosophers,[11] that the Deity doth not at all
mind the businesses of this world; but their opinion is so far
from truth, as the slightest things (or at least many of them) seem
to be decreed. Saul was chosen by God to be King of Israel, and
was not the straying of his father's asses designed a means of bringing him to the presence of Samuel, for the effecting of it?[12] A
seeming casual spark falleth into a magazine of gun-powder, which
is occasion of the loss of a kingdom, and can this be thought to
pass without a divine providence? Some men understand it as a
thing derogatory to the Deity to order trivial things (which caus-
eth the scoff of profane Lucian[13] upon Jupiter, as entertaining
himself with the painting of butterflies), but the consequences of
things trivial are not always slight, though conceived so by us,
who are no less ignorant of effects as they relate to their causes,
than of causes as they relate to their effects. And certainly to order
and govern the universe, with all the seeming casualties in it,

can be no derogation to the Deity; for to say truth, we cannot conceive rightly of God, without believing his infinite wisedom and power to comprehend and penetrate all things, together with their causes and effects, and also that his government of the whole is effected with more facility, than the wisest man can order the clearest and easiest matters. The truth is, that this providence is always at work, and that humane wisedom and folly do but cooperate with it. As for us, these may either yield us a justification, or aggravate against us, but the effect is always steered by providence. *The race is not to the swift,* saith Solomon, *nor the battel to the strong,* etc., but time and chance (or the effects of providence) come alike to all. It is more evident among gamesters, that the money is many times lost by playing that which is clearly best; and so it falleth out in matters of greatest concernment. And fit it is that it should be so, for humane wisedom might justly boast it self against providence, if the common saying were true, *Sapiens dominabitur astris, A wise man shall over-rule the stars.* What is then to be said, shall we omit the using of those parts[14] which God hath given us, because the issue of things is not in our power? This were *to heap up condemnation to our selves against the latter day.*[15] Rather let us, but in a more general sense, take up the resolution of Joab,[16] captain of David's hoast, who spake thus to his army before a battel (which exhortation of his hath always passed with me for most precious, and shall be the conclusion of this discourse.) *Be of good courage, and let us play the men for our people, and for the cities of our God, and let the Lord doe what seemeth him good.*

NOTES

1. *an Italian writer:* The allusion seems to be to Machiavelli, *The Prince,* chapt. 6. 2. *the Luciferian presumption:* Devilish pride, illustrated in Milton's account of the war in heaven, *Paradise Lost,* Books V–VI. See also Manley, med. 51. 3. *For that power . . . their own:* Compare Romans 13:1; also Spenser, *Faerie Queene,* I, x, 1: "If any strength we have, it is to ill, / But all the good is Gods, both power and eke will." Compare also Tuke, "Of the Law," final sentence. 4. *the true proprietary:* the true owner, i.e., God. 5. *extirpation of one . . . cut off:* Illustrated by Spenser, *Faerie Queene,* V, ix, in Mercilla's (Elizabeth's) execution of Duessa (Mary, Queen of Scots). 6. *with Pilate sells:* Com-

pare Mark 15:15; and, more at large, John 18–19. 7. *him, who hath said:* I.e., God; compare Romans 12:19. The italicized statement translates the Greek quotation. 8. *fortune . . . by the fabulist:* This seems to refer to some illustrated version of Babrius's fables; compare Fable 49 (Loeb). 9. *Among the heathens . . . goddess:* See Howard R. Patch, *The Goddess Fortuna* (Cambridge, Mass., 1927); and, for the relation of providence and fortune, Boethius, *Consolation of Philosophy.* Behind Boethius lies the Stoic treatment of providence, fate, and fortune in Seneca's *De Providentia.* 10. *St. Paul's expression:* Paul uses the "vessel" image on several occasions (and in several senses). North may here have in mind Acts 9:15.

11. *opinion of some philosophers:* One of whom was Pliny the Elder, who says (*Nat. Hist.,* Book II, sect. 20): "It is ridiculous to suppose that the great head of things, whatever it be, pays any regard to human affairs." 12. *Saul was chosen . . . of it:* See 1 Samuel 9:3–18. 13. *the scoff of profane Lucian:* "Scoffing" Lucian, usually somewhat cavalier in his treatment of the gods, gives Zeus his worst thumpings in "Zeus Cross-Examined" and "Zeus Tragoedus"; see *Works,* tr. H. W. and F. G. Fowler, 4 vols. (Oxford, 1905), III, 71–104. 14. *parts:* aptitudes, special gifts. 15. *to heap up . . . latter day:* Perhaps in reference to the parable of the talents, Matthew 25:15–28; or to Deuteronomy 31:29, the chiding by Moses of his followers. 16. *the resolution of Joab:* 2 Samuel 10:12.

Works Cited

Aelian (Claudius Aelianus). *On the Characteristics of Animals*. Edited and translated by A. F. Scholfield. 3 vols. Cambridge, Mass., 1958–1959. Loeb Classical Library.

Augustine, Saint (Aurelius Augustinus, bp. of Hippo). *The City of God*. Translated by John Healey; first published in 1610. 2 vols. Edinburgh, 1909.

———. *De fide et operibus*. Venice, 1534.

———. *Select Letters*. Edited and translated by James Houston Baxter. London, 1953. Loeb Classical Library.

Babrius (Valerius Babrius). *Babrius and Phaedrus*. Edited and translated by Ben Edwin Perry. London, 1965. Loeb Classical Library.

Bacon, Francis. *Apophthegms*. Works edited by Basil Montagu, vol. 2. London, 1824.

———. *Selected Writings of Francis Bacon*. Edited by Hugh G. Dick. New York, 1955. Modern Library.

Bartlett, John. *Familiar Quotations*. 13th ed. Boston, 1955.

Black, Matthew W. *Richard Brathwait: An Account of His Life and Works*. Philadelphia, 1928.

Boethius (Anicius Manlius Severinus Boethius). *The Consolation of Philosophy*. Edited, with the English translation of "I. T." (1609), revised, by H. F. Stewart. London, 1956. Loeb Classical Library.

Boswell, James. *The Life of Samuel Johnson, LL.D.* New York, 1931. Modern Library Giant.

Brydges, Sir Samuel Egerton. *Archaica*. 2 vols. London, 1815.

Bush, Douglas. *English Literature in the Earlier Seventeenth Century 1600–1660*. 2d ed. Oxford, 1962.

Calamy, Edmund. *Nonconformist's Memorial*. 3 vols. London, 1802–1803.

Calphurnius (C. Calphurnius Siculus). *Buccolica*. Paris, 1503.

Cassiodorus (Flavius Magnus Aurelius Cassiodorus, Senator) *Opera Omnia*. Geneva, 1650.

Chambers's Cyclopaedia of English Literature. New edition by David Patrick. 3 vols. London and Edinburgh, 1903.

Chrysostom, Joannes, Saint. *In Evangelium secundum Matthaeum*. Paris, 1545.

Cicero (Marcus Tullius Cicero). *De oratore*. Edited and translated by E. W. Sutton. Cambridge, Mass., 1948. Loeb Classical Library.

Congreve, William. *The Old Batchelour, a Comedy*. London, 1693. (Wing C5863).

Cornu, Donald. "A Biography and Bibliography of Owen Felltham."

Ph.D. dissertation, University of Washington, 1928.

Cornwallis, Sir William. *Essayes by Sir William Cornwallis, the Younger*, Edited by Don Cameron Allen. Baltimore, 1946.

Cotgrave, Randle. *A Dictionarie of the French and English Tongues: Compiled by Randle Cotgrave*. Reproduced from the first edition, London, 1611. Introduction by William S. Woods. Columbia, S.C., 1968.

Daniels, R. B. *Some Seventeenth-Century Worthies*. Chapel Hill, N.C., 1940.

Dictionary of National Biography. Edited by Leslie Stephen and Sidney Lee. 21 vols. London, repr. 1908–1909.

Dio (Cassius Dio Cocceianus). *Dio's Roman History*. Edited and translated by Earnest Cary. 9 vols. London, 1914–1955. Loeb Classical Library.

Diogenes Laertius. *Lives of Eminent Philosophers*. Edited and translated by R. D. Hicks. 2 vols. London, 1942. Loeb Classical Library.

Duff, J. W. *A Literary History of Rome*. 3d ed. New York, 1960.

Feltham, Owen. *The Poems of Owen Felltham*. Edited by Ted-Larry Pebworth and Claude J. Summers. University Park, Pa., 1973.

———. *Resolves*. Edited by Oliphant Smeaton. London, 1904. Temple Classics.

Guazzo, Stefano. *The Civile Conversation of M. Steeven Guazzo*. Translated by George Pettie and Bartholomew Young. With an Introduction by Sir Edward Sullivan. 2 vols. London, 1925. Tudor Translations, 2d series.

Hall, Joseph. *Works*. Edited by Josiah Pratt. 10 vols. London, 1808.

Heywood, Thomas. *The First and Second Parts of King Edward IV*. With an Introduction and notes by Barron Field. London, 1842.

Holinshed, Raphael. *Holinshed's Chronicles of England, Scotland, and Ireland*. 6 vols. London, 1807–1808.

Horace (Quintus Horatius Flaccus). *Satires, Epistles, and "Ars Poetica."* Edited and translated by H. Rushton Fairclough. London, 1929. Loeb Classical Library.

Jamieson, John. *An Etymological Dictionary of the Scottish Language*. New edition. 4 vols. Paisley, 1879.

Justin Martyr. *The Writings of Justin Martyr*. Translated by Marcus Dods. Edinburgh, 1867. Ante-Nicene Christian Library.

Juvenal (Decimus Junius Juvenalis). *[Satires of] Juvenal and Persius*. Edited and translated by G. G. Ramsay. New York, 1928. Loeb Classical Library.

Lievsay, John L. "Daniel Tuvill's 'Resolves.'" *Studies in Philology* 46 (April 1949) 196–203.

Livy (Titus Livius). *Livy['s Roman History]*. Edited and translated by

B. O. Foster et al. 15 vols. London, 1919–1950. Loeb Classical Library.

Lucan (Marcus Annaeus Lucanus). *Belli Civilis libri decem.* Edited by A. E. Housman. Oxford, 1950. (Commonly known as *The Pharsalia*).

Lucian of Samosata. *The Works of Lucian.* Translated by H. W. and F. G. Fowler. 4 vols. Oxford, 1905.

Machiavelli, Niccolò. *The Prince and Other Works.* Translated by Allan H. Gilbert. Chicago, 1946.

Martz, Louis L. *The Poetry of Meditation.* New Haven, Conn., 1954.

Mills, Laurens J. *One Soul in Bodies Twain.* Bloomington, Ind., 1937.

Milton, John. *An Apology against a Pamphlet.* The Works of John Milton, edited by F. A. Patterson et al. 18 vols. New York, 1931–38. *Apology* in vol. 3, Part 1 (1931).

———. *Complete Poems and Major Prose.* Edited by Merritt Y. Hughes. New York, 1957.

Montagu, Henry, First Earl of Manchester. *Contemplatio Mortis, et immortalitatis.* London, 1631. (*STC* 18024).

Montaigne, Michel de. *The Essayes of Montaigne.* Translated by John Florio. Introduction by J. I. M. Stewart. New York, 1933. Modern Library Giant.

New Catholic Encyclopedia. 14 vols. and Index. New York, 1967.

[*OED*] *A New [Oxford] English Dictionary on Historical Principles.* Edited by J. A. H. Murray et al. 10 vols. Oxford, 1884–1933.

Ovid (Publius Ovidius Naso). *Metamorphoses.* Edited and translated by Frank Justus Miller. 2 vols. Cambridge, Mass., 1939. Loeb Classical Library.

Owen, John. *Epigrammatum.* 1st and 4th pts. London, 1612. (*STC* 18987).

Oxford Classical Dictionary. Edited by N. G. L. Hammond and H. H. Scullard. 2d ed. Oxford, 1970.

Oxford Dictionary of the Christian Church. 2d ed., revised by F. L. Cross and E. A. Livingstone. Oxford, repr. 1978.

Patch, Howard R. *The Goddess Fortuna in Mediaeval Literature.* Cambridge, Mass., 1927.

Pepys, Samuel. *The Diary of Samuel Pepys.* Edited, with additions, by Henry B. Wheatley. 3 vols. London, 1928.

Pliny (C. Plinius Caecilius Secundus). *Natural History.* Edited and translated by H. Rackham. 10 vols. Cambridge, Mass., 1938. Loeb Classical Library.

Plutarch of Chaeronea. *Parallel Lives.* Translated by John Dryden. Revised by Arthur Hugh Clough. New York, 1932. Modern Library Giant.

———. *The Philosophie, commonlie called, the Morals.* Translated by Philemon Holland. London, 1603. (*STC* 20063).

Pollard, A. W., G. R. Redgrave, et al., compilers. *A Short-Title Cata-*

logue of Books Printed in England, Scotland & Ireland, and of English Books Printed Abroad 1475-1640. London, 1926; repr. 1946. (*STC*).

Rich, Barnaby. *The Honestie of This Age.* London, 1614. (*STC* 20986).

Robertson, Jean. "The Use Made of Felltham's 'Resolves': A Study in Plagiarism." *Modern Language Review* 39 (April 1944): 108–15.

Sallust (Caius Sallustius Crispus). *The Conspiracy of Catiline and the War of Jugurtha.* Translated by Thomas Heywood. Introduction by Charles Whibley. London, 1924. Tudor Translations, 2d series.

Sandys, Sir Edwin. *A Relation of the State of Religion.* London, 1605. (*STC* 21715).

Seneca (Lucius Annaeus Seneca). *Moral Essays.* 3 vols. Edited and translated by John W. Basore. Cambridge, Mass., repr. 1958. Loeb Classical Library.

Smith, G. C. Moore. *Henry Tubbe.* Oxford, 1915.

Smith, Henry. *Works.* Edited by Thomas Smith. 2 vols. Edinburgh, 1866–1867.

Spenser, Edmund. *The Complete Poetical Works of Edmund Spenser.* Edited by R. E. Neil Dodge. Boston, 1908. Student's Cambridge Edition.

Terence (Publius Terentius Afer). [*The Plays of*] *Terence.* Edited and translated by John Sargeaunt. 2 vols. London, 1925–1926. Loeb Classical Library.

Tilley, Morris P. *A Dictionary of the Proverbs in England in the Sixteenth and Seventeenth Centuries.* Ann Arbor, Mich., 1950.

Tillyard, E. M. W. *The Elizabethan World Picture.* New York, 1944.

Tuke, Thomas. *A Treatise against Painting and Tincturing of Men and Women . . . Whereunto is added the Picture of a Picture, or, the Character of a Painted Woman.* London, 1616. (*STC* 24316).

Tuvill, Daniel. *Essays.* Edited by John L. Lievsay. Charlottesville, Va., 1971. Folger Documents of Tudor and Stuart Civilization.

Valerius Maximus. *Dictorum factorumque memorabilium libri novem. A Sebastiano Corrado emendati et illustrati.* [n.p.], 1559.

Virgil (Publius Vergilius Maro). *Aeneid.* Edited by J. W. Mackail. Oxford, 1930.

———. *Virgil's Georgicks.* Translated by Thomas May. London, 1628. (*STC* 24823).

White, John ("Century"). *The First Century of Scandalous, Malignant Priests.* London, 1643. (Wing W1777).

Wing, Donald G. *Short-Title Catalogue of Books Printed in England, Scotland, Ireland, Wales, and British America and of English Books Printed in Other Countries, 1641-1700.* 3 vols. New York, 1945–1951. Index Society.

Index

www.Ingramcontent.com/pod-product-compliance
Lightning Source LLC
Chambersburg PA
CBHW060358030726
47497CB00003B/760